Do Not Go QUIETLY

A Guide to Living Consciously and Aging Wisely
for People Who Weren't Born Yesterday

George and Sedena Cappannelli

Agape Media International

Published by Agape Media International, LLC
5700 Buckingham Parkway, Culver City, California 90230
310.258.4401   www.agapeme.com

In Association With
AgeNation, LLC
119 W. Sunlit Drive, Santa Fe, New Mexico 87508
505.982.5753   www.agenation.com

Distributed by Hay House, Inc.
P.O. Box 5100, Carlsbad, CA 92018-5100
(760) 431-7695 or (800) 654-5126

Hay House USA: www.hayhouse.com®   Hay House South Africa: www.hayhouse.co.za
Hay House UK: www.hayhouse.co.uk   Hay House India: www.hayhouse.co.in
Hay House Australia: www.hayhouse.com.au

Book Credits
Executive In Charge of Publication: Stephen Powers
Editor: Laurel Airica
Copy Editor: Nicolette Salamanca
Cover Design: Benjamin Cziller
Interior Design: Julie Melton, The Right Type Graphics
Author photo: Lisa Law

Printed in USA on recycled paper.

Hardcover ISBN: 978-1-4019-4249-6   Digital ISBN: 978-1-4019-4250-2

Library of Congress Control Number: 2013932250

Not Quietly,
No, we will not go quietly,
Not meekly into this or any other night.
We who cheered when Martin marched
And who first heard Rachel Carson's call;
We who lost our heroes to hate
And tried to find ourselves in love;
We who died at Kent State
And cheered when the wall come down;
We who contributed to the loss of America's grace
And then celebrated the rebirth of hope
We will not go quietly
Not meekly
Into this or any other night.

We will harvest our experience
And bay at the moon of new possibility.
We will dance to life's mysteries.
And forge a path of renewed promise
For ourselves and those
Who come after us.
We who hold in our hands and hearts
The power to resurrect the dream.
We who stood on the front lines before
And who are called once again
Will not go meekly
Not quietly
Into this or any other night.

~ George Cappannelli ~

Dedication

We dedicate this book to those on whose shoulders we stand and there are many. Specifically we thank Carl Jung, Elisabeth Kubler-Ross, Ram Dass, Stephen and Ondrea Levine, Jerald Jamploski, Angeles Arrien, Michael Meade, and Jean Houston. We also thank Zalman Schachter-Shalomi whose book, *From Age-ing to Sage-ing,* opened our eyes and the eyes of so many to the challenges and opportunities of "spiritual eldering" and conscious aging. And we are deeply grateful to our parents George and Mary Cappannelli and Bill and Betty Spivey, not only for the gift of life and the lessons and support they shared with us along the way, but for the final lessons they shared with us during the closing chapters of their lives. It was these lessons that prompted us to write this book.

We also honor those who spend their lives in the trenches each day working to develop new systems, procedures, technologies, and alternative strategies for people in the second half of life. And we especially celebrate those who have the courage, compassion, and grace to care for the elderly, to serve the dying, and in this way to remind us all of our duty to those who need us now and to those who will come after us.

Finally, we dedicate this book to you and celebrate your willingness to keep your dream alive and to do the courageous and necessary work of learning to live the life you were born to live.

PART FOUR
Here and Now — Your Next Step on the Road to Living the Life You Were Born to Live   142

PART FIVE
Charting a Remarkable Course for Your Future   201

The Beginning

"Everything has to do with loving and not loving."

~ Rumi ~

Breakdown or Breakthrough

We are entering a time of demographic revolution that will, over the next several decades, result in a large number — some say half of our population — being 50 years of age or older for the first time in history. Although this revolution is still in its early stages, it is clear from the conversations and conflicts being acted out in the chambers of government and in the boardrooms of our institutions and corporations that this "graying" of the world's population is ushering in a time of unprecedented social, political, cultural, economic, technological, and environmental change for all of us who are passengers on this train called Humanity and especially for those of us who are older GenXers, Boomers, and Elders. And this, as they say, is only the beginning.

Couple this reality with the fact that many governments, institutions, and businesses at all levels and in all parts of the world, as well as the vast majority of us — and even the organizations that are supposed to advocate for us — are unprepared for the substantial challenges and unprecedented opportunities that lie ahead. Only then does one begin to understand that this confluence of factors represents either a recipe for disaster or fertile ground for a historic breakthrough.

Do Not Go Quietly weighs in on the side of those who believe that the time ahead will provide the fertile ground for breakthrough. It advances the proposition that many of us who are older GenXers (40 to 45), Boomers (46 to 64), and Elders (65+) not only have the opportunity but the time, resources, talent, and experience. And all of us have the need to revisit the values and priorities that have guided our individual lives. Through such an essential and periodic reassessment and in other important ways, we can contribute our wisdom and experience to help steer the ship of state onto a course that promises greater well-being, environmental sustainability, social responsibility, and financial stability for ourselves and those who come after us.

So if you fall within one of these demographic categories and are interested in living more consciously and aging wisely you are, as they say, on the right page at the right time.

If you are under 40 and want to better prepare for your own road ahead — as well as to better understand the road your parents, older friends, and relatives may now be on — then you have also come to the right place.

If you want to use the time you have remaining — whether years or decades — to make right your relationship with yourself and with others, if you want to connect with greater meaning, passion, and joy and, in the process, contribute to a more positive and compassionate future, then *Do Not Go Quietly* is a good book for you.

We have written *Do Not Go Quietly* to remind all of us to use this precious gift of our lives to harvest the fruits of our past and turn them into gold that we can invest in the present and future. For only by living in each present moment with greater mindfulness can we fulfill the dreams we have come here to manifest.

Yes, we have written this book because we believe that no matter what religious beliefs or political philosophies we hold, what economic strata we belong to, what our educational background may be, or what we do or have done in the world to earn our daily bread, when we come to the end of our lives none of this will matter as much as the knowledge that we alone will hold in our hearts as to whether we have done our best to use our time, skills, heart, and resources to lead a life of genuine value and contribute to the "Common Wealth."

Here at the outset, we want to be clear that *Do Not Go Quietly* is not one of those candy-coated self-help books full of pithy sound bites, designed to appeal to everyone without disturbing anyone. As we — and a number of others "who weren't born yesterday" — already know, genuine transformation is not possible without experiencing some bumps and disturbances on the road. In fact, in our experience, without these bumps many of us would not learn the essential things we have come to Life to learn.

So you will not find "The 10 Effortless Steps to Easy Street" between these covers. Nor will you find promises of easy wealth, continual happiness, good health, the perfect waistline, and a no-cost timeshare on Maui without having to get up off the couch and work up a little sweat. So if you still believe in free rides or a life free of challenges, this is probably not your book.

Instead, *Do Not Go Quietly* is for those who understand that a life of genuine quality and accomplishment is most possible if we remember Helen Keller's good advice — "life is either a daring adventure or nothing."

Do Not Go Quietly is also for those of us who recognize that we may not have always done as good a job as we could have — as individuals, parents, friends, colleagues, leaders, lovers, and stewards of our planet. But now, with the wisdom of experience and the gift of hindsight, we still have time to do some things — both large and small — to change some of that and to leave behind a legacy that makes a positive difference in the lives of our loved ones and the larger community.

So if you believe, like we do, that you are never too old or too young to learn what you do not know, and if you find value in stories about people who have accomplished things of genuine value — particularly if you are open to being surprised that many of these people did these things when they were in their 50s and, in some cases, in their 60s, 70s, 80s and even 90s — then please join us for what we hope will be a journey that reminds you that it's never too late to live your dreams.

If you are open to digging a little deeper into some of the larger questions that lie at the heart of life's mysteries and exploring alternative life strategies, if you have unfinished dreams and new territories you want to explore and are interested in opening your heart even wider so that Life can have its way with you, then welcome to *Do Not Go Quietly*.

While we can't promise you those "10 Effortless Steps to Easy Street," we can promise to help you remember how remarkable you are, what extraordinary things you are still capable of expressing in this lifetime, and how much joy and satisfaction this expression will bring to you and to others.

In Part One, we will identify and explore some of the challenges and opportunities we face — individually and collectively — as a result of the graying of the world's population. As you will see, we also issue you an invitation to do one of the most important things you can do to inherit your individual dreams and contribute to the world around you.

In Part Two you will have the opportunity to explore some concepts, questions, and recommendations we believe can help you better prepare for the road ahead.

In Part Three you will have a chance to review your past, revisit some of your beliefs and basic values, and harvest some of your valuable experiences and wisdom and turn them into real gold that you can invest in living the life you were born to live in the present and future.

In Part Four you can experience the freedom that comes from learning to put down some of the burdens of the past and avoid worrying about the future so you can live more joyfully and successfully in each present moment.

And in Part Five you can take some important steps in envisioning and mapping a future that is brighter, more engaging, and more extraordinary than you can currently imagine. For as they say, "the best is yet to come."

Finally, throughout the book, you are given encouragement, support, and inspiration. **Life Inspirations** are short, motivational stories about people who demonstrate some of the best principles of conscious living. Each chapter also concludes with a section that has some **Life Rules, Life Achievements,** and **Life Tools** that will provide you with some prompts and some practical techniques to create greater balance along with enhanced physical, emotional, and mental well-being.

At the back of book, you will find a description and link to P.E.P., the valuable and restorative Portable Energy Process that Sedena has created. Originally we included some of her easy-to-do, powerful processes in the pages of this book, but realized that it would be much more helpful to you if, rather than reading them, you could follow her as she demonstrates and leads you through them. So if you would like to give your body the same kind of attention you will give your mind, emotions, and spirit as you take this journey you may want to turn to the back page or go to www.donotgoquietlythebook.com and arrange to get your copy of P.E.P.

One final note: In his inspiring work, *The Book of Awakening,* poet and author Mark Nepo has this to say about turning the dross of our lives into gold:

> But it is too late for me, you might say, I am already full-grown. Not so, for in the world of our inwardness, we are always growing.... We can return and begin again by facing ourselves. In this way, we can go below our hardened ways to the soft impulses that birth them. Instead of breaking the bone of our stubbornness, we can nourish the marrow of our feeling unheard.... Instead of counting the scars from being hurt in the world, we can find and re-kiss the very spot in our soul where we began to withhold our trust.

PART ONE
As It Is Now

"There lies before us, if we choose, continual progress in happiness,
knowledge, and wisdom, but we must appeal as human beings
to human beings, remember our humanity, and forget the rest.
If we do so, the way lies open to a new Paradise."

~ Albert Einstein ~

Unsinkable

Molly's Story

The large manila envelope contained a copy of the front page of the <u>Cleveland Plain Dealer</u> neatly folded in quarters. The page featured a photograph and lead story about a demonstration for senior rights on the steps of city hall. In the center of the photograph, arms raised, with an expression of determination and enthusiasm on her face, was Molly Brown. A short note was clipped to the article. "Thank you," it read. "I feel like a new person."

Molly and I had met three weeks before. I was facilitating a personal trans-formational seminar in Philadelphia for some 400 social, environmental, and political activists who had assembled there from around the country for this five-day event. I had flown in the previous afternoon from Los Angeles and had a very comfortable night in one of the city's best hotels. Molly and a group of five other activists, on the other hand, had driven most of the night in a van from Cleveland after a hard day's work to be part of this gathering.

I noticed Molly right away. She was sitting in the front row with a bright, no-nonsense look on her face. It was clear she was committed to learning whatever we had to offer, but would be quick to let us know if she could not separate the chaff from the wheat — the essential and the authentic from the ordinary and the usual.

As the training progressed it was also clear that she was an original. Her enthusiasm and honesty were apparent as was her courage. She participated wholeheartedly in all of the processes, even in the more challenging ones in which additional personal disclosure and transparency were required that some of the younger people in the room were resisting. Still, every once in a while, in quiet moments between sessions when I would catch a glimpse of Molly, it appeared that something was troubling her.

On Saturday afternoon, the fourth day of the program, Molly approached me during the lunch break. She wanted to thank me, she said, for facilitating processes that had allowed her to let go of some of the guilt and resentment she had been holding on to for years. As she spoke there was a glint in her eye and I could hear a sense of confidence in her voice.

From comments she and others had made during the preceding days I knew she was a real spark plug in her work on behalf of the elderly in Cleveland. During this Saturday afternoon conversation, however, she admitted that over the course of the previous few days she had come to realize that she had also been hiding her own fear of growing old and dying behind her work. She also talked about some of the anger she had been directing toward people in government and in the general public who did not seem to get the seriousness of challenges the elderly faced or the personal suffering these challenges caused.

But what she said next surprised me even more. She said she was coming to see that her anger, in the end, wasn't a very effective tool and that she had to remember that her real job was to educate others about the challenges, explore solutions with them, and above all encourage their compassion. Finally, leaning in close with that glint in her eye, she told me that her anger had also been preventing her from admitting that she simply did not know how to deal with the reality that she was losing her ability to do things she had been able to do all of her life.

Later that night as part of a process that marks the beginning of the final phase of this training, I watched Molly celebrating with some of her younger compatriots. Her eyes were shining. Her smile was inviting. And in those moments, I saw right there beneath the lines and wrinkles that gave such character to her face, glimpses of the young woman she had once been. And I understood in a new way that when someone connects with their truth and passion, beauty never fades. Molly was 88 at the time.

Except for a brief good-bye I did not to talk to Molly at the end of the seminar; but when the brown manila envelope with the article arrived, I knew she was doing just fine. And while I cannot say that I thought a lot about her in the years that followed, occasionally an image of Molly would pop briefly into my mind and I would wonder how she was doing.

Of course, little did I know then that Sedena and I would one day be devoting our lives to the same work that Molly was doing. And today as Sedena and I look out upon the divisive and conflicted political landscape in America, as we listen to a public dialogue that continues to treat aging and death as if they were inconvenient alternatives rather than realities, as we listen to the foolish and the greedy advance so-called solutions that are more about profit and not nearly enough about compassion and heart, we find ourselves sometimes getting angry. Then that image of Molly's courage and commitment, and her honesty about her fears, comes into our minds. That and the realization that she was clearly way ahead of her time in recognizing the crisis our world would face as 50% of our population moves toward a time when they will be 50 or older for the first time in history.

So if you are experiencing any of these same concerns and awareness in these awkward times we hope Molly's story, her sparkle and her willingness to separate the chaff from the wheat, will help you as well. Yes, we hope that Molly's commitment will help you to stay in touch with your greater love and compassion and to live the life you were born to live.

The Whole Story

*"[Elders] are wisdomkeepers who have an ongoing
responsibility for maintaining society's well-being
and safeguarding the health of our ailing planet."*

~ Zalman Schachter-Shalomi & Ronald Miller ~

The Up Side

Few dispute that these are challenging times. Many, in fact, claim that the challenges we face are game-changers, and there is certainly mounting evidence to support some of these claims. These challenges, in turn, are being exacerbated by a confluence of political discord and by the growing ease with which some people with power and influence are willing to sacrifice truth in the interest of private political agendas and personal financial gain. As a result our progress in very critical areas is being delayed while a number of those to whom we look for leadership seem content to strut about in an increasingly tawdry carnival atmosphere that is, to quote the good Mr. Shakespeare, "full of sound and fury and signifying nothing."

At the same time, beneath this surface tumult, a remarkable and unstoppable bubbling up seems to be happening. New energy and new levels of awareness are being demonstrated in unexpected ways, and new levels of courage and activism are emerging from the hearts and minds of people in cities and towns all across the globe. This bubbling up is bringing with it unprecedented opportunities and extraordinary possibilities for people of all ages — and especially for the 150 million Americans and billions more throughout the world who are already in or will soon be joining the second-half-of-life crowd.

Yes, those of us who make up this over-50 crowd have at our disposal greater resources, more information and technological knowhow, better health options, and, for some, more leisure time than the generations before us. Some of us also have decades of direct experience in creating substantive social and political change. Through the human potential movement many also have a growing understanding of how our thoughts and intentions influence the shape of our lives. We also have available to us an almost endless array of positive life strategies distilled from spiritual and religious traditions around the world. And all of this experience and learning can help us achieve higher levels of individual and collective consciousness as well as greater effectiveness in pursuing our personal and shared goals.

In our lifetimes we have witnessed and been the beneficiaries of tremendous advances in science and technology, communications and transportation, and our knowledge of the physical universe — advances that would have astounded those who preceded us by only a few generations. We are also privileged to have witnessed and encouraged the birth of the environmental movement; the initial stages of world disarmament; and the coming of age of the civil rights, human rights, women's rights, gay rights, animal rights, and anti-war movements. Indeed, we are fortunate to be alive during a time that will, we believe, be viewed as the start of one of the more conscious and expansive periods in human history.

We have also been present as the boundaries of medicine have been advanced with so much success that the average human life span is now approaching 80 years of age and will soon, if we believe the predictions of some futurists, reach and exceed 100. Indeed, according to some studies, within the next several years more than 5 million people in the U.S. alone will be over 100 years of age (centenarians) for the first time in history.

We also have a broad new menu of alternative health and wellness practices available to us: new diets and exercises and an army of new types of healers and coaches to support us in implementing these and other practices into our daily lives. Within several hours we can reach many places on this planet, and in a few seconds with only a slight tap of a touch screen we can access more information about this planet, its species, and the universe at large than many of us thought possible just a few years ago.

Quite extraordinary, don't you think?

The Other Side of the Coin

On the other side of the coin, however, we face the challenges previously identified. And while these challenges impact the lives of everyone on this planet, the graying of our population — one person every seven seconds joins the 50-and-older crowd — is exacerbating them and presenting those of us who are GenXers, Boomers, and Elders with immediate threats.

Among these threats are those being advanced by people and groups that appear more committed to defending the frailty of an unbalanced economic model than in creating, articulating, and implementing truly effective strategies, policies, and methods that can better support the well-being and greater good of the majority. Their efforts include serious attempts to dismantle the social safety net by altering or eliminating Medicare and Medicaid and privatizing Social Security. And unfortunately for the majority of us, some of these attempts are gaining purchase in some quarters. If successful, the road ahead for older citizens around the world will be increasingly challenging indeed.

A number of us are also dealing with efforts to reduce our retirement and pension benefits, if not by those intent on advancing flawed theories of fiscal austerity then by organizations that seek to avoid responsibility for their past ineffectiveness by reorganizing under the protection of bankruptcy laws.

The cost of health insurance and of health care in the U.S. for individuals as well as those covered by group plans is going up dramatically. Workers' rights to collective bargaining, which have substantially eroded over the last several decades, are now under frontal assault; and proposals to increase the retirement age are being seriously considered. Even with the recent changes to the healthcare laws, the cost of healthcare and drugs in America is spiraling out of control with no realistic or achievable solutions in sight. And this is only a partial list of the challenges we who are 50 and older face.

While some of the blame for these challenges can, at least in part, be assigned to special interest groups, lobbyists, and the politicians and legislators whose votes have been purchased by them, the reality is that each and every one of us must take full personal accountability for these conditions.

During our time at the helm, although some of us have done our best to explore alternatives and others have tried mightily to bring greater light to the shadows, many of us have witnessed, contributed to, or allowed some of these less-than-laudable conditions and practices to come into being. For example, on our watch, many of the greatest advances in science and technology have also cast long shadows that threaten some of our most cherished values, raise more than just the specter of the loss of personal privacy and human rights, and create levels of toxicity that are turning many of our homes and our places of work into places of danger.

Along with their substantial benefits and breakthroughs our medical advances have increased our dependence on artificial drugs, further distanced us from our capacity to self-heal, and ushered in a time when we are often asked to choose between a plethora of detrimental side effects (some of which include death) and the illnesses these drugs have been created to address. In short, we are asked to choose a cure that is sometimes as bad or worse than the disease.

The technology we celebrate — while making our lives easier and dramatically increasing our ability to connect with each other — has also turned many of us into media voyeurs who too often experience life vicariously rather than directly and who, as a result, appear to be losing our ability to think for ourselves.

Although we have witnessed the growth of collaborative world bodies like the UN, we continue to allow our own and other governments to practice war as the habitual though futile response to dealing with our differences. And under the guise of nationalism we continue to allow a number of our elected officials and religious leaders to fuel the fires of bigotry and hatred both at home and abroad, fires that serve as the breeding ground for ignorance, violence, and terrorism.

And while progress is being made in support of some environmental initiatives, our efforts to reduce the impact of climate change are timid, at best, and almost always limited by the gospel of short-term economic need rather than guided by a genuine commitment to protect our habitat now and for future generations.

Finally, on our watch we have abdicated too much of the primary control of our society to others, especially to a new breed of philosophically biased legislators and judges, to a privately owned and biased media, and to a strange new entity called "the corporatocracy." With this abdication a subset of political and financial operatives now manipulate the public trust in the pursuit of self-serving religious and financial agendas. This abdication has, in turn, contributed to a number of practices that threaten the foundations on which this great experiment in democracy called America was founded.

The Tale of the Tape

Quite a picture, isn't it? Challenges and opportunities of historic proportions are tugging at us from seemingly opposite directions and threatening to spin our world off its axis. But what has all of this got to do with our "not going quietly" and with the goal of this book, which is to invite, inspire, and encourage those of us "who weren't born yesterday" to live more consciously and age wisely?

We believe it has everything to do with it. *Do Not Go Quietly* advances this primary premise:

Before we will be able to truly create and implement new solutions to our external challenges, those of us who make up this second-half-of-life crowd would be wise to first do some additional and essential inner work that will help us to continue to refresh and heal our minds, balance our bodies, and enliven our spirits.

And, in our opinion, this applies equally to those of who have already done a lot of inner work and to those who may have been more focused on the world at large. In our opinion, each of us can always raise the level of our game and demonstrate greater consciousness, and in this way live more successful and joyful individual lives. We will also contribute more constructively to the road ahead for those who come after us.

In short, if we agree that our time at the helm is not over and that our job is not done, if we remain committed to continuing our quest to uncover and demonstrate what makes us even more authentic and unique, if we get out of our heads and into our hearts or at the very least give both of these intelligence centers equal attention, then we believe we stand a really good chance of becoming even more responsible human beings and more effective citizens of this nation and of the world.

Otherwise we run the risk of living out our lives in increasingly smaller circles of influence and at the mercy of those who appear to have lost touch with their compassion and who, in their haste for personal gain, seek to acquire more than their fair share. Or worse yet, from a place of personal imbalance and disharmony, we ourselves will visit or allow others to visit upon the world and future generations more of the wounding, pain, and suffering that has marked much of the past.

We also believe that another essential step those of us "who weren't born yesterday" can take is to initiate a more effective dialogue with younger generations. Yes, we believe part of our responsibility is to build better bridges of understanding with young people, bridges that will allow us to be more receptive to their unique gifts, understandings, and contributions and that will invite them to be more open to the fruits of our experience.

The Next True Frontier

This commitment to more conscious living and wise aging is, in our opinion, the next true and great frontier. It is also the best and highest use of our time and energy.

Unfortunately, from our perspective, it is this step that a lot of us have avoided committing to as deeply as we could have in the past — with results that are clear. But if we make this commitment to put our own individual houses in order first; if we agree that this is not an intellectual exercise, not a question of theory and concept, but instead a matter of acknowledging and following the wisdom of our hearts as well as our heads; if we focus on bringing greater love and meaning back into our lives, then our ability to influence and impact the world house can, at last, move beyond repetitive half measures and missteps, beyond the disassociated acting out and visiting of our individual frailties on the world at large. In short, if we continuously explore and demonstrate our willingness to be better at being human we can, as poet Mark Nepo has so eloquently said, "unlearn our way back to God."

While this commitment to lead a more conscious life can and, we certainly hope, will become the goal of every being no matter what their age, we believe it is a particularly important goal for those of us who may have more years behind us than we do ahead of us.

The Hands of Time

As an added encouragement to those of us who fall within these age groups, we ask you to remember one unalterable fact — that each of us is only here on this Earth for a limited period of time. So please do not take the time you have remaining for granted. Consider one question a lot more often and with much greater awareness. This question is a paraphrase of one that the poet Mary Oliver often asks:

What am I doing of genuine value with these relatively
few and precious moments called my life?

While this question is critical at every phase of life, it seems especially significant for those of us who have lived long enough, failed and been victorious often enough, to have at least glimpsed the difference between what matters and what does not.

We know this is not an easy question and that depending on the stage and circumstances of your life your answers will vary. But in our experience, when each of us commits to improving our individual skills and bringing our mind, body, emotions, and spirit into greater harmony, the larger changes that so many of us want to see occur in our world will become truly possible.

Indeed, from our perspective among the remarkable opportunities those of us in the second half of life have, as Alice Walker so beautifully reminds us, is "to reclaim our right relationship to the world."

When framed in this context, this appears to be the only sane choice any of us can make. But the fact that this choice is sane in no way guarantees that we will make it. And this, in large part, is why we have written this book and why we ask ourselves and you to "not go quietly"!

Life Rule
"To harvest our lives successfully we must come to terms with our mortality."
~ Zalman Schachter-Shalomi

Life Achievement
Carl Jung, one of the fathers of modern psychology, completed his book *Memories, Dreams, Reflections* in his 80s.

Life Tool
Questions are like lights we can shine on our beliefs and practices that are habitual and perhaps limiting. "Questions," as Clarissa Pinkola Estes said, "are the central keys to transformation. Questions are the keys that cause the secret doors of the psyche to swing open." So what are the questions that can make today new and more alive for you? What are the questions that can help you to hear the wisdom of your heart?

These Awkward Times

"If we always do what we have always done,
we will always get what we have always gotten."

~ Anonymous ~

These Awkward Times

Joseph Campbell, noted mythologist and author, said, "Opportunities to find deeper powers within ourselves come when life seems most challenging. So I choose faith over fear!"

Well, as many of us agree, we are certainly living in a "most challenging time" — especially as a result of the giant demographic wave that is coming. These statistics bear repeating: In the United States alone one person every seven seconds joins the second-half-of-life crowd. Every day 10,000 Boomers retire. Every 72 seconds someone is diagnosed with early onset Alzheimer's.

As a result of the latest financial implosion, only 1 out of every 8 or 9 Americans who are old enough to retire have enough money to live out their remaining years in dignity. And as if this information alone is not enough to astound, the average American spends between 70% and 90% of all of the money they spend during their entire lifetime on healthcare in the last year of their lives.

Our current world economic condition is also being made worse by those who deny the wisdom of John Maynard Keynes, the man who advanced the premise that economic recessions/depressions are best weathered through a combination of fiscal responsibility and incentive spending. Instead, they appear intent on hurtling full speed down the path of only making draconian budget cuts — a path that has failed over and over again to produce viable solutions to economic challenges.

Add in a few other facts — people are living longer and fewer children are being born in many of the world's developed countries with the result that we have a shrinking tax base and fewer public dollars to support the commons — and one begins to better understand the scope of our dilemma. So when we say this demographic shift will impact many aspects of life we are not exaggerating.

It will alter:

- ⊛ Our ability to support the commons.
- ⊛ The kind of healthcare and medical services we require.
- ⊛ The size and type of the organizations needed to deliver these services.
- ⊛ The way we pay for them.
- ⊛ The way we design and make thousands of everyday products.
- ⊛ The kind of public buildings we construct.
- ⊛ The forms of transportation we require.
- ⊛ The kinds of private residences and communities we design and build.
- ⊛ The number of people who will require life-care services.
- ⊛ The number and types of life-care workers we will need.
- ⊛ The kind of training they require.
- ⊛ The kind of life-care communities we build and how we operate them.

The demographic revolution will also significantly change our definition of "the commons," put a substantial strain on our financial system, require new levels of "compassionate" technology, and alter the type of public services we will need to deliver. It will require that we reevaluate the kinds of foods we eat, the type of exercise we do, the way we organize our lives, the way we plan for the future, and many of our priorities and core values. In short, it will change the way we structure our society and, ultimately, if we are wise, the way we redefine the purpose of life.

Surf or Sink

So, "there's a wave a comin'," a rip-roaring mother of a demographic wave and unfortunately, as we've already said, most of us are unprepared for it. In fact, not only are we unprepared, the majority of us are living out our daily lives as if the lives we have known up until now will continue indefinitely. And while all of this is happening, far too many of our leaders, following in the tradition of another great republic, appear to be more committed to fiddling than to addressing the fact that Rome is at risk of burning.

As a result of our growing awareness of these realities — and because, as card-carrying members of this second-half-of-life crowd we will be among those most immediately affected by this inattention and denial — we have decided we can no longer stand on the sidelines. Instead we are getting back onto the field where we can do something about this situation.

For us "doing something" involves first putting our own houses in order. It also involves remembering to exercise the enormous power that those of us in the second half of life have — financial and electoral voting power to influence the kinds of companies that exist, the kinds of products and services they deliver, the kind of political office holders who are elected, and the priorities we address and the power to use our experience to help inform and engage those in younger generations in a new kind of dialogue. And above all it involves our remembering that genuine power, the power that can make a positive difference going forward — in fact the only power that everyone has is the Power of One — the power each of us as individuals has to continue doing the important and essential work of separating the chaff from the wheat and then having the wit and the courage to act on what we discover.

If we are to exercise this precious power we hold with greater consciousness and greater clarity, we must take our cue from Joseph Campbell and "choose faith over fear" and awareness over denial. We must also not be dissuaded from this path by the transitory events that occur around us. And above all, we must also be wise enough to always seek to live our lives more authentically — especially in regard to committing more deeply to the development of the spiritual side of our lives.

And while we cannot claim that our individual search has given us all of the answers, at the very least it has shown us some possible paths we can follow to stay more awake and become more responsible for our own lives. These paths include:

⊛ Admitting what we do not know and do not yet understand.

⊛ Being willing to experiment with mind-expanding and heart-opening life strategies.

⊛ Reaching out to others who are faced with these same challenges so that we may find ways to better cooperate and collaborate in discovering and implementing solutions.

In fact, we believe that only by working together in these ways can we learn how to turn the "wave" that is coming toward us from one that threatens to engulf us all to one we can learn to accept and perhaps even surf with greater presence and effectiveness. Since the tide is clearly turning in our favor — at least in terms of numbers — let's find ways to use the power of numbers to advance a more humanistic social agenda.

More than Enough Justification

From our perspective, these objectives alone justify our writing this book, but we have also been motivated by compelling, personal reasons. Starting in the late 1990s and continuing into the first years of this century, we found ourselves facing the challenge of helping to care for our parents as they entered the final stages of their lives. In short, we found ourselves moving from being the children of our parents to being more and more responsible for their well-being.

It was during this time that we were surprised and stunned to discover the limitations in our healthcare and life-care systems — limitations that our own good health and relative youth had prevented us from experiencing directly. These experiences and the resulting emotional turmoil they caused also caught us by surprise because until that time we were willing members of the Great Army of the Youth Obsessed and Age Averse.

Suddenly we found ourselves having to deal with a confusing series of government regulations and insurance industry double talk. Suddenly we found ourselves facing the difficulties of finding and ensuring quality private care for our parents in their own home. We were also shocked by the lack of an available blueprint to guide us in our efforts to support and care for our parents and by the enormous costs associated with paying for this care. In short, we discovered that even in this age awash in information and advanced technology, most of us — whether as caregivers or those involved in our own end-of-life journey — often find ourselves struggling to make sense out of things and discovering that there are often few acceptable, affordable, and humane options.

In making this later stage of the life journey with our parents we did, however, thankfully encounter a small army of remarkable, talented, generous, and committed individuals who spend their lives in the service of others. Indeed, were it not for their courage and kindness, their willingness to do the right thing even when they often had to defy or circumvent the rules of the systems they worked within, we and our parents would have been lost. Without these good and caring souls we believe our society as a whole would be in much greater trouble than it is. Life-care nurses, doctors, counselors, spiritual guides, volunteers, hospice workers, and so many others — what a dedicated army they are!

Despite this support, however, we often found ourselves deeply troubled. And this experience was very visceral — not intellectual. It kept us up at night wondering and worrying over what to do. It brought up levels of sadness, confusion, and despair we had not previously encountered.

The people at the center of this drama were, after all, not just two elderly couples whom we were witnessing from afar. We were dealing with our mothers and fathers, the people who had given us entry into life, who held us, nurtured us, protected us, and aided us in finding our way in the world. These were the people who cared for us through sicknesses and our early stumbles. They were the ones who cheered for us in our victories and did whatever they could to be certain that our lives would have more opportunities and greater scope than their own.

So to arrive at a point in our lives where we felt we could not do as much for them as we knew in our hearts that they had done for us was more than disturbing. When the challenge of keeping them comfortable and safe and providing them with appropriate care in their own homes became not only physically challenging but cost-prohibitive, it was also very hard to accept. To discover that even when this cost could be met, there was a scarcity of quality private caregivers was even more discouraging. And even when such people could be found, to learn they could not provide our parents with the kind and range of care they eventually required was also very unsettling.

Then, of course, there was that troubling search for a nursing home that was, if not perfect, at least qualified, safe, clean, and competent. In the process we experienced that terrible sense of sadness and guilt when we and our families had to leave these kind and gracious and increasingly more helpless souls who had cared for us in the care of strangers. This was something for which no one or perhaps nothing could have prepared us. Indeed, to walk away after visits that never felt long enough or frequent enough and yet, in all honesty, were always challenging and difficult, only added to our guilt and sadness.

And this is just part of the story — the end-of-life story that more and more of us who are now in the second half of life are finding ourselves passing through either with our parents and older relatives or with ourselves.

These are some of the reasons this subject of conscious living and wise aging got our attention. But this is not just a personal story. It is, we believe, a larger one that exposes who we are and where we are going as a nation and as a world at large. This is also a story that will, if we do not do something to change it, become a tragedy of unprecedented proportions. And many of us will find ourselves at the center of it. Indeed, it will be a story that we and those who come after us will look back upon and find as unacceptable as it is unconscionable, especially for a nation that was birthed out of the promise of freedom, justice, and equality for all.

We realize that some of us may still be in denial. "Can't be!" you say. "Not in America, not in this land of opportunity! We will make it better!" Those of us who are in particularly good health and financially comfortable may have a different mindset. "Not us. That will not happen to us!" And in truth, were it not for our personal experience, were it not for our study of emerging trends and demographic, were it not for the conversations and meetings we have had with a number of national and international leaders and experts — we might be saying the same thing.

Finally, were it not for ill-advised actions many of the world's governments are taking in proposing those draconian cuts in spending on social services without raising the substantial revenues needed to sustain a compassionate and appropriate commons, we would probably still hold some of the same beliefs.

But in the face of these and other realties we know that unless we raise our individual consciousness and change some of our beliefs about aging and dying there will be very challenging times ahead. Unless we begin to act more compassionately toward elders, and unless our governments, our institutions, our businesses, and we as citizens get to work now, it is not just likely but inevitable that a large majority of us will find ourselves facing an endgame in which the norm will be medical warehouses understaffed by overworked caregivers struggle under the burden of delivering services at greater and greater costs that fewer and fewer of us can afford.

From the Personal to the Societal

As a result we believe that those of us who are older GenXers, Boomers, and Elders are the ones — perhaps the only ones — who have enough motivation to actually do something about the challenging conditions that exist in our society.

Why are we "the ones"? As we pointed out earlier, we are either already experiencing or are next in line for the scenarios discussed above. We were also born before the dawn of the digital age and therefore know that many of the overamped, excessively medicated, digitally preoccupied, entertainment addicted, economically driven, and relatively unconscious practices that constitute life in the modern world are not our only choices. Many of us remember a time when we utilized our time and invested our energies differently.

We remember when life was more about seeking connection and not about creating division; more about meaning and purpose and less about making a profit; more about caring and courage and less about fear; more about honor and less about being right; more about building a future and less about hiding from an unacceptable, terrorized present. We remember a time when the nuclear family still existed and when grandparents and older relatives were cared for primarily by family members. We also remember when public office was more about governance than about political positioning, more about finding solutions and less about gaining advantage.

Of course it is true that the world we remember was simpler and slower. Families tended to remain in the geography of their birth. Income was generated primarily by one breadwinner so there was at least one individual in the family who could act as the caregiver to elder parents and to other members of the extended family. In fact, it was considered natural to care for these individuals in this way.

Our world has changed and we cannot simply snap our fingers and reverse time, nor do we wish to. Those of us who still remember what this other world looked and felt like, however, have the opportunity to ensure that the "brave new world" we are entering will still offer genuine opportunity, as well as sufficient care and compassion, for all members of our human family and especially for our elders. This care and compassion may have to be delivered differently and by a predominance of non-family members. But it cannot and should not be less loving and humane, nor offer less dignity.

We Are Not Broken

No matter how passionate we are about encouraging change, or how critical we are of our current political process and the failure of many of our institutions to address these challenges; and no matter how outspoken we are about the need to reevaluate some of our fundamental values and how impatient we are to create a more sane and sustainable way of life, we also want to be clear that we do not believe we are broken or that the world situation is hopeless.

Asleep and unconscious may be two adjectives that apply to a lot of us. In jeopardy and off-course are two phrases that apply to some of our governments, institutions, and businesses. Still, we remain hopeful that as a gloriously complex, courageous, and talented species, we can still wake up in time and smell the roses. There is still hope that we will remember that although we are responsible for the things we have done or failed to do, there is still time to make our individual choices more conscious, our society more compassionate, and our world a better place in which to live.

So we close this chapter with a few questions by M.C. Richards and hope that more and more of us will soon be willing and able to answer them in the affirmative:

Am I willing to give up what I have in order to be what I am not yet? Am I willing to let my ideas of myself, of man, be changed? Am I able to follow the spirit of love into the desert? To empty myself even of my concept of emptiness?

Life Rule
"Life is a school. Every experience and encounter offers us a gift and a tailor-made opportunity to discover exactly what we need and precisely what we are here to learn for the next step of our journey."

~ Sedena Cappannelli

Life Achievement
Morihei Ueshiba, the founder of Aikido, was still evolving his practice as a martial artist in his 70s.

Life Tool
Since this day will never come again, we invite you to let two simple questions guide you as you go through your day. Try asking yourself:

- Am I spending this moment wisely?

- What other choices can I make that will enhance the quality of my life and contribute to the lives of others today — most especially the lives of my older relatives and friends?

Lifestyle Revolution

"We are members of a vast, cosmic audience
in which each living instrument
is essential to the complementary
and harmonious playing of the whole."

~ J. Allen Boone ~

The Brave New World

One of the most daunting and yet exciting aspects of this dawning demographic revolution is that the world ahead — especially for those of us who are in the second half of life — will be not just incrementally but radically different from the world into which we were born, matured, had families, and participated in careers from which unprecedented numbers of us are now retiring — by choice or forced by circumstance.

Kelly Greene, former staff reporter for *The Wall Street Journal,* once described aspects of this new world in this way. "Cell phones that monitor your body temperature and sleep patterns. Cruise ships that take the place of retirement communities. 'Brain gyms' where you sharpen your wits with computer games. Video autobiographies and interactive cemeteries. The baby boom is about to enter its golden years — and getting older will never be the same." And this is only the beginning.

What are others saying about this "brave new world"? Some futurists suggest that over the next several decades, longevity will increase to a possible average age of 120. Some claim our profit-based healthcare system, the only remaining holdout in the entire industrial world, will implode under the weight of increasing numbers and skyrocketing costs. Other futurists predict that the majority of public services will shift to the private sector and experience significant reductions in quality and much higher costs — especially for the shrinking middle class, the elderly, and the poor. Meals in a pill and other artificial forms of nutrition may become commonplace. Office space may become obsolete. Fully computerized and automated forms of transportation, homes, and commercial buildings will be standard.

Others suggest that new forms of cooperative residential communities will become commonplace and that a united global economy will be the only sensible choice. Robotic communities where manufacturing and other forms of work are performed by robots only, time travel, space communities, telepathy, bubble cities, underwater cities, and much more are all projected as a part of our landscape. And these extraordinary changes, as farfetched as they may seem at this moment, will only be the beginning.

As if these predictions are not already enough to boggle the mind, it is becoming more and more apparent that no matter what governments or political parties say, we cannot wish our individual or collective problems away nor can we look for solutions from the private sector alone. Indeed, as the graying of the world's population becomes a reality it will become increasingly clear to everyone that we ignore these challenges only at our own peril.

The Part We Can Play

In the face of these and other changes and challenges, we believe those of us in the second-half-of-life crowd will, out of necessity, need to become even more engaged in influencing the course our world takes. Indeed, as we said earlier, older GenXers, Boomers, and Elders may be the only ones who can actually turn the ship of state in a saner and more meaningful direction.

In the U.S., Boomers alone earn approximately $2 trillion annually. Boomers and Elders control a very significant percentage of this nation's financial assets and have almost $2 billion in annual spending power.

Those of us in the second half of life also spend about three times more per capita in discretionary dollars than any other segment of the population. We spend about $80 billion on health insurance and purchase more than 62% of all new cars. We purchase about one-third of all apparel and almost half of all personal care products, and we account for over two-thirds of the $850 billion spent annually on leisure travel and $170 billion in healthcare spending. In short, we are the wealthiest and among the most educated population segments, and over the next few decades we will oversee the largest transfer of wealth in the history of the world.

Astounding numbers! Astounding implications! Yes, the bottom line is that those of us who belong to this second-half-of-life crowd have the power to make a real difference, but only if we commit to put our own houses in order and to exercise our power by voting with our attention and our dollars as well as with our political ballots. Indeed, in addition to supporting more conscious, credible political candidates, we must support more conscious companies and products, those that contribute to our well-being instead of just to their own profit margins. After all, without our attention and resources, these political candidates, companies, banks and brokerage houses, and media organizations will be gasping for breath.

Something else we need to stop doing is waiting for our politicians, our government, our institutions, and businesses to do what needs to be done for us. And what exactly is that? We believe GenXers, Boomers, and Elders need to initiate another lifestyle revolution, one that echoes and continues what we started 50 years ago and one in which each of us reclaims our sovereignty, redefines our priorities, redirects our resources, honors our own wisdom and experience, and contributes our significant array of gifts and talents to our own well-being and that of society as a whole. To do this we will, of course, have to set aside our obsession with youth and reclaim our rightful place as elders (keepers and transmitters of wisdom).

The Right Trajectory

As contemporary writer and spiritual teacher Eckhart Tolle indicates in his book, *The New Earth,* if each individual life is a microcosmic model of the universe then it must hold that the same rules that apply to the life cycle of the universe apply in our individual lives as well. So if the universe, which is estimated to have begun around 15 billion years ago, has a cycle that includes an outward thrust and expansion and then an eventual inward direction and return, it must follow that our individual lives also go through a cycle in which a first half of life is outer directed and the second half more inner focused.

Please pause and consider the implications of this statement. First half — primarily outer directed. Second half — more inner focused. Indeed, if we pay attention to this natural cycle then it follows that what we do and value and the strategies we employ in the second half of life need to be different from those we practiced in the first half of our lives. This, we believe, can become an important yardstick we can use to evaluate our needs and revolutionize our lives going forward.

Life Rule

"The secret to living a successful life lies in the practice and mastery of the basics."

~ Anonymous

Life Achievements

Dame Judi Dench, one of the world's most acclaimed actresses, is in her 70s as of this writing and continues to astound and delight audiences around the world.

Life Tool

Like a great dancer, learn more about balance so that you can live life more fully and joyfully. Ask yourself: "Is my life in balance or out of balance?" If your answer is "out of balance," you might want to identify specific aspects of your life — physical, emotional, intellectual, or spiritual, in your career, your relationships, or in the pursuit of your personal dream — where you may be out of balance. Then identify at least one thing you can do in each of these areas to regain and maintain your balance.

Do Not Go Quietly

"What we reach for may be different
but what makes us reach is the same."

~ Mark Nepo ~

An Invitation to Conscious Living and Wise Aging

The title of this book and this chapter take their inspiration in part from Dylan Thomas's well-loved poem, "Do Not Go Gentle into that Good Night." The opening stanza of his poem reads:

Do not go gentle into that good night,
Old age should burn and rave at close of day;
Rage, rage against the dying of the light.

"Old age should burn and rave at close of day." What a line! What a powerful and essential message for this time of demographic revolution. Indeed, as part of our efforts to better prepare for the tumultuous and remarkable time ahead, we invite you to consider this raving and raging from a different perspective. We know that Dylan Thomas, as artists often do, used this poem to express his anger and regret over his father's diminishing capacities, limited resources, and unfulfilled promises as well as some of his own unfinished dreams.

These experiences are, of course, things that all of us encounter some of the time and some of us encounter a lot of the time during the second half of life. However, rather than be saddened or troubled by Thomas's words, we believe we can instead use his lines as a reminder to take full advantage of the time remaining in our lives to do what our hearts know will allow us to complete our journey with greater dignity, originality, and honor.

Instead of regret, we think these lines can help us to remember to let our passion burn and lead us into the deeper inquiry into why we are here and what we still have left to discover. We especially believe they can help us to honor and celebrate all of the stages of life, even and particularly the last. For without this honoring, we believe we run the risk of arriving at the end of our journey having missed important opportunities and essential lessons that contribute to life's meaning.

Instead of letting Dylan Thomas's words trouble us, let them stimulate the awareness that there are unique and valuable gifts that each of us have to give and receive in each of life's stages and that we should not treat these gifts lightly or be dissuaded from their expression. Yes, we believe these powerful words can serve all of us who are willing to listen and courageous enough to hear.

As we take our next steps on this journey of learning to live more conscious and meaningful lives, the lives we were born to live, let us remember to be true to our dreams, learn from our stumbles, and celebrate our breakthroughs. In the process, let us each reaffirm our commitment to a deeper level of healing for ourselves, for those we love, and for those who will come after us so that they will be blessed by the gifts we leave behind!

Let us make a collective declaration of faith and hope that each of us who is part of this second-half-of-life army — which will eventually number 150 million Americans and billions more around the planet — will not fade meekly and invisibly into the background. Instead we will do what is possible to ensure a legitimate legacy of promise and not one of regret.

Let us be encouraged to step more fully into our daily lives, not in anger or frustration with a system that is badly in need of repair or with those who labor under the illusion that they are in charge, but with genuine compassion for ourselves and for those who, in so many ways, have lost their compass.

Let us remember that none of us can afford to fritter away the time we have remaining — whether that is years or decades — on some of the inconsequential pursuits our society promotes as appropriate for those of us who are or should be, at least in society's opinion, retired. Instead we invite all of us to ask what exactly we are being asked to retire from. From life? From the continued pursuit of our dreams? From the constructive use of our experience and talents? From the deepening and unfolding of our spiritual promise? Or are we being asked to retire from the things we still have time to make right so that we can complete the promise we made long before we began this life's dance?

Of course, many people are being forced to work longer and many must now find employment at lower-paying jobs. In the corporate sector more and more people who are 50 and older are being laid off and forced out. In many instances what used to be called a "buy-out" is no longer even being offered. Now people are being "right-sized," "down-sized" and in truth, simply discarded.

But as pained as the feelings behind Dylan Thomas's words may be, let them not discourage us or make us afraid of the time ahead. Instead, let them prompt us to open our hearts and pay attention to the wisdom that has been transmitted to us by humanity's wisest teachers — the very wisdom that is available to each of us when we listen to that "still small voice" within.

May we remember our rights and especially our responsibility to leave the world better than the one we inherited. May we remember our accomplishments and those made by others who have been way-showers — like Rachel Carson, Dwight David Eisenhower, Martin Luther King, John F. and Bobby Kennedy, Gloria Steinem, Rosa Parks, Cesar Chavez, Nelson Mandela, and Bishop Desmond Tutu. May we also remember some of our troubadours — Bob Dylan, Janis Joplin, Joan Baez, The Beatles, and so many more.

May we remember the discoveries of mind-expanding drugs, the energy and spirit of rallies and peace marches, of heart-opening encounters, of sit-ins, protests, and civic engagement. Remember that during our lives we have witnessed and contributed to the birth of a popular movement toward higher consciousness, a movement that has placed at our fingertips wisdom and tools from many ancient cultures as well as a number of great spiritual teachers who can help us reach higher individual and collective levels of consciousness marked by greater sanity, balance, and compassion.

Yes, may we remember to model a new vitality, a new form of transparency and honesty, one that does not look to physical accomplishments alone as the measure of our success, but instead to the quality and character of our being and to the amount of compassion and consciousness we express in our every interaction. We hope these finer qualities will help us to remember that it is not our material possessions or our financial wealth that matters most, but the wealth of our experience that we share each day in our many small encounters with each other. And may each of these encounters help us to remember the gift that life is. Let them also invite us to turn inward where we not only come to better know ourselves and discover more of our truth, but where we can remember the unique note that each of us is born to sing in the great song that is life.

For those who are still in the first half of life (39 and younger), we hope this poet's words move you to look beyond your sometimes easy acceptance of and preoccupation with the technological fads and transient social furies of the day. Instead, let them motivate you to seek a fuller understanding of your connection to history — to its frailties and follies as well as its victories — so that you can better prepare for the challenging future that lies ahead. Let them also prompt you to encourage those of us who are older to do the work for which the second half of life is intended so that they can make your path ahead a little clearer.

So young and old, we encourage an agreement — as individuals and as members of this collective called humanity — to let joy be our guide and to participate in the future more gracefully, presently, and compassionately than we have in the past. And in doing so, let us remember that to be successful in this effort we would be wise to be guided at least as much by our hearts as by our heads and to turn the spotlight of our attention first upon ourselves so that we can better align our thoughts, words, and actions with our higher principles. We would be wise to apply the balm of understanding and forgiveness to the wounds we may be carrying from the past and that we may still be inflicting upon others and on our habitat for it is these unhealed wounds that distort our vision and limit our ability to manifest our dreams.

In short, may we be inspired to write a new, more appropriate, and valuable third act for our own lives, one that can lead to a more sane and sustainable future for all.

Easier than We Imagine

While this may seem to be a lot to ask, we sincerely hope that it is not. Instead we hope that we will all have the willingness and the courage to reconnect with the love we have for ourselves, for all other life forms, and for this planet that is our home. Yes, let us remember that taking this path toward more conscious living and wise aging is what we were all born to do and that if we do it with integrity and honesty, years from now those who come after us will look back on this moment in human history and will be able to say that when we were called — we answered.

Life Rule
"Young, old, just words."

~ George Burns

Life Achievement
Jeanne-Louise Calment lived 122 years and 164 days. She lived longer than any other person thus far documented. Jeanne was still riding her bicycle at 100 years of age.

Life Tool
There is one rule we value above many others, "To thine own self be true." So please consider ways in which you can be more true to yourself today. What can you do to express more of what is distinct, authentic, and original within you so that you can contribute to making your own life — and the lives of those around you — more joyful, engaging, and rewarding today?

PART TWO
Concepts, Questions &
Encouragements
for the Road Ahead

"How can you follow the course of your life
if you do not let it flow."

~ Lao-Tzu ~

The Portrait Artist

Sidney's Story

Sidney Mersky was forced to leave home when he was 11 years old. His parents — afraid he would be conscripted into the Russian army and too poor to bribe local officials — could not offer him an alternative. So they sent him away with a small bundle of possessions draped over his shoulder.

When Sidney first told me this story I thought it was pretty harsh treatment for an 11-year-old boy, but he assured me that it was not as bad as the treatment he and his family feared he would receive if he was forced to fight for the Red Army during the Russian Revolution.

Life on the road for an 11-year-old boy was, of course, extremely difficult, especially for someone who had never before been away from the protection of his family. Following the instructions of his father, however, he generally travelled at night and hid during the day. As a result Sidney was hungry a lot of the time. Occasionally he earned a little food in trade for some work, but since he was small for manual labor, he was often forced to take what he needed to survive.

His size, however, proved to be an advantage. Lacking the strength for larger tasks, he had to find other ways to survive, and so Sidney relied on his talent for drawing. Although it had been treated as an indulgence by his family, which needed him to perform tasks to help them survive, his skill with a pencil actually made it possible for him to earn a little money. In fact, he would make little sketches of people he met along the way and this, in turn, would sometimes lead to longer stays. It also led to the opportunity to paint other things — signs, for example.

Eventually, against remarkable odds, Sidney made his way across Russia, into Europe, and eventually to the United States. And all along the way he drew, sketched, and painted. Without any formal study of the theories of light, texture, and volume, Sidney used the landscapes, buildings, and the remarkable array of faces and forms that surrounded him as his classroom.

As a result, by the time he arrived in America, Sidney had managed to become a reasonably accomplished artist.

During his early years in America he continued to earn his keep doing odd jobs and manual labor, but he always had his sketchbook handy and whenever the opportunity arose he drew. In addition to pencil, pen, and ink, he also became proficient with Conté crayons and charcoal. He learned to etch and to make prints, and began to paint with watercolors as well as oils. He even tried his hand at sculpting. It was during this period Sidney came to understand that if he wanted to survive, especially as an artist, he needed to learn to express his skill in as many different art forms as possible.

This was one of the first things Sidney told me when I met him in the lobby of The Art Students League on West 57th Street in New York in 1979. I was there to enroll in my first formal drawing class and Sidney was there awaiting the start of what at the time was called The Members Life Drawing Class.

We were sitting beside one another on one of the wooden benches in the lobby. His thinning white hair was parted in the center and combed neatly to both sides. His frameless glasses accented intelligent eyes that had more than a glint of humor in them. He had on a pair of old but pressed pants and a blue dress shirt. Sidney was a small man, just a little over five feet tall. In fact, sitting there on that bench his feet did not even rest on the floor.

What was the first of many conversations to come began when he asked me what I did. I told him I was a sculptor. "Are you any good?" he wanted to know. I looked at him trying to decide if he was serious. I mean no one had ever asked me anything quite as directly. From the look on Sidney's face it was clear that he was very serious so I told him I was relatively new to sculpting but believed I had a gift for it. He nodded, apparently satisfied with my answer. He then told me about his belief that an artist needed to experiment with and master many mediums. That moment, that question, and his comments were the beginning of our friendship.

From that day on we fell into the habit of saying hello whenever we met at the League. One day he told me that if I paid a relatively modest fee, I could become a member and join him for the free drawing class that was held every afternoon at 4:30. Hungry for every chance I could get to draw, I paid my fee, and that afternoon and every weekday afternoon after that I joined him in one of the studios where the members of The Art Students League would gather for life drawing.

I was just beginning to learn to draw so I felt awkward and clumsy, especially during the shorter one- and five-minute poses. By comparison, with just a few strokes Sidney could capture the essence of the pose and especially the unique qualities of the various models. Indeed, although Sidney's hand shook and his eyesight was failing him, his mastery of the medium was astounding. As a result there were a number of occasions when I wanted to get up and walk away, but Sidney, sensing this, would shake his head and smile. In these moments I would put down my own pencil and sit there beside him in quiet awe of this old man whose hands, although limited by age, exhibited magic with pencil, charcoal, and Conté crayon. Eventually, after weeks of sitting beside him, just a little bit of his magic began to rub off and my drawings began to have a little more life and energy.

One afternoon after drawing class, Sidney invited me to his apartment. He lived alone, his wife having died eight years earlier. From the way he talked about her, it was clear she was never far from his thoughts.

The walls of his apartment were filled with portraits he had done over the years. One of them was a portrait of his beloved wife, but there were many others of people I recognized. That was when I learned that Sidney had, at one time, been one of New York's most sought-after portrait artists.

After a while he asked me to help him drag two large cardboard boxes out of a nearby closet and then proceeded to show me a collection of notebooks containing drawings and sketches he had done over the years. The covers of many of the notebooks were worn and stained and some of the bindings had been reinforced by tape, but the contents were amazing. One of the boxes contained a collection of notebooks in which he had recorded images from memory of his childhood in Russia and his odyssey across Europe and the Atlantic. The work in pen and then later in watercolor was remarkable. As I flipped carefully through them he told me stories about the places he had traveled and about a world that had changed so very much over the course of his life.

Sidney was 92 when I met him. We were daily companions until I moved to Los Angeles two years later. Sidney was the grandfather of the novelist and poet Erica Jong, author of <u>Fear of Flying</u> and other well-received works. I will never forget him — not just because of his skill as an artist, but because of the courage, commitment, and passion that continued to motivate him in the final years of his life, and which still inspires me.

The Ruts of Ordinary Perception

"To be shaken out of the ruts of ordinary perception,
to be shown for a few timeless hours the outer and inner worlds,
not as they appear to [one] obsessed with words and notions,
but as they are apprehended, directly and unconditionally,
by [our souls] — this is an experience of inestimable value."

~ Aldous Huxley ~

Time & Perception

"To be shaken out of the ruts of ordinary perception..." Is it possible? Aldous Huxley clearly thought it was. So have other pioneers and adventurers who have experimented with the boundaries of human consciousness by using mind-altering drugs, breathing techniques, meditation, fasting, and even just the power of undiluted observation. Do you think it is possible? As we begin this next stage of our journey toward more conscious living and wise aging, we invite you to step out of the boundaries formed by some of your current beliefs and practices. We invite you to take a few days, just a few out of a whole lifetime of days, to experiment with some thoughts, beliefs, and behaviors that can help you make the rest of your life the best, most precious, and valuable time of your life.

It has been said that our perception of life changes with each passing year. That time closes old doors and opens new ones. So in this time together we invite you to open new doors and embrace the changes that are a natural part of your life. We also invite you to do your best to honor whatever stage of life you are now in, whether young or old, by looking at your life — past, present, and future — with new eyes. In this way we know you can make sense of your experience, master some of the life lessons that are still unlearned, and apply the wisdom you gain to the time ahead so that it can be filled with greater joy and touched by mystery and grace.

New Challenges in the Game of Life

As we have said, those of us who are in the second half of life — and please remember this group includes everyone who is 40 and older — are challenged as few generations before us. Our world is moving at such an enormous speed and with what sometimes seems like a reckless disregard for the consequences of our actions. So even though it does not always recognize or willingly acknowledge it, our world today needs the experience and wisdom that we who are elders and elders-in-training can offer. Yes, this wisdom drawn from the victories and failures of our lives when combined with the innocence and energy of youth can bring enormous strength and nurturing to our world today. Indeed, as author Marianne Williamson reminds us, "The light at the center of things is who we are. And our mission in life is to uncover this light."

So we invite you to begin this next stage by "moving outside the ruts of ordinary perceptions," or if this is already a part of your practice, by turning the heat up on this process. How do you do this? By experimenting with the beliefs that you hold. For your beliefs determine the boundaries of your life.

Napoleon Hill, author of *Think and Grow Rich* said, "Whatever the mind can conceive of and believe in it can achieve." Valuable guidance. Indeed, on the upside this statement offers genuine insight and an important clue as to how we can experience a more creative, satisfying, and successful life. On the downside, this same statement contains a caution that our beliefs are very powerful and can as easily confine us in a limited world as they can free us to explore new horizons.

Henry Ford said it differently. He said, "Whether you believe you can or you can't, you're right." And Marcel Proust, the great French writer, said, "The real journey of discovery is not in visiting new landscapes, but in having new eyes."

Although stated differently, the members of this diverse group are all saying the same thing — that the beliefs we hold are the primary determiners of the scope, rhythm, quality, and boundary of our lives. And if we return to the quote by Huxley that opens this chapter, we find a few other valuable keys to succeeding on this journey toward more conscious living and wise aging.

Huxley reminds us that we need, "to be shown for a few timeless hours the outer and inner worlds, not as they appear to [one] obsessed with words and notions, but as they are apprehended, directly and unconditionally, by [our souls.]"

"To be shown." This is an essential clue to getting beyond the ruts of

ordinary perception. Yes, we need to be willing not just to look but also to see. We need to be willing to observe and experience what is actually happening rather than what our words and notions (our beliefs) tell us is happening.

A second important key found in Huxley's quote is that in order to get outside the ruts of ordinary perception we have to experience life, *directly and unconditionally.* In short, to be free of our perceptions it is essential that we spend at least as much if not more time on the right side of our brain where insight, imagination, intuition, and creativity reside as on the left side of our brain where rational, linear thought and analysis have their home. This right side of the brain is where envisioning, reflection, prayer, meditation, and flights of daydreaming and fancy can be experienced. This is the realm where "being" is at the very least as important as "doing."

A Primary and Limiting Belief

Among the beliefs many of us hold, one in particular determines the amount of freedom or limitation we experience in the second half of life. This is the belief that is prevalent in our society that there is something wrong with getting old. When we couple this with a second limiting belief — that if we focus primarily on youth and deny aging, we will somehow avoid aging or, at the very least, not be subject to its consequences for some time — then we more fully understand the dilemma many of us face in the modern world.

Strange, isn't it, that when we are very young most of us can't wait to be older? We want to be able to do the things our older siblings and friends can do — go off with friends without a babysitter, play sports, stay up later, etc. Then we want to be older still so we can get our driver's license, and then older still so we can live on our own and do what we think we want to do without adult interference.

When we get to this stage, however, many of us believe we are still not old enough. We want to be settled and successful in our careers, involved in more meaningful and lasting relationships, and have the financial freedom to acquire the things we believe are important. When we get to this stage many of us — particularly in our society where so many of us work at things we "have to do" rather than those we *want* to do — continue to look forward and plan for the time when we no longer have to do these things: the time when we can retire.

Yes, we live in a world in which most of us go from one stage to the next anxious to experience whatever we think the next stage offers until, of course, the next stage is about getting old. Then suddenly we don't like the transition very much. In fact, as earlier mentioned, most of us deal with this essential and unavoidable reality by trying to deny or prevent it. And yet getting older is not only inevitable, it is also natural; not only natural, but — and here's the kicker — valuable!

Yes, getting older is like the third act of a play, the final chapters in a book, or the concluding movement of a symphony. Without these final chapters, acts, or movements there can be no summation, no conclusion, no way to put all of the earlier experiences that have unfolded in our previous acts, chapters, and movements into perspective so we can graduate to higher levels of learning. Without the third act or the final chapter there is no way to capture and then communicate the unique and individual lessons we have learned along the way. And since these lessons are one of the main reasons we came here to this school called Earth in the first place, trying to deny or avoid the final chapter, act, or movement only prevents us from adding our distinct and unduplicatable note to what musical troubadour Michael Stillwater and others call "The Great Song."

So contrary to the ruts of ordinary perception that keep many of us trapped in illusion, getting old is not something to be denied, avoided, or feared. Instead with new eyes and a little honest observation and experience, getting older can become something that is accepted, experienced, and even honored and celebrated. Please try on this sentence a few more times! *Getting older is not something to be denied and avoided, it is something to be accepted, experienced, honored, and celebrated.*

Of course, in our youth-obsessed and age-averse culture this requires that we go against the grain of conventional beliefs and not only recognize and accept the reality of our aging but also our eventual exit — and the implications this exit involves. Indeed, just as we celebrate our entrance, we would be wise to acknowledge and learn to celebrate our exit. Not such an outlandish request considering that our exit is an essential and unavoidable part of our price of admission.

So if we want to get beyond the ruts of ordinary perception that may be restricting our lives, we would be wise to explore the belief we may be holding that a life of endless youth is the only desirable one. We may want to consider that there is a lot more to life than material accumulation and self-gratification. Indeed, if we are willing to deepen our experimentation with various practices such as observation and reflection, yoga, prayer, and meditation to name a few; if we are willing to try different breathing techniques and even some consciousness-expanding drugs; if we are willing to experiment with our diet, various forms of exercise, and different amounts of sleep — we may just find that it is possible to go beyond our fear of aging and dying and accept both as natural parts of the flow of life.

Indeed, in experimenting with these concepts and practices we will be taking some very important and critical steps toward making peace with our lives and finding a path toward a more expansive and engaging next stage of our journey.

Celebrating Life and Accepting Death

We could, of course, spend hours exploring how it is that so many of us have been lulled into accepting the illusion of eternal youth and some of the misperceptions and false beliefs about growing older that we hold. But to occupy ourselves with an analysis at this point in our process and to go on denying the reality of aging would, in our opinion, be a poor use of our precious time. And while we can't speak for you, we know that we have certainly wasted enough time already in our lives. So we encourage you to use these next, potentially extraordinary chapters of your life living in celebration and exploration rather than in analysis, regret, or denial. For to do the latter would be like taking a wonderfully aged wine that comes from a special vineyard in a really terrific year, a wine that we have kept at just the right temperature for just the right amount of time, and then uncorking it and drinking it hurriedly on a busy street out of a paper cup with a cheap hot dog we purchase from a street vendor.

No, we do not believe we have come all this way, through the many twists and turns, the ups and downs, failures and victories of the first half of our lives to end up in some stagnant backwater of denial or regret. Nor have we made this long journey to become invisible and relegated to inconsequence.

Instead, we believe it is our right, privilege, challenge, and — of particular consequence — our time to live out the final chapters of our lives helping to redirect the current of cultural consciousness into a more positive river of awareness rather than shuffling quietly and meekly off to some senior facility never to be seen or heard from again.

Dreamers and Revolutionaries

"Not us," you say. "We will never do that! We belong to the powerful generations. We are dreamers and revolutionaries who changed the world. We are the freedom marchers and anti-war protestors, the political activists, the soldiers, the 'love children' and spiritual warriors, and we will not settle for going out with a whimper rather than a roar."

Well, we certainly hope this is true, but we would be less than truthful if we did not say that we are concerned that unless each of us willingly chooses to renew our commitment to move beyond the ruts of ordinary awareness; unless we are willing to continuously look our beliefs about life, aging, and death in the eye and keep learning how to make a deeper peace with and acknowledge each of these stages with greater acceptance, understanding, and compassion — then shuffling off may, even for those of us who believe we are dreamers and revolutionaries, become more of a reality than we realize.

So let's be aware of our responsibility — first to ourselves and ultimately to the rest of humanity — to rewrite the missing third act of life's drama. Let us more fully accept that aging and death are realities. Let us acknowledge that these realities change us. They strip away the veneer and get us closer to the essence. They challenge us to let go of our illusions and cause us to surrender to that which is greater than we are. And while aging and dying are not always pretty and stylish, they are real and essential. So let us remember that our work is not done and that it's never too late (or too soon) to live out the promise we made a long time ago.

Life Rule
"Nothing splendid has ever been achieved except by those who dared to believe that something inside them was superior to circumstances."

~ Bruce Barton

Life Achievement
James Earl Jones continues to astound theatre and film audiences into his 80s.

Life Tool
As you go through your day today, we invite you to pause occasionally and ask yourself a few simple questions: "What beliefs about aging am I holding that prevent me from moving 'beyond the ruts of ordinary perception'? Do these beliefs advance or retard my ability to experience more passion, engagement, and joy in this moment?"

It's Never Too Late (or Too Soon)

"It doesn't interest me what you do for a living.
I want to know what you ache for, and if you dare to dream of meeting
your heart's longing. It doesn't interest me how old you are. I want to
know if you will risk looking like a fool for love,
for your dreams, for the adventure of being alive."

~ Oriah Mountain Dreamer ~

One Day...

Do you remember believing that one day you would be a great writer, painter, or composer? Do you remember wanting to invent a remarkable new product or social system, find the cure to a debilitating illness, be the one who rallies the troops to save the day, enters the courtroom to right an injustice, or throws your hat into the political ring to make a difference? Do you remember wanting to bring a brood of children into the world and raise them with genuine love and consciousness, wanting to play the music or sing the songs that echoed in your heart? Do you remember wanting to be a coach or a teacher, a dancer, actor, choreographer, cook, carpenter or fisherman, an astronaut or mountain climber, a religious or spiritual leader, a humanitarian or a healer?

Perhaps in your case, you did not know exactly what you wanted to do with your life but you did feel a longing you could not name, a restless tug to do or manifest something more and different than others around you were doing or manifesting. Perhaps that is still true for you. And so in this section we invite you to examine some beliefs you may be holding, answer some questions, and explore some recommendations that can make the next stage of your journey not only more satisfying and rewarding, but also more in alignment with the dream you came here to manifest.

If you are willing to take a little time to do this, to listen to your own inner voice, we believe you will discover that this longing is still present and that by paying attention to it you will rediscover a pathway that can — no matter how old or young you are — lead you to live the life you were born to live.

The Power of Your Dream

Our personal experience confirms the fact that when we are in touch with our personal dream and stay true to its call — stay true to what is called our destiny — we are not only more creative, impassioned, and energetic, but we are more involved in our own lives and connected to others and to the natural rhythm of life. We are also more connected to the well-being of our planet and to all of the species that reside here. In short, we know that our personal dreams are keys to not only living more consciously and aging wisely, but to fulfilling our spiritual heritage.

Over the course of the last 30-something years we have tested this premise in our personal lives as well as through our work with hundreds of major organizations and with thousands of individuals who have attended both our organizational and public programs. As a result we have confirmed that following our dreams is one of the most important keys to living the lives we were born to live. In fact, our dreams hold the blueprint for a unique and successful life. And this blueprint is very much alive in each of our hearts whether it has been days or decades since we have last paid it any attention.

If you have been faithful to your dream you know this to be true and we applaud your efforts. But then again, our applause is unnecessary for you already know the value of the journey that was written indelibly in your heart long ago.

If you have not yet been as faithful to your dream as you have wanted to be then you are at least familiar with what is called the "still small voice," for all of us experience it periodically asking us to pay more attention.

So we invite you to pause and remember our friend Molly Brown and her journey. Pause and take a little time to touch that place in your heart where your dream still resides so that you, too, can once again regain that glint in your eyes and raise your arms in joyful celebration on the front steps of the city hall of your life.

No matter what your experience has been — whether it has been the hot pursuit of a dream that has been clear and compelling or the turning away and living with that restlessness of knowing that there was or is something else or something more inspiring that you want to do — we invite you to lean back in your chair, close your eyes, and go to that quiet place inside you that is not limited by the boundaries of physical time or practical considerations. Yes, go to that place where you keep your secrets and listen and remember what you once wanted to do with "these relatively few and precious moments called your life."

Please do not just read the last paragraph and move on. Take a few deep breaths and give yourself the gift of getting back in touch with your dream. You will, we know, be grateful for this experience. There are, of course, numerous techniques that can be used to assist you in having this greater present-moment experience. There are many forms of yogic breathing, various reflective and meditative practices, the use of mantra and simple phrases spoken on the out-breath and the in-breath, and a host of emerging technologies that assist one to more easily enter the alpha state or to find what Doc Childre at the world-renowned Institute of HeartMath calls "coherence."

Even if it is only a vague sense of a direction, a hint, or a passing image, allow yourself to feel it. Yes, touch into that special energy, that sense of hope, purpose, and passion. And then perhaps you may feel the impulse to blow the dust off those paintbrushes; open the cover of the piano or of your toolbox; or dig out that notebook you tucked away on the bottom bookshelf that is full of ideas for that humanitarian project, that business venture, or the novel you once wanted to create.

What If?

No matter how old you are or what you have chosen to do thus far in your life to earn your daily bread, we are sure that when you touch the dream that lives inside you, you experience that sense of rightness, of alignment with something that is deeply familiar. You may also experience some pangs of regret for not listening to your muse more often and listening instead to those who told you that you had to be reasonable and responsible, that you needed to find a practical and proven way to support yourself, and eventually, perhaps, a family. Can you feel some of that sense of alignment and naturalness and perhaps a little of that regret?

Many of us, especially those of us who weren't born yesterday, have followed a script that is different than our dream script, haven't we? Having been told that life was about practical things — logical, predictable, acceptable, responsible, mature and material things — and that this practical path was the one we needed to take if we wanted to find our rightful place in society, that is what we did.

"Put aside those foolish dreams and schemes," many of us were told. "They're unrealistic and impractical! Go to school, study something practical, and then take your place in the great army of the gainfully employed."

We don't have to dwell on this "real world" script! Millions of us know it by heart — at least some version of it. As a result for the last 10, 20, or 40 years or more we have, for the most part, done our best to live within its pages. Diligently, decently, responsibly, we have been doing our best to speak our lines and follow the stage instructions notated in the margins. Yes, that's been our ticket! And it's been the ticket for most of humanity throughout history and especially since the dawn of the Industrial Revolution and the Age of Enlightenment. That's when the Gods of Productivity, Materialism, and Reason took center stage. Economics became the primary religion and intuition, imagination, individuality, and creative expression were relegated to minor supporting roles in the human drama.

"Do your part! Play the game and you'll get the rewards!" This has been the primary mantra since the 19th century and so this is what most of us have done. And some of us have, in fact, been pretty successful at being diligent, decent, responsible, and hardworking. Some of us have also been lucky or crafty or done whatever it has taken to get that bigger house and more stuff, and tuck away what we think is enough in our savings and investment accounts to protect us from what are called the vagaries of life.

Some of us have also risen to the top of our professions or somewhere close. Some of us, in addition to financial rewards, have also received accolades and recognition from our peers and even, in some cases, the adoration of the public. In short, "we've made it," as they say. Whoever "they" are and whatever "making it" means!

The Other Side of Making It

According to a number of recent studies, however, a significant number of us who have followed these practical, logical, and responsible paths have been able to manifest some of the things that we set out to achieve, enough generally to keep us motivated to keep going. But in today's topsy-turvy financial landscape, many of us have found that the script has changed. Indeed, a number of us are still chasing the promise of financial independence and security, and the rewards we were promised still elude us. As does the promise of the day when we will be able to finally turn away from this job, that financial obligation, or this somewhat awkward but necessary path we chose and finally begin to enjoy the fruits of our labors.

Strange turn of phrase, isn't it? *Enjoy the fruits of our labors.* But that's what the golden years are supposed to be for, aren't they? That's when we are supposed to be able to hang up our cleats, put away our toolboxes or briefcases, and start doing the things we've worked so hard all of these years to do. Yes, time finally to retire and enjoy those years of golf and antiquing, those years of traveling, gardening, and puttering. After all, this is the American Dream!

Sadly enough, however, as the full weight of the graying of the world population becomes clear, many of us are discovering that the world we were promised is not real. Many of us have discovered that the money we worked so hard to earn so we could invest in the stock market and in real estate, the money we have set aside in hard-earned pensions and severance packages, our company retirement accounts, and even our Social Security and Medicare benefits are neither as secure nor anywhere near as much as we thought they would be.

In addition to these basic financial concerns, many of the people we have met through our consulting practice, our public programs, and in our private lives have also verified the fact that no matter where on the spectrum of "making it" they find themselves, they still find themselves trying to scratch an itch they can't quite reach, yearning for something more, something else, or different. They often report finding themselves feeling that old restlessness and wondering what that something more is — that something that was not in the script — that keeps tugging at the fabric of their consciousness.

In short, no matter what path many of us have chosen or how seemingly successful we have been at our doctoring, lawyering, family raising, company running, political-office holding, financial manipulating, administrating, accounting, selling, or more, there is a look of longing that comes into our eyes when we are asked what we would be doing if we were not doing these logical and practical things. Yes, we get that wistful look and that melancholy tone in our voices when we find ourselves wondering "what if?"

And that's generally the point in the conversation when most of us begin to talk about our dream. Yes, right there below the surface of our practical and regular lives, that dream of being a poet, musician, actor, adventurer, teacher, athlete, coach, explorer, film maker, writer, singer, artist, or social change agent is still very much alive even after decades of doctoring or computing, selling or financial manipulating.

Is that true for you? Can you still feel that dream burning brightly in the recesses of your heart? And when you do feel into that dream can you remember what made you decide that it was, as the realists around you claimed, too impossible, impractical, and selfish a dream to pursue?

Please give yourself the gift of exploring these questions! Please take the time to look honestly into the mirror of your life. We know it may be a little challenging. We know that once you open that door to your past you may encounter feelings of regret that you turned away from that small inner voice that was urging you to hold on to your dream.

In other cases, you may be among those of us who actually made a sincere effort to pursue your dream only to discover that the road toward your mountain top was more costly, arduous, or lengthy than you imagined and that when confronted by doubt and encouraged by that chorus of the nay-sayers who sang the practicality song, you turned away. How were you to know that doubts and obstacles are essential parts of the game Fate arranges in order to test our mettle and assist us in developing the skills, the grit, and the courage to fulfill our destiny?

So while looking back on some of this may not be easy, at least not at first, we encourage you to stay with this process because we know you will find something of inestimable value by doing so. So now, without thinking too much about it, please pick up your pen and write whatever comes to mind about your dream.

Life Rule
"Dreams come true; without that possibility, nature would not incite us to have them."

~ John Updike

Life Achievement
Carl Sandburg, one of America's great poets, wrote some of his most inspired poetry in his 80s.

Life Tool
Consider that each moment, each encounter, each thought, word, and deed could be your last. If this is true here are some questions you might want to ask:

- Is this truly the best and highest use of this moment, this energy, and this interaction?

- Is what I am doing contributing to improving my life and the lives of others or am I just going through the motions?

- Am I still interested in developing and contributing my unique gifts to the world around me?

- Am I being true to the authentic and original dream I was born to manifest or am I following a script written for me by someone else?

The Hero's Journey

"The tragedy of life is not that it ends so soon,
but that we wait so long to begin it."

~ W.M. Lewis ~

We are encouraging you to reconnect with your dream because we know this reconnection is essential to your personal well-being and to fulfilling the agreement you made long before you arrived here on this earth. In fact, in our experience your dream is your doorway to what throughout history has been called The Hero's Journey.

Based on the experiences of many people we had the privilege to work with, we also know that it is not in our individual interests or that of the world at large — although the world may proclaim it to be so — for us to set aside our individual dreams for the sake of collective goals that are measured too exclusively by the amount of our economic accumulation and the number of our material possessions.

Indeed, we know the world today with all of its environmental, social, economic, political, and cultural challenges is in jeopardy not because we have not been practical, acquisitive, and rational enough, but because many of us have been *too* practical, acquisitive, and rational. Yes, we have subjugated our individual dreams in pursuit of goals that are the illegitimate offspring of the Age of Reason and the Industrial Age. And as a result, we and our world are paying a very high price.

So from our perspective if each of us is to take full advantage of the years we have remaining — whether that number is 5 or 75 — and if each of us is to fulfill the purpose we have come here to fulfill, then getting back in touch with our individual dream and with the unique and essential energy it contains is of paramount importance.

In Search of Innocence

Anthony de Mello, a writer and Jesuit priest who lived and taught primarily in India, believed that our dream — our unique, individual dream of what we are here on Earth to accomplish — is also a key to innocence. Innocence in terms of *"lest you be as children you will not enter the kingdom of heaven."* And if we take a little liberty with de Mello's definition, we believe innocence includes authenticity and originality, two primary keys to living lives of true meaning and purpose.

De Mello writes, "The first quality that strikes one when one looks into the eyes of a child is its innocence, its lovely inability to lie or wear a mask or present to be anything other than what it is. In this the child is exactly like the rest of nature."

Notice that de Mello equates innocence with naturalness! He then goes on to say:

"When grown-ups punish a child for telling the truth, for revealing what it thinks and feels, the child learns to dissemble and its innocence is destroyed. Soon it will join the ranks of the numberless people who say helplessly, 'I do not know who I am' for having hidden the truth about themselves for so long from others, they end up hiding it from themselves."

What a powerful statement and what a telling critique of the beliefs that shape so much of the world today. We who are now grown-ups have learned from other grown-ups and then, in turn — often unconsciously — passed on to our children the socially acceptable dishonesties that rob them, ourselves, and the world at large of genuine innocence. And with this loss of innocence we lose direct contact with meaning and purpose and our ability to fulfill the destinies we have come to this Earth to accomplish that we and only we can accomplish.

There is additional gold in de Mello's words including the key, we believe, to a revolutionary path each of us can take to rediscover our innocence and fulfill our destiny through the resurrection of our dream.

"[In our world] the child is infected by the desire to become somebody. Contemplate the crowds of people who are striving might and main to become, not what nature intended them to be — musicians, cooks, mechanics, carpenters, gardeners, inventors — but somebody successful, famous, powerful; to become something that will bring, not quiet, not self-fulfillment, but self-glorification, self-expansion. You are looking at people who have lost their innocence because they have chosen not to be themselves, but to promote themselves, to show off, even if it be only in their own eyes. Look at your daily life. Is there a single thought, word or action untainted by the desire to become someone…?

"Here is another way that grown-ups corrupt [themselves and] the innocence

of childhood: They teach the child to imitate someone. The moment you make the child a carbon copy you stamp out the spark of originality with which it came into the world. The moment you choose to become like someone else, however great or holy, you have prostituted your being. Think sadly of the divine spark of uniqueness that lies within you, buried under layers of fear. The fear that you will be ridiculed or rejected if you dare to be yourself and refuse to conform mechanically in the way you dress and act and think. See how you conform not only in your actions and thoughts, but even in your reactions, your emotions, your attitudes, your values. You dare not break out of this prostitution and reclaim your original innocence. This is the price you pay for the passport of acceptance by your society and organization. So you enter the world of the crooked and the controlled and are exiled from the kingdom that belongs to the innocence of childhood."

The Path Forward

For a man of the cloth Anthony de Mello certainly did not pull his punches. In fact, one might call him ruthless in his championing of truth, courage, and the pursuit of individual dreams. Indeed, to read his words, to allow them to enter our consciousness, is to feel the unavoidable and unquestionable power of his unswerving commitment to what is authentic about each soul.

So what do we do with this understanding? Do we avoid it, telling ourselves it is too late for us and, as a result, walk away again from that unique, divine spark that burns deep inside us? Do we walk around feeling guilty and regretting our loss of innocence and our missed opportunities? Do we try to take our entire world apart and start over, walking away from our current careers and accomplishments to pursue our dreams?

As much as we are in favor of remaking our world as quickly as possible along much more sane, sustainable, and individually ennobling and innocent lines — although we are in favor of encouraging ourselves and others to live lives that are based on the rhythms of the natural world and the agreements each of us made long before we arrived on this planet — it would be impractical to assume that we can do all of this in a single leap. For it is no small challenge to reverse hundreds of years of habitual servitude to Gods of Reason and Economics or the thousands of eons of habituated behaviors that have accustomed human beings to trade sovereignty and innocence for acceptance, recognition, and a pittance of security and safety that is promised but rarely delivered by the collective.

So if we cannot change the world in one leap, what can we do? As we discussed in the previous chapters, we believe the first step in bringing about genuine and necessary changes in our world requires each of us to look closer to home and begin or deepen the work of understanding our-selves. And in this we will be not only aided but also empowered by our individual dreams.

Yes, instead of following the old habit of trying to be someone else and instead of projecting the dissatisfaction we feel inside us out onto the world around us and trying to recast the world in our image — a practice that has led largely to the mess we now find ourselves in — our sugges-tion is always to first practice creating true alignment within ourselves, alignment that only comes from getting in touch with our dream and the unique wisdom it contains.

So let your dreams lead you into and through the maze of the chal-lenges and obstacles that fate has placed or will place in your path. For this is the surest, truest, and ultimately the only way to create sanity and harmony in your inner world and then, ultimately, in the world at large.

George Leonard, the author of *Mastery* (among other books and arti-cles on human potential), describes this experience in this way: "There is a human striving for self-transcendence. It's part of what makes us human. With all of our flaws we want to go a little bit further than we've gone before and maybe even further than anyone else has gone before."

Doctor Reverend Michael Beckwith puts it this way, "Pain pushes until the vision pulls."

Sedena has her own unique way of describing the process of finding and living our dreams. She uses the symbolism of old-time "spectacles" and believes that dreams can be discovered if we are willing to see in a new way; to "re-spect," to re-look, and discover those things that taught us to be loving, those people who made us smile and feel just right. This is a valuable way of "re-specting" our gifts and talents. By remembering people who influenced us in a positive way, we can discover some of the courage that will help us follow our dreams and be all that we can be.

In a world as seemingly sophisticated and complex as ours it is easy to dismiss the premise about the importance of following our dreams. It may seem too simplistic. After all, how can challenges as significant as those we face possibly be solved by each of us returning to what others called the unrealistic dreams some of us had as children?

But please do not be too quick to dismiss this premise. Instead, ask yourself the following questions. You might want to use your journal or a blank pad of paper to capture some of your answers for they may prove helpful to you later on.

❋ What feelings do I experience when I get in touch with my dream?

❋ Do I experience joy, passion, enthusiasm, or an increase in my energy level?

❋ Do I experience greater clarity, hope, and a sense of renewed purpose?

❋ What would my life be like if I went forward into the world each day with this kind of joy, passion, enthusiasm, clarity, hope, and energy?

❋ What could I contribute to the people I love and to the world around me each day from this place of joy, passion, enthusiasm, and energy?

And remember, the purpose of getting in touch with that quiet place inside you where you hold your dreams is not to feel bad about not following them, but instead to help you to remember that it really is never too late or too soon to do so. And if you doubt this you need only look at the Life Achievements that are included at the end of each chapter and take the time to explore the stories that are associated with them. Many of these individuals whom we admire did not discover the fullness of their dreams or their next steps on the path to manifesting them until they had taken many other paths or until late in their lives.

Perhaps you are already discovering that having touched briefly into your own dream again you are sensing some of the unlimited potential and possibilities that George Leonard refers to or Reverend Beckwith describes. Having a dream that you pursue — even if only in your spare time — can insulate you from a lot of the pain and frustration that accompanies every life.

Of course, we know that a number of questions arise when you consider your dream.

❋ How can you follow your dream and still propitiate the Gods of Economics and Reason?

❋ What about the needs of your family?

❋ If you do this or that what will happen to your financial security?

❋ How do you make peace with lost opportunities?

Fortunately we cannot answer these questions for you. We say "fortunately" because no one should rob us of our individual and authentic discoveries. Yes if someone gives us an answer we could very well end up in the same dilemma we may be in now — that of following someone else's path. It is equally true that if we take the easy way and try to answer these questions in our heads rather than let our dreams lead us to our answers, we may end up throwing in the towel long before we reach our goal.

In the end, the pursuit of your dream takes trust, determination, and courage. It involves effort and both the meeting and overcoming of the obstacles that life presents. It is "the hero's journey;" and if it was an easy path to travel, most of humanity would have taken it long ago. But easy or not, it is what we are all born to do. And only the doing of it will get it done. Only the doing will enable us to overcome the doubt and confusions that sometimes threaten to overwhelm us — and allow us to learn from our experiences. As Matthew, the Apostle, once said: "For what will it profit a man if he gains the whole world and forfeits his Soul?"

A Stevie Wonder Story

We invite you to keep this question about the value of dreams in mind as you read this short story that Stevie Wonder told on the occasion of receiving an award for Personal Integrity from a Los Angeles–based foundation. This is a paraphrase of what Stevie said to an assembled crowd at the Beverly Hilton Hotel on that occasion:

When I was a little boy, after I lost my sight, I would often hear sounds in my head and try to reproduce them by banging on various objects that were around me. Sometimes in my enthusiasm I would break the objects that I banged on. Because I was both little and without sight, I did not know at the time that we were very poor and that most of the objects that I broke could not be replaced. But I remember that my mother would simply take away the broken pieces and put another object in its place. Never during all of that time did she ever scold me or punish me for breaking the thing.

Imagine what the world would be like today, your individual world as well as our collective world, if all of us received the kind of unselfish support, encouragement, and love Stevie Wonder received from his mother. But even if the world around you did not or does not offer you support and encouragement, you can support yourself. You can nurture and grow that spark of hope that lies in your heart that is waiting to be ignited. You can also ask for guidance and courage through prayer, reflection, and meditation to assist you in staying in touch with your inner wisdom. And, above all, you can trust your dream. After all, you and only you have the ability to discover and fulfill the agreement you made before coming here. And one day, in looking back, you will be amazed to see how all the challenges that obstructed your path ultimately worked together to assist you in achieving it.

Life Rule
"It is never too late (or too soon) to live the life you were born to live."
~ George and Sedena Cappannelli

Life Achievement
Joseph Chilton Pearce, noted author and expert on the human heart as a center of intelligence, continues to write, lecture, and expand the horizons of human experience in his 80s.

Life Tool
You have the opportunity today to remember that you can use this precious gift that is your life in any way you choose. You can spend your time in the push, pull, and noise of the outside world. You can listen and be influenced by the often confusing suggestions and demands others make; or you can go into the quiet of your own heart, to the place inside you where you hold your dream, and let the wisdom of this dream guide you.

Who Are You & What Are You Doing Here?

"The real challenge of old age is to risk all habitual frames of reference and to open the mind to another field of possibility that lies beyond the physical. Having gained a foothold in the inner world, we can encounter death with calm anticipation rather than fear."

~ Joseph Chilton-Pearce ~

A Few Essential Questions

We have been told about a British philosopher who has a rather provocative message on his answering machine. The message seems rather ordinary — at least, at first. "Who are you and what do you want?" the answering machine asks. The message, however, does not end there. It goes on to say, "If you think these questions are simple, think again! Most people come to this planet, live out a certain number of years, and never answer either of them."

So as your next step on the road to living more consciously and aging wisely, we invite you to take your lead from this British philosopher and explore these and a few other questions. *Who are you? What do you want?* And a third question that is certainly as important as the first two — *What are you doing here?* We believe, in fact, that your answers to these three vital questions will serve you extraordinarily well on this journey toward living the life you were born to live.

Of course, in the push and pull of daily life these questions are sometimes treated casually or even dismissed as being inconsequential — particularly by those who measure success by following the dictates found within the Zones of Productivity and Profitability. They are questions, at least according to these folks, that only occupy the romantics among us, those who live in somewhat rarified academic environments or those who do not attend to the daily rigors of earning a living. Yes, according to the pragmatics, these questions are only for those who have the luxury of pondering them while the rest of us have to go about the "real" business of earning money, raising a family, and doing the necessary things that make life manageable.

But please do not make this same mistake with our words. We live in the same "real world" that you live in, and we certainly do not underestimate the challenges of surviving and thriving within it. At the same time, as we look around at the enormous challenges humanity faces, it becomes increasingly clear to us that it is highly probable that far too many of us have been far too focused on doing all of these practical and productive things and not focused enough on the philosophical and spiritual bedrock that lies beneath them. We believe, in fact, that our world would be much saner and more effective if each of us took the time to answer the two questions posed by the British philosopher and the one we have added.

We also believe that if more of us followed George Burns's good advice — *I honestly think it is better to be a failure at something you love than to be a success at something you hate* — more of us would be living the lives we were born to live.

We also believe that if we dig more deeply into the consequences of our thoughts, words, and deeds and especially into our relationship to the personal dream and the longings that live in our hearts, then our individual lives and the well-being of the world around us would be remarkably improved.

What Do You Believe?

You may be the leader of a major organization or someone who simply spends time tending to your garden. You may be self-employed, a volunteer at your local church or community organization, or in charge of an army. You may be responsible for the well-being of a large family or simply doing whatever you can do to deal with the challenges and opportunities that come up each day in your individual life.

No matter what your level of responsibility to others or to yourself, or what your age or your role in the world may be, if you are reading these pages you probably have days in which you feel as though your life is going reasonably well and others in which you wonder how it could have gotten so completely out of balance. On these out-of-balance days you may feel that you have wandered off your path or indeed never found it. You may feel certain you are out of touch with your purpose and what gives your life its meaning.

We all have days like this, of course, both the in- and the out-of-balance ones. Indeed we are all in the same boat and some days the sea can feel pretty choppy.

That's why in this chapter we invite you to explore these three questions as well as some of the beliefs that may underlie them. Why? Because an ancient spiritual law suggests that: *energy follows thought and manifestation follows energy.*

If you are willing — even briefly — to allow for the possibility that this law might be true, then it would hold that the physical universe as we experience it is largely the result of our thoughts and intentions and the actions that issue from them. In short, if you follow this chain of cause and effect a few links closer to the source, you may come to the conclusion that the shape and scope of your world is to some important degree determined by what you think about and the amount of attention you give to your beliefs.

For example, you may believe you are just one of many billions of physical organisms residing on this planet at this time, simply the byproduct of an evolutionary process. You may believe that you are a life form that was birthed, will live out a certain number of years, and will eventually die and return to the Earth to serve as the basic stuff from which other life forms will grow. On the other hand, you may believe that you are a unique divine spark that issues from the heart of God and that you take up temporary residence here in a physical body for a specific period of time to learn, expand in consciousness, share your gifts, and then return with the wisdom gained to your original Source. Of course, depending on where on this gamut of beliefs you stand, your experience of life will be fundamentally different.

Perhaps you believe life is a test with unlimited potential and endless opportunities, or instead that you are born with an indelible stain you must carry all of your life and from which you can never be free. Perhaps you believe that when your life is over you will be judged on the basis of how well you dealt with this stain, and as a result you will either be granted permanent rest in a glorious place or sent into some lower realm to be punished forever. On the other hand, you may believe that you reincarnate as a physical being in as many as 8,400,000 lifetimes in one cycle and that each lifetime will be an opportunity to experience the dance of life differently and to expand the scope and reach of the divine consciousness you carry.

Yes, you may believe that you are a physical being on a physical journey or a spiritual being temporarily occupying physical form. You may believe you are a vital energy who brings unique qualities and characteristics, individual purpose and meaning, an energy that has never been here in quite the same way before and never will be again — or that you are just a collection of random characteristics that nature has assembled organically but randomly and without further purpose, direction, or intent.

As to your wants and desires, we believe they are also determined largely by your beliefs. Indeed, some of us know what we desire and what some of our dreams are. Others of us by virtue of the difficulty of our life experiences and challenges, and the absence of hope these experiences have given rise to, believe that our path and our limits are set in stone. Others who hold particular religious or political beliefs may not even believe they have the right or ability to dream.

What about you? What do you believe? Is it even acceptable for you to dream or do you believe that dreams are the doorway to sinful thoughts and immoral behaviors? Do your dreams pit your longings against those of others? Do your dreams threaten to interfere with all the practical stuff we talked about — making a living, raising a family, etc.?

And if you allow yourself to dream, are your dreams focused primarily on material things (a new house, new clothing, some special car, particular amounts of money, or attaining certain physical characteristics) or do your dreams lead you toward less tangible experiences (happiness, love, laughter, good health, goodness, higher consciousness, etc.)?

The Core Question

See what we mean? The questions on that British philosopher's answering machine can be a lot tougher than we at first imagine. And this, perhaps, is the reason so many of us go through life avoiding them.

In our experience the first two questions — *Who are you and what do you want?* — are important stepping-stones to answering the third — *What are you doing here?* Or as we have said earlier, they go a long way toward answering the question the poet, Mary Oliver asked — *What are you going to do with this one wild and precious thing called your life?*

So if you are to live a life of greater consciousness and if you are to age wisely, this third question will become vitally important. So what is your purpose in being here? In short, why were you born — what did you come to share with your world?

We believe that when each of us truly wrestles with these questions, everything will change. Indeed, when each of us answers these questions we know it will no longer be acceptable for anyone to pollute the world; to eliminate vital and essential species; to violate the rights of others; or to slaughter fellow human beings in the name of one religious, economic, or political philosophy. We will no longer allow our brethren to die of starvation while others live in excess — to let some live in despair while others frivolously pursue meaningless activities and purely ego-flattering goals. We will no longer accept systems that deny basic healthcare, medicines, and education to some while others overmedicate and overprescribe; or to accept limited and outmoded definitions of what it means to be a success and a true elder in our world.

Do you see what we mean about this "belief" thing? So what do you believe?

Life Rule
"Success is the child of audacity."

~ Benjamin Disraeli

Life Achievement
Geronimo, the storied Native American warrior and chief, completed his autobiography at 77.

Life Tool
We invite you to spend the next few days asking and seeking to answer these questions — *Why am I alive? What am I doing with the precious gift that is my life?* You do not have to change or do anything. Just let these questions live inside you. Let them guide you and illuminate your thoughts, words, and deeds. In this space of openness, you may be surprised by the thoughts that come to you, and you may want to write them down so you can continue to reflect on them in the time ahead.

The Myth of Youth

*"You gain strength, courage, and confidence by every experience
in which you really stop to look fear in the face. You are able to say
to yourself, 'I lived through this... I can take the next thing that
comes along...' You must do the thing you think you cannot."*

~ Eleanor Roosevelt ~

A Misguided Siren's Song

The media, playing its awkward role as the pied piper for today's corporatocracy, trumpets the Myth of Youth above all else. In fact, as a
culture, we have become so obsessed with youth that we have, even if
unintentionally, marginalized everything and everyone else, including a
large number of young people who do not fit within the arbitrary standards of what is young, hip, beautiful, and compulsively thin.

This focus on youth is, of course, not offensive to the "corporatocracy."
For the message promotes and sells products and services by appealing to
the young and the restless and to those of us who are still desperately pretending we belong in this group.

Unfortunately this focus on youth has some detrimental side effects.
For example, many in our culture believe that we have to get "it" done
(whatever "it" is) before we are 40 or it will be too late. And this "it"
of course, most often involves acquisition of status; accumulation of possessions; and now that we are in the social-networking phase, aggressive
self-promotion.

Our obsession with youth also contributes significantly to the denial
of some of life's unavoidable and natural stages — as we've mentioned,
aging and dying are two essential ones. As a result we have become a
culture addicted to tucking in, trimming down, covering up, tanning over,
building up, augmenting, and liposuctioning and, when all that fails, simply denying aging and death as if our denial will prevent these natural
stages from occurring.

Yes, there is a lot of push and pull in our youth-obsessed, age-averse, 24/7, medicated, media-addicted culture and a lot of it seems to issue from the belief that only the young have value. And unfortunately, in a world in which the Gods of Economics and Consumerism rule, this illusion too often becomes true.

Another place our obsession with youth shows up is in the work environment, where intelligence, superior performance, and genuine experience are often no longer enough to ensure a reasonably stable place in the great army of the employed. Instead, youth has become a sought-after commodity, not only because youth can be persuaded to work at significantly lower prices, but because we have come to believe that young leaders are essential to attracting young buyers; and in our consumer-driven world the rest of us, particularly those of us who are no longer consumption-driven, are often written off as members of the over-the-hill gang. Of course, if marketers were not so blinded by these illusions, they would realize that the real buying power remains with those of us who are part of the second-half-of-life crowd.

None of this is to say that being young, vibrant, and still under the illusion that one is invincible is a bad thing. Indeed, youth is an incredible and valuable stage in the life cycle. Without it there could be no middle and ending chapters; no second and third acts; no chance to engage vigorously, make mistakes, and learn from them. So youth is certainly well worth celebrating.

The Great Rebalancing

The trouble comes when we start believing that youth is the only part of the cycle worth celebrating. So let us put a pin in the bubble of this myth by championing a much more egalitarian focus on all of the stages of life! Let us move beyond youth mania and relearn to honor the contributions, experience, values, and wisdom those of us in the second half of life have to offer. Let's also remember that although the young challenge us with new ideas, motivate us with their exuberance, nudge us with their impatience, and prompt us to adopt new options, their contributions have the greatest value when they are compared and contrasted, blended and integrated, with all that has been experienced by those who have come before them.

So we think it is time for a much needed "rebalancing" — by those of us "who weren't born yesterday" and by the rest of humanity as well. It is also time to be aware that the physical standards we used to measure earlier stages of life simply cannot apply. For example, aging won't ever be desirable or even acceptable if we insist on evaluating it using the same standards we use to evaluate youth. Aging is not about perfectly smooth skin and the absence of wrinkles. It is not about continually striving to match all of those PhotoShopped images of taut and toned bodies. These images are the products of the commercial dream makers who intentionally overlook the obvious truth that a large number of Americans in their 20s and 30s are far from taut and toned.

We also believe that we would be wise to include the quality of one's character, the depth of one's life experience, the mastery demonstrated over life's major challenges, the strength of one's values, the amount of balance and inner peace one demonstrates, and the level of one's inner focus and spiritual evolution among the standards we use to evaluate a successful life.

If we follow this same line of thought a little further, we believe it will be important to reevaluate our addiction to change — at least change for its own sake. While there is a great deal to be said for change and innovation — not the least being that change is unavoidable — neither come exclusively from the young, and not all of the changes and innovations that young people so quickly champion are positive. In fact, one need only look around for a moment or two to understand how wholeheartedly the young adopt technology even if it is moving them away from a direct experience to a virtual experience of life and to an addiction to a 24/7 wired, interconnected, web-based, data-deluged, game-minded, media-mad world.

Indeed, as a result of these technologies the traditional impatience with and lack of exposure and support that young people have for "being" and "silence" is exaggerated and "doing" and "noise" come to define the landscape.

We know, of course, that similar types of criticisms have been leveled against each generation by those who have preceded them. Still no one can deny that the world has speeded up and is changing in ways previous generations did not even dream of. And, if we subscribe to Moore's Law of doubling, which predicts the astounding rate at which computers will increase their efficiency and impact on our world, this speeding up has only just begun.

You Ain't Seen Nothing Yet

So what exactly are we suggesting we do about this all-pervasive myth of youth and some of the less-than-constructive behaviors that go along with it? Our advice is for those of us who are in or moving toward the second half of life to start telling the whole truth and nothing but the truth about life as we know it.

In "Four Quartets," T.S. Eliot suggests that we would be wise to pay attention not just to "the wisdom of old men, but rather of their folly." Well, from our perspective, our frailties and follies add up to a lot of experience; and this experience, when processed correctly, can add up to a lot of wisdom. And it is precisely this kind of wisdom that we believe our youth-obsessed, noise-filled, media-mad world appears to need at this time.

How do we process and share this wisdom? We can start by telling the truth about our frailties and our follies, our victories and our breakthroughs, our indifference and our insensitivities, our discoveries and our perceptions. Yes, if we want to find genuine solutions and reengage and enlist the attention and respect of younger generations, we have to stop telling them what they should be doing and instead start sharing our truth, and nothing but the truth so help us God. We can also share our experience, model alternative paths for the road ahead, and celebrate the significance and importance of living consciously and aging wisely.

We can use our collective energy and power to make America age-friendly. To celebrate the wisdom we have gained from those who have come before us, to reinfuse within our culture an understanding of why honoring our elders is important. We can encourage our governments — national, state, and local — to create new Departments of Longevity to support the needs and rights of older Americans. We can expand the reach of the Older Americans Act that was passed originally in 1965. We can also require our businesses to become age-friendly by ensuring that their products and services meet the needs of elders.

One additional way we can move beyond the myth of youth is to stop focusing so exclusively on the temporary and transitory interests we practice in the first half of life, and start focusing instead on the more immutable traditions and wisdom that can be gained on the inner journey. This then can help us prick the bubble of the myth of youth — not for the young who should be encouraged to celebrate every minute of their youth, but for those of us who may be laboring under the delusion that we should never allow ourselves to look or act older. In the process of doing this and other things, we can discover and model a legacy of truth and wisdom that can make a significant difference in the future of this planet.

Life Rule

"Hold fast to dreams."

~ Langston Hughes

Life Achievement

Don Robitaille, a committed elder, rode his bicycle from Bar Harbor in Maine to Washington state, a distance of more than 3,000 miles, over the course of six months at the age 70.

Life Tool

In a world in which many of us learn to say no, we invite you to start experimenting with saying yes. Say yes to new opportunities, new ideas, new people. Say yes to living the life you want to live. Say yes to the truth — the truth about life, about aging, and about death.

The Persistent Provider

Leah's Story

Leah Waterman was born in Pivla, a small town in Poland, in the early part of the last century. She was an Orthodox Jew at a time when holding such beliefs in that part of Europe was a dangerous thing. Leah was my great grandmother and a dynamic teacher in my life.

At 15, Leah went to work in the kitchens of the czar of Russia, baking 80 loaves of bread a day. She soon married my great grandfather, Isaac, who was a tailor. Leah then became a seamstress. Their daughter, Dora, was born in Poland before they fled from the pogroms — the organized massacres of innocent people inflicted by the Russian army on the Jews.

I remember early stories my mother told, repeating the stories she'd heard from Leah's first cousin, Liala, who later also fled Poland. Most of my great grandmother's remaining family was killed by a different threat. Liala would say, as she showed me pictures of my relatives, "Hitler killed them all."

Leah and Isaac and my young grandmother, Dora, landed first in London, England, where they stayed a few years before moving to Seattle, Washington. There was a gold rush in Seattle at the time, so my great grandfather opened a saloon to attract the miners' gold, which he kept for them in his safe.

Leah was resourceful in her determination to find a better life in America. She and Isaac later moved to Los Angeles, where Isaac opened a tailor shop and Leah worked as a seamstress. When my great grandfather could no longer sew due to bronchitis, they moved to a farm in Los Angeles between Compton and Linwood, where my Mother, Betty, and her four siblings would stay for most of the year. Their grandparents sewed all their clothes and the farm provided all their food. The farm provided turkeys, geese, chickens, and milk from the cow that Leah would use to make butter, cheese, and buttermilk, when she was not canning vegetables from their garden. The farm was the home of some of my mother's, aunt's, and uncle's favorite memories.

Some years after my great grandfather Isaac passed away, I remember seeing my great grandmother for the first time in her Boyle Heights home in Los Angeles. She had remarried a man named Morris. I remember what a magnificent cook she was. Although I was a young girl at the time, I can still remember the smell of the kosher pickles fermenting in large crocks all around her house.

My mouth watered every time my family came to visit, because of the smell of fresh rye bread, those amazing pickles, and an assortment of delicious dishes she always prepared for my family's visits. As the oldest of eight children, I was in awe of her talents and infectious positive attitude. Our great grandmother had her hands full cooking for such a large and hungry bunch. Like her, my mother was a great cook, and it is no accident that cooking is one of my passions. This is just one of the legacies she left me.

When Leah was in her 80s she came to live down the street from my Auntie Fran and Uncle Ernie in the hills of Berkeley, California. This was where my family would visit on holidays from Southern California. Grandma Leah would come over to their house and we would all laugh and eat and listen to her stories. When I played the piano she would come over and whisper in my ear, "You are such a talented girl, Sedena my darling, you will do great things in your life." She had such belief in me, and needless to say I loved her very much.

One day while we were visiting I remember walking down the street to her house and walking in on her in the bathtub with her candles lit, praying out loud. She stopped praying and invited me in as she explained the ritual and fed my curiosity about the meaning of her faith. Another great memory was showing her how to dial the phone with the large numbers. She did her best to dial my aunt and uncle's number although she couldn't read. We laughed as she performed this feat, and yelled into the receiver, "Hello, hello, can you hear me? This is Leah, I'm calling you now!"

I will also never forget when my great grandmother had her 84th birthday. She blew out her candles, stood up, and crossed her arms in front of her *as she bent down into a squat and performed a Russian-style dance for a couple of minutes. She ended with a big smile as she exclaimed, "L'chaim" — to life!*

This amazing woman, who fled from tyranny when she was young and never gave up, was never afraid to say how she felt and freely shared her light with those around her. Her intention was to be the best she could be: fully alive, kind and loving, responsible to her talents, committed to her faith. She was a provider of nourishment, from her food to her inner beauty and wisdom. She gave me many gifts — a longing for the Great Mystery, a light-heartedness about making mistakes, courage in following my dreams and believing in where they lead, and joy in celebrating life regardless of its challenges. She continues to nourish me with the legacy of her love and inspiration.

Tomorrow...Tomorrow

"If all I have is Now
Where will I look for joy?"

~ Mark Nepo ~

Waiting for Life to Happen

Like the lyrics from the title song from the Broadway musical, *Annie*, "Tomorrow! Tomorrow! I love ya, tomorrow! You're always a day a way!" and the characters in Samuel Beckett's classic play, *Waiting for Godot*, an awful lot of us spend an inordinate amount of our lives waiting for tomorrow or for whatever the next something, someone, or somewhere is.

We wait for the phone to ring, the weekend to arrive, the invitation to come, the workday to end, the next program to start, or the trip to begin. We wait for this job to be completed and the next one to start, for the new position to open, the stock market to go up, that special person to come into our lives, and often and especially for someone else or the world we live in to change.

Yes, we live in a world of online calendars, smartphones, and touchscreen tablets on which we dutifully record or search for upcoming events — events and experiences we believe will bring us more joy; entertain us more; or make us more important, wealthier, stronger, or safer. We want what we believe will make our lives more meaningful or, at the very least, different and hopefully better. In short, a lot of us spend a lot of our time waiting for something other than whatever is currently happening, something that we hope will be more interesting or more significant than whatever we perceive to be happening now.

Our hope seems to stem from the belief that these future somethings, someones, or somewheres will not only be better than whatever is going on now, but they will somehow relieve us of the underlying discomfort, anxiety, confusion, pain, suffering, and even the terror that many of us in the modern world live with either on or beneath the surface every day. Sometimes we wait for something to happen because whatever is going on feels boring or dull, ordinary or uninteresting. Fritz Perls, the father of Gestalt Psychology, used to ask his students and clients who reported being bored: "Why are you boring yourself?"

At other times, whatever is happening is not boring but seems painful, complicated, challenging, or frightening and so we assume that there is another something/someone/somewhere that will be less painful or complicated, more interesting or exciting, or simpler or easier to deal with.

In short, we have a lot of assumptions and a number of expectations about that something/someone/somewhere and yet these expectations rarely, if ever, materialize. Still, like the folks who keep buying lotto tickets year after year against incredible odds and without any sign of a return, we continue to expect, assume, and wait for that something/someone/somewhere that is better and different to show up.

There is another aspect of this practice that author Eckhart Tolle includes in his explanation of this "waiting for something to happen" syndrome, which says that in most of these periods of waiting, we assume there is someone out there who knows more than we do or has more energy or courage or ability to take on whatever is currently troubling us. In these instances, we believe that as a result of finally finding or meeting this someone who can do this something better than we can, we will feel better, bigger, more important, safer, happier, saved, or whatever.

Perhaps you are familiar with Tolle's "waiting for something to happen" syndrome or our version of the "tomorrow, tomorrow" complex. Perhaps you occasionally or frequently find yourself gazing longingly at the future and hoping it will be better and different than your present moment. That is certainly true for us, especially in particularly challenging or trying moments. Our anecdotal research demonstrates that this is also the case for many other people, especially people who are in the second half of life. So if it is true for you, we have a strong and clear piece of advice for you.

Stop Waiting!

Yes, stop waiting for the doctor, the lawyer, the government official, your boss, your minister, rabbi, imam, priest, guru, your exercise instructor, your best friend, parent, lover, husband, wife, or even God to save you or show you the way. Stop waiting and start paying attention to what you know and don't know, to what you can and cannot do, and most especially, to what is occurring right now in your world. For your world has within it the answer to whatever questions you may be asking. It also reminds you that "you are the one you have been waiting for," the one and only one who will make you feel better or different. So please stop waiting and remember that all you have to do to find this answer is to have the willingness to look for it inside yourself, the wit to recognize it, the courage to trust it, and the sense to allow it to guide you.

Beyond Tough Love

We do not offer this advice as a form of tough love and certainly do not want to preach to you. Instead, we hope you will stop waiting because we care enormously about you and about our world, and we know that if those of us who are already in or are approaching the second half of life do not stop waiting for something/someone/somewhere to happen or someone else to show up to fix things, the probability is very high that whatever is happening now will keep on happening or perhaps get worse before it gets better. And this is as true in our inner emotional landscapes as it is in the world at large.

For example, our planet is currently suffering, and rather dramatically we might add, from years of our indifference and downright insensitivity. We have, as we discussed earlier — if not directly then by proxy or failure to act — allowed others in the service of the Gods of Short-term Economics to pollute the air, the water, and Mother Earth herself. We have also created, promoted, or allowed others to take much more than their fair share of the Earth's natural resources and to design lifestyles that require absurd amounts of energy and thereby require others to suffer levels of poverty and hunger that are unconscionable.

On the more personal side, many of us have personal habits or patterns that we know are not good for us and/or for others; and yet rather than do something about them, we wait for something different to happen. We eat foods that are not good for us; hold and express limited or negative emotions that hurt ourselves and others; and demonstrate behaviors that are troublesome, dumb, dangerous, insensitive, indifferent, selfish, or harmful. And no matter what the pattern or habit, many of us keep doing it over and over again while waiting for something different to happen, oblivious to the old rule that says:

If you always do what you have always done
you will always get what you have always gotten.

So what are you waiting for? Are you really waiting for the day you will actually quit whatever the bad habit is? Are you actually waiting for someone to invent a pill to neutralize the effect of whatever harmful things you are doing to your body? Are you waiting for someone to come along and either do it for you or help you to get it done? Do you really think it is likely that someone else will change? Are you waiting for the unpleasant condition — that pain or that fear — to magically go away in complete defiance of physical laws? Are you hoping that someone will finally come along and eliminate these inconvenient dilemmas like aging and dying before they impact you?

The Alternative

Fortunately or not, depending on your point of view, there is only one cure for this "tomorrow, tomorrow" condition. We need to stop waiting and start acting! We need to stop thinking negative thoughts; stop holding limited beliefs; stop practicing outmoded attitudes; and stop exploitive, repressive, unconscious behaviors toward ourselves and others.

"Easier said than done!" you say. Yes, that's true! After a reasonable number of years spent waiting and hoping for any number of things, we know how true that is. But remember what we said at the beginning: living consciously and aging wisely are not always easy, and they're certainly not for sissies. But neither is the alternative. If we never do anything different, if we only think and talk about making changes, change will eventually occur anyway and it will likely be a form of change we will not find particularly to our liking. Indeed, whatever is currently troubling us or prompting our fears will only get worse; and so we strongly suggest that we all wake up and smell the roses before it's too late.

In order to experience more joy, a greater sense of peace and acceptance, and more sanity, each and every one of us must roll up our sleeves and get involved in life — not some theoretical, philosophical, or virtual version of life, but this life! Your life! Today! This very moment! Yes, we must decide, right here and now, that this or that condition, fear, situation, or relationship needs to be healthier, more uplifting, more supportive, more constructive, or better and different.

And if what has got to change has something to do with the world around us, then we suggest that helping it to change is a part of our job. We have to take action, real and specific action, that contributes to solutions.

Poverty, disease, pollution, war, crime — whatever the condition that disturbs or troubles us, we must decide if and how we may be contributing to it, even if it is only by insensitivity and inattention. If what has to change has something to do with what goes on inside us, then we would be wise to begin to express enough love and compassion for ourselves and enough concern for those who are impacted by us to take charge of ourselves and work to alter our habits and beliefs. And this is not to say that that we need to attack whatever is out of alignment inside us or in the world around us. We do not have to be Hercules. We only need to tune in to our original, compassionate, and grace-filled hearts and let them lead us.

If we are wise, each of us will make peace with whatever is out of balance first. We will show genuine compassion and understanding. We will then make a shift in our perceptions, understandings, beliefs, thoughts, and practices — one step, one action, one breath at a time. In this way we can stop waiting and start being who we were born to be. In the process, we will bring greater light and love and wonder to our world. If we take Dr. David Hawkins's good advice that he illustrates in his book *Power vs. Force* — and raise the level of our thoughts, words, and actions to a higher, more positive frequency — then we will be able to contribute to raising the frequency of our world as well.

Life Rule
"Life is too short to be small."

~ Benjamin Disraeli

Life Achievement
Willem de Kooning, one of the 20th century's most recognized artists, painted significant work in his early 80s.

Life Tool
We invite you to get into the habit of asking questions that can help you get in touch with your authentic Self. You can do this in a journal; while you are out for a daily walk or run; or even in conversations with friends, colleagues, and loved ones. You may find it interesting to compare your answers to theirs.

- Why was I born?
- What am I doing with the gift of my life?
- What am I going to do with the rest of my life?
- What actions can I take today to express my unique gifts and talents?
- What do I really believe happens when I die?

Celebrating Life —
Befriending Death

"Seduced by our technological successes, which have given us unparalleled control of the physical world, we hope that genetic engineering, anti-aging chemicals, and bionic research will eliminate death...[But] death is not a cosmic mistake. Woven into the warp and woof of existence, the presence of death deepens our appreciation of life."

~ Zalman Schachter-Shalomi & Ronald Miller ~

Setting Ourselves Free

As we make our way toward the end of Part Two of this book and prepare for the next stage of our journey together — during which we will have the opportunity to harvest the experience and wisdom of our past and turn it into gold we can spend in the future — we invite you to consider one more topic. In some ways it is, as they say, "the Mother/Father of all topics." And as a result it often brings up, especially at our age-averse society, a number of concerns, confusions, and illusions. The subject, of course, is death.

To set ourselves free from the greatest illusion of them all — the illusion that prevents so many of us from fully living the lives we were born to live — we encourage you to pay close attention to the sage advice that the writer and spiritual warrior Carlos Castaneda shared with us. He suggests we not only befriend death but allow it to become our ally.

So if you are serious about wanting to inherit more joy and a fuller, deeper, and more vibrant experience of life, we encourage you to open — even if only a little more — to remembering that death is an essential and unavoidable part of this life. Yes life — intricate and beautiful in its design, a whole system that represents the unique handiwork of Source — includes an entrance, the experience, and an exit. When you learn to accept death as a natural part of your journey, understand the important role it plays in enriching and deepening your life experience, and consider it as a kind of graduation from one level of experience to another, it allows you to appreciate another good piece of advice that Castaneda shared with us. He suggests we all consult with death often during our lives, that we turn toward it as one would a mentor or coach and ask for its advice.

After all, isn't that one of the things we often hear from those who have had what are called near-death experiences? They often report that after one of these experiences life suddenly becomes more precious to them. They begin to see things — even some of the most mundane — with new eyes. They remember how valuable their ordinary moments of connection with the people who make up their daily lives are. They report being motivated to reevaluate their priorities and values, and identify new metrics they can use to determine what is important and what is not. And they report something else, as well — that death ceases to be something they fear and instead becomes something natural and understandable.

Unfortunately, the majority of us who have not had a near-death experience get caught up in the everyday push and pull of life and as a result tend to do the opposite. We focus on what we think are the important things — our career, making money, gaining status and recognition, satisfying our material wants, and accumulating the things we believe make our lives better. As a result, we view death as an unwanted intrusion, an end to our independence, and we do our best to deny it, which does us as much good as going out on a rainy day without an umbrella and hoping to not get wet. But we do it anyway.

Indeed, as Elisabeth Kubler-Ross, one of the 20th century's most courageous guides in the journey of life and death, wrote:

> It is the denial of death that is partially responsible for people living empty, purposeless lives; for when you live as if you'll live forever, it becomes too easy to postpone the things you know that you must do.

The poet, Mary Oliver, another true champion of greater awareness concludes one of her beautiful poems about death, "When Death Comes," with this stunning line — "I don't want to end up simply having visited the world."

An Extraordinary Idea

What a remarkable closing line! "I don't want to end up simply having visited this world." Even if only in that place deep in our hearts, most of us know what Mary Oliver means. In fact, how many times during the first half of our lives have we wondered if what we were doing was serving us and others or if were just taking up space, just shuffling along on that road from birth to...

Yes, this is certainly what some of us have been and are still doing. We entered this world full of audacity, kicking and screaming for breath and hungry for life. We entered this world as daring voyagers who passed through the ritual of birth seeking the opportunity to unfold a unique destiny. We came in still wet with amniotic fluid, still attached to our mother by the umbilical cord. We came in full of vim and vigor, innocence and courage, and then somehow, slowly for some of us, all too rapidly for others, that vim and vigor, that enthusiasm and curiosity, that distinct, original hunger for meaning and purpose was challenged, dulled, dampened, discouraged, and perhaps finally, almost forgotten.

How does this happen? "Education," some call it. "Socialization," others name it. Don Miguel Ruiz, author of *The Four Agreements,* calls it "domestication." We call it "mimicry." Yes, we are domesticated, socialized, educated; and in so many steps along the way we are seduced by the gods of Acceptance and Recognition who dole out approval like alms to the poor — through our parents, teachers, religious leaders, and friends. We are also domesticated and kept in line by the gods of Opinion and of Economics.

The Great Denial

One of the most powerful domestication methods results from the masking of the experience of aging and death in our daily landscape. Death is talked about, of course, especially when someone famous or someone close to us dies. The topic is also covered ad nauseam in the media, especially if there are gory details associated with its occurrence. However, death is not actually talked about, but rather the way in which death happens is explored. The actual and unavoidable condition, that state of no longer being here in physical form, is not talked about or reflected on very much, if at all. Nor is there — with the exception of beliefs promoted by religions — much conversation about what really happens after we die. And when this conversation does occur, it often involves fanciful tales of heaven and threats of eternal punishment.

The actual, natural, and unavoidable condition of no longer being in the physical realm is something we pretend to know little about. We say "pretend" because after having dropped the veil when we entered life and then denying some of the glimpses we occasionally get into the unknown during moments of heighted experience or deep inner quiet, we tend to stay pretty much between the lines, clinging to what we call reality and avoiding that which we cannot explain. As a result, this state of no longer being, which we call "death," scares the heck out of most of us. In truth, however, the level of fear we experience over what happens after we die is nowhere near as great as our fear about the way in which we will make our exit.

And who can blame us? We spend our lives working to stand out; to succeed; to be special, separate, and independent; to accumulate and accomplish. No wonder in a world that has come to value these things above all others the idea that all of this will disappear in an instant frightens us. Yes, what scares us — in addition to the idea of possible physical pain of disease or accident — is the invisibility. What scares us — in addition to all of those images from disasters and wars, horror films, TV shows, and the real-life tragedies that the media trumpets — is the idea that all we struggle so hard for during our lives will, in the end, have very little if any lasting value to us.

In our culture, death, at best, is considered an inconvenience, an interruption in the flow of what we like to think is normal. At worst, death is considered the end of the line and of the game. That's why — at least here in the West — the bodies of the dead are taken away quickly, mummified with formaldehyde, and painted with rouge and lipstick. Then the rest of us stand around talking about how good old Uncle Harry or Aunt Tilly looks, and what a long and terrific life he or she led, or what a blessing it is that they finally passed on. Many times, of course, we know that what we are saying it is not true. Uncle Harry and Aunt Tilly may not have really had such terrific lives, especially in their old age. As for the "what a blessing" part, that may be a little more true.

Perhaps we visited them in that senior residence or sat in their room at the nursing home. Perhaps we felt some of their loneliness or despair, their sense of being left out and left behind, their confusion and fear over what lay ahead, or maybe we were just projecting our own fears. Perhaps the melancholy and sadness we experience in these moments comes from the knowledge that they may not have kept faith with the agreement they made before they were born. And perhaps the reason we glimpse this fact is that it is true for us as well.

Or perhaps when we visited them we did not linger long enough to open our hearts wide enough to feel what was happening. Or perhaps, perhaps they were much more content and accepting of the final stages of their lives than we were. As a result, most of the time, especially here in this country and among those cultural and ethnic groups who no longer live in multi-generational family units, we neither witness nor participate in the steps leading up to death. The old are often isolated from the rest of us, first in retirement communities where children and animals — except for occasional visits — are generally excluded. Then, when seniors have progressed beyond self-care, they are tucked away in assisted-living environments, nursing homes, and then eventually in the dying wards in hospitals so that their approach to death does not remind the rest of us in the general population of what many of us mistakenly believe is the awkwardness and inconvenience of the final stage. And in this way the elderly and dying do not intrude on the productivity that the rest of us are expected to maintain. No reason to disturb those of us who make up the great army of the employed. No reason to screw up a perfectly valid run on the stock market or impact a good golf game with truth about life and death. Hell, it might cause us to question how we are spending the days of our own lives!

Defying Trends and Realigning with Truth

We suggest that we do ourselves a really gargantuan service by breaking out from the confines of these limiting beliefs and faulty traditions! Instead of denying the existence of death, let's look it in the eye. Yes, let's welcome death back into our world and find out for ourselves — knowing rather than believing — whether death is our ally or our adversary. Let's find out if Castaneda, Elisabeth Kubler-Ross, Mary Oliver, Ram Dass, Stephen and Ondrea Levine, and so many other wise guides have been telling the truth. Let us understand what Kabir, the Indian poet and mystic, meant when he asked, "If you can't cross over alive, how are you going to cross over when you are dead?"

As a way of getting started on welcoming death back into our world, we recommend a little brainstorming to identify some of the names we use to refer to Death. Here are a few of the names participants in some of our seminars have come up with. As always, we invite you to add other names to the list.

Death

The Specter
The Grim Reaper
The End of the Line
The Judge

The Terminator
The Executioner
The Final Solution

What do you think would happen in our world if, instead of using these names, we began to give death a different set of names:

The Reward	The Doorway to a New Dimension
The Great Reliever	The Graceful Exit
The Blessing	The Graduation
The Next Step	The Opening
The Rebirth	The Holiday

See what we mean? Doesn't it help to change your attitude and refer to death by one of these more positive names?

Why We Fear Death &
Why We Are Talking about It

As we've already discussed, most of us fear death, but we especially fear the possible pain that may be associated with our death. Depending on our religious beliefs, some of us also greatly fear the projected consequences we will experience at and following the end of our lives.

There are other very natural fears associated with death. We fear the loss of loved ones, of opportunities, and of what we think of as control over our lives. But the bottom line is that most of us fear the manner and consequences of our death far more than we fear the state or condition we call death. And this, of course, is one of the human frailties the media exploits by dwelling on the goriest possible details of accidents and tragedies. Indeed, if we have a phobia or weakness or a fear, that is precisely what the media plays upon.

Compound this with all of the "fire and brimstone, hell and damnation" ranting that goes on in a number of churches turned television studios and entertainment centers. It is no wonder the majority of us live in fear of what is one of the only two natural, unalterable, uncontested facts about life. Just as in-breath follows exhale, just as light follows darkness, so eventually death follows birth. It is a non-negotiable reality!

If this is the case, if death is so natural, so inevitable, perhaps it is time that we begin looking at why so many of us are in such denial of its existence and the essential role it plays in our lives. Here's a short list of some of the reasons participants in our seminars have said they are afraid of death. Perhaps it will help you in your process.

Loss of control
Loss of opportunity
Loss of loved ones
Possibility of punishment
Fear of pain
Loss of security
Elimination of accomplishments
Loss of possessions
Suffering
Loss of self
The Great Unknown
The end of the game
Loss of identity
Getting stuck in some horrible place
Punishment for what I've done or failed to do

Please take a moment and add a few of your own fears to this list.

Incidentally, we are including this subject here in Part Two because we hope it will assist you in the process of befriending death. We believe it will serve you well as you explore ways in which you can harvest the wisdom of your past, learn to live more fully in the present, and chart a course of greater meaning for your future.

We close this chapter with a quote from Reverend Chariji, an Indian teacher, whose wisdom has served us on a number of occasions.

"Death is really a holiday from life. Babaji [his teacher] has used this beautiful analogy — that even the prisoners in the dungeons are let out for one or two hours every day to go up in the sunshine in the courtyards, to have fresh air, to have some exercise, so that they can face the next period of incarceration in the dungeon. Therefore, death is not a punishment. Neither is death an end. Some Occidental writers on the subject treat death with contempt, with fear. And many people have been educated into thinking that death is to be avoided, even by committing suicide, which is ridiculous. You cannot avoid death by dying. You can only avoid death by living properly."

Life Rule
"You know quite well deep within you, that there is only a single magic, a single power, a single salvation and that is called loving."

~ Herman Hesse

Life Achievement
Helen Keller, writer, activist, way-shower, and first deaf/blind person to earn a bachelor of arts degree, was still writing at 75.

Life Tool
Although it may feel awkward and uncomfortable at first, we invite you to experiment with having a conversation with death. Yes, give death a body and a personality, and then invite it to sit with you for a few moments.

Do not try to avoid your discomfort by talking to death right away. Just sit there and feel whatever you are feeling. After a while, ask death whatever you would like to know, and then listen. You may feel a little foolish or awkward at first. You may wonder if the answers you are receiving are just answers you are making up in your own mind. But don't worry. If you trust the process and listen, you may be surprised and pleased with what you will learn.

Not for Sissies

"Am I willing to give up what I have in order to be what I am not yet?
Am I willing to let my ideas of myself, of man, be changed?
Am I able to follow the spirit of love into the desert?
To empty myself even of my concept of emptiness?"
~ M. C. Richards ~

Not Always Easy

As is probably clear to you by now, living consciously and aging wisely is a valuable but not always an easy path to follow. But then again, as author Etta Clark, television host and humorist Art Linkletter, and many others have said, growing old is not for sissies. Indeed, those of us who are interested in making the best of the rest of our lives — who want to age with greater grace and awareness — find that there is a certain amount of attention we need to direct to some primary areas of our lives. This certainly includes diet and exercise. It also includes the need to clarify and recast some of our thoughts, beliefs, and actions in order to heal fissures and breakdowns in our relationships. We need to redefine priorities and values and spend sufficient time on our inner landscape in reflection, prayer, and meditation. If we do some of these things with greater awareness than we have up to now, in the days ahead, our lives will be healthier and have greater meaning, purpose, joy, and satisfaction. We will also find that we will have a greater chance to make a positive difference in the lives of others. And we will certainly be a lot closer to completing the destiny we have come here to manifest. Not a bad list of outcomes, is it?

When the rigors of life are intense or you forget why living consciously and aging wisely are so important, here are a few things that may help you get back on track:

⊛ Look a little deeper and listen a little closer to the wisdom that speaks through you.

- ⊛ Explore and make greater peace with some things that may scare you — aging, death, after death.

- ⊛ Experiment with different beliefs, behaviors, and attitudes.

- ⊛ Practice living in the present by simply turning your focus away from the past and the future.

- ⊛ Explore your inner landscape more often and with greater commitment.

Ram Dass, contemporary author, spiritual teacher, and expert on aging, encourages us to realize that "we are not isolated life forms but essential parts of a deeply aligned and interconnected whole." When we make this adjustment in our thinking and move away from believing that we are independent and isolated organisms in a dangerous and threatening world; when we move toward knowing that we are interdependent, interrelated, constantly evolving parts of this whole, then a more genuine and satisfying life becomes possible.

If we are willing to do this — at least some of the time — we may finally begin to admit that whatever happens in our lives, including aging and dying, is part of the natural, organic process called life. And the more we come to understand this, the more we focus on cultivating our inner wealth, the more our fears about changes in our physical form and our interaction with the external world can be seen as less important.

This is not to say that there are not very real challenges we face as we age. Nor is it to understate the impact of physical changes in our bodies, the physical pains that show up along the way, some of restrictions in our movements and energy levels, and other changes that most of us experience some of the time and some of us deal with a lot of the time as we make our transition to being older.

However, even a cursory look at our lives to date, including all of the earlier stages, helps us to remember that there are a number of steps that are a part of the natural process of being a human being that are not all that easy.

Indeed, if we are honest with ourselves, making the journey through the birth canal, taking our first breath, adjusting to early stages in the physical world when we learn how to make our needs known, learning to walk and talk, and making sense of the early rules of social behavior are all rather complicated and challenging steps.

In fact, when we slow down our observation of each of these steps and study them physiologically, emotionally, and intellectually; if we track the biochemical changes that occur in our bodies during and as a result of each, we discover that each of these passages is pretty staggering and miraculous in their complexity and in the challenges they impose upon us.

Travel a little further on in your mind and consider the experience of going to school, of making the passage through puberty, and your first sexual encounters. Consider the physical, emotional, and intellectual complexities associated with leaving home for the first time, entering college, or going into military service. Reflect on the process of developing new adult skills and learning the rules of new jobs and relationships. Consider the challenge of giving birth, parenting, and then all of the other changes associated with the loss of a loved one, accidents, emotional and physical spiritual losses, betrayals, illnesses, new discoveries, new geographies, career setbacks, personal achievements, financial ups and downs, caretaking parents and dealing with their deaths, etc.

You see, life — every single stage of it — is not easy! So why then would we assume that getting older is supposed to be without challenges or be offended because these difficulties exist? Why, indeed, would we expect aging to be different from all of the other stages and why are so many of us so disappointed or discouraged or concerned about this stage — more concerned than we have been about all of the other stages?

The changes that come from shifting from a lifelong focus on work and career to more self-generated interests and activities, and getting used to different levels of physical energy and abilities, are not easy transitions. But are they really all that different from hundreds of earlier transitions we have made?

Dealing with the loss of a regular salary and the realization that the time remaining to generate income or make up for losses in one's stock portfolio can be very challenging. Coming to terms with changes in our physical appearance and in the way the world relates to us; with the loss of loved ones, family, and friends; learning to accept less mobility and more isolation; and many more such challenges — none of these passages are easy. But are they really the first time we have dealt with some of these experiences?

Of course, the challenges associated with aging vary in pace and consequence for each of us. But no matter who we are or how we age, some or all of these consequences are simply unavoidable parts of being a human being and wearing this human body. In fact, challenge is simply the unavoidable price we pay for entering, experiencing, and exiting the game of life.

Compounding the Difficulty

So if aging is just as complicated, but no more complicated, than the other stages of life, why do so many of us make things even harder by pretending that aging and dying are different or worse or not natural parts of life? Why do we choose to struggle against the natural, organic, and inevitable shifts and changes that come after a certain number of years spent inhabiting a physical body? Wouldn't it be better, wiser, and ultimately easier to be honest about all of the stages in this spectrum that stretch from being born to maturing, growing older, and ultimately dying? Wouldn't it make more sense to let go of the illusions and limiting beliefs that we use to defend against reality and instead look life in the eye?

One day Grandfather was walking along with his grandchildren when they saw a wolf standing on a rock cliff high above them. Pointing toward the wolf, he spoke to them about life, "A battle is raging inside me...it is a constant struggle between two wolves.

"One wolf represents ego with all of its fear, anger, envy, sorrow, regret, greed, arrogance, self-pity, guilt, resentment, inferiority, lies, false pride, and superiority. The other stands for joy, peace, love, hope, sharing, serenity, humility, kindness, benevolence, friendship, empathy, generosity, truth, compassion, and faith."

The old man looked at the children with a firm stare. "This same fight is going on inside you, and inside every other person, too."

They thought about this for a minute, and then one of the children asked his grandfather, "Which wolf will win?"

"The one you feed," said Grandfather.

In Part Three you will have a chance to spend a little time reviewing the life you have lived to date from an objective standpoint and learn some things about who you have been and what you have done. So we encourage you to look your experiences in the eye, begin to make more peace with them, and to benefit from them. Then you can decide which wolf you are going to feed from now on.

Life Rule

"In art, as in life, everything is possible so long as it is based on love."

~ Marc Chagall

Life Achievement

Mack Sennett, comedian and one of America's early filmmakers, appeared in an Abbott & Costello movie in his 70s.

Life Tool

Experiment with going to breakfast or lunch today with a friend or, even better, someone at work you do not know as well — or even someone you meet for the first time in a restaurant. During your meal take the time to share at least one story from your past — something you previously had assigned to the "negative" pile. Tell your lunch companion the lesson you learned from this experience and how it has impacted your life or provided you with opportunities you otherwise would not have had.

As you are telling your story, see if you can answer this question regarding your challenge. "What did I contribute that was helpful or positive to this situation and what did I learn?" If someone shares their story with you, ask them this same question. And then at the end of your story, express your gratitude for the challenge.

PART THREE
Harvesting the Wisdom of Your Past

"One would not think of throwing out the juice from a freshly squeezed orange and saving only the skin. So we might not want to focus exclusively on the images and memories from the past and miss the wisdom they contain."

~ George Cappannelli ~

The Sculptor

Michelangelo's Story

Michelangelo Buonarroti is one of our personal heroes. He is without dispute one of the greatest artists in the history of world. Some proclaim him to be the greatest sculptor who ever lived.

Born to a middle-class family in a small village in Tuscany in 1475, he became an apprentice in the workshop of Domenico Ghirlandaio when he was 12. His earliest surviving piece of sculpture, <u>The Madonna of the Steps,</u> dates from 1491 when he was 16. After that the talent he was to share with the world really opened up: he created many works of art, including <u>Bacchus</u> in 1497, and between the time he was 23 to 25, he carved the <u>Pietà.</u>

Anyone who has ever had the privilege of viewing the <u>Pietà</u> in person understands the scope of Michelangelo's creative genius. To experience the beauty and harmony of the composition, to see the subtlety of the emotions, the sensitivity of the textures, the accuracy of the anatomy, and the energy that radiates from the piece almost defies the notion that a human being carved it.

From 1501 to 1504 Michelangelo carved <u>David</u> from a single, flawed block of marble 19 feet high — a block that had been started and abandoned by another sculptor. <u>David</u> has literally become the most universally recognized symbol of sculpture in the world. His unfinished sculptures often referred to as the slaves were begun in 1506 and the ceiling of the Sistine Chapel in 1508. At the age of 66 he completed the <u>Last Judgment</u> in the Sistine Chapel. In 1546, at the age of 71, he was named chief architect of the Vatican. He completed overseeing the building of Saint Peter's Basilica in Rome in his 80s. He was working on a piece called <u>The Rondanini Pietà</u> in the last week of his life in 1564. Michelangelo was 89 at the time of his passing.

While history has certainly applauded his many talents, few are familiar with some of the human frailties he possessed and some of challenges he faced. A man of below-average stature and relatively awkward features, his entire life was impacted by the political intrigue he dealt with under various popes, the jealousy he endured, and the family burdens he faced. In many ways, of course, these life challenges helped forge his artistic talents.

Still when one walks, as we have, in the galleries that make up the Accademia in Florence, and one spends time exploring what are called his unfinished pieces, the true nature of his work begins to reveal itself. When one glimpses the extraordinary power of these pieces which he carved with only four chisels — a point chisel, a tooth chisel, and two different kinds of flat-bladed chisels — when one experiences, as he the artist experienced, this remarkable uncovering of these forms from within their massive blocks; and when one finally turns and lifts one's eyes toward the <u>David</u> sitting in its majestic setting at the far end of the gallery, one can only hold one's breath in wonder at this genius who walked among us and the legacy of enduring brilliance that he left behind.

Backing into the Future

*"If we looked back on our lives with complete honesty,
many of us would conclude,
'I was lived by my parents; I was lived by my teachers;
I was lived by society.'"*

~ Zalman Schachter-Shalomi & Ronald Miller ~

Truth Telling

Our journey back in time does not, of course, begin here in the beginning of Part Three. Many of us, no matter how young or old we are, have spent a reasonable amount of our time living in the past.

It is, as they say, one of the two primary strategies the majority of us select — we either live in the past or we live in the future. While it is not a hard and fast rule, it appears that those who are younger tend to spend more of their time in the future; while those of us who are further along in years tend to spend more time in the past. After all, not only is there more of it to pay attention to, but spending time in the past also means we have less time to spend thinking about the challenges of the moment and what is ahead.

As a result, as some of the clichés about older people suggest, a number of us spend a lot of our time talking about what we did, who we were, and what we accomplished when we were younger. These same clichés also suggest that we are very set in our ways, somewhat stubborn about our beliefs, and often unflinching in the opinion that we know the right way of doing things. Not a very pretty picture but unfortunately even the most outrageous caricatures — like Archie Bunker and George Jefferson — often contain a certain amount of truth.

So what's wrong with this looking back and living in the past? Isn't this section of the book about the past? Yes, it is. But we have found that there is a distinct difference between a periodic and intentional visit to the past and the inclination to take up permanent residence there. The first situation allows us to reflect and process our experiences so that we can put the lessons we have gained in the past to work in the present. The second approach is literally like walking backward into the future. And as you know, no matter how agile one is, walking backward is never the easiest of experiences nor does it allow us to take maximum advantage of all of the remarkable opportunities that facing forward offer.

As we take these steps into the past in *Do Not Go Quietly*, there is one other thing we feel inclined to say. Executed with the right intention — the intention to better understand oneself and capitalize on the lessons and experiences of the past — this part of the journey can prove to be one of the most rewarding you will ever undertake.

And while it will include exploring some important and relevant things, it will not involve your languishing in nostalgia about the "good old days"; nor will it involve applying that brand of selective memory that allows all of us to keep telling the same old stories with the same old deletions and distortions over and over again.

Instead, your task, if you choose to accept it, is to revisit your past with new eyes (to go beyond the ruts of ordinary perception) so that you can make peace with some of its more awkward moments, squeeze the juice of experience and wisdom from other moments, make use of your stumbles and failures as well as your victories, and then use what you have culled from it all to set a course in the present that will allow you to live the life you were born to live.

If this invitation brings up any feelings of trepidation, please know they are natural. For when we revisit the past we generally encounter at least some memories that are awkward or painful because they involve some of our less than stellar past actions.

Selective Encounters with the Past

There are, of course, other reasons many of us have only selective and carefully controlled encounters with the past. Having lived through a number of cycles in our lives we are aware that not all of them were a bed of roses. Yes, in between the pages of our past — right there alongside, between, and under the joys and the accomplishments — are some old wounds, disappointments, failures, losses, moments of despair, betrayals (of self and others), and disillusionment. So it is not at all surprising that we are not all that enthusiastic about revisiting some of these less-than-pleasurable experiences.

And yet, unless we are willing to do precisely this, the pain we are holding in our bodies, in the pathways of our minds, and in the etheric stuff that is called our "consciousness" will remain trapped there. And this pain — as well as some of the guilt, shame, resentment, and regrets associated with the pain — will continue to weigh us down, obscure our sight, limit our access to our passion, reduce our sense of self-worth and self-confidence, lower our levels of physical energy, and block our curiosity and our access to joy. And ultimately, if not released in a constructive way, this trapped emotional, intellectual, and spiritual energy can lead to a wide range of debilitating circumstances, illnesses, and diseases.

By comparison, if we are willing to take an honest look at our past — the joys as well as the pains, the failures, and the victories — we will give ourselves the opportunity to truly experience new levels of freedom and new pathways of creative expression, and the opportunity to explore new dimensions, both external and internal.

Our willingness to delve into the past with new eyes and open minds also allows us to heal the wounds that may be troubling our hearts so we can open them and celebrate our connection with others and move into the realms that only the wisdom of the heart can ever allow us to reach.

Let's Talk a Little about Pain

So delving into one's past may involve re-experiencing some pain, but we can assure you that the pain you may experience will be far less than you imagine and certainly far less than the pain some of us currently experience as a result of holding on to the unnecessary and excess baggage from the past.

To prove this for yourself, we invite you to take part in a very simple experiment. It will only take a few moments, and if you do it with genuine commitment, we know this experience will assist you greatly in a variety of ways for the rest of your life.

If you have done this exercise before, we ask you to do it again and with a beginner's mind.

The Closed First Exercise

Just lay the book down on a flat surface in front of you or on your lap in a way that allows you to read these words. Then take your right hand and form a clenched fist.

Now take your left hand and clench it as well and then begin to squeeze both hands tightly — tightly enough to feel some discomfort.

Pay attention to what is going on with your hands. If you are squeezing tightly enough, you should find that some parts of your hands are red and others, where the blood is not flowing as easily, are turning a little white. Also notice that your fingernails may be adding to your discomfort because they may be digging slightly into the palms of your hands.

We know this is uncomfortable, but please keep squeezing. There is a very valuable payoff if you stay with this exercise.

So keep squeezing — even a little tighter, if possible.

Now ask yourself, *"What can I do with hands that are so tightly clenched?"*

Some of you may think you can hit something with your hands. But the truth is that if you were really squeezing tightly you would hurt your hands more than the object they hit.

Please hold on just a little longer.

When your hands are clenched so tightly, notice that it would be impossible to hold some object or pick up something else. Also notice that your hands may be feeling a little numb or cold.

This is what happens when our energy is not allowed to flow. We get numb, cold, and distant.

Okay, in just a few seconds we are going to ask you to open our hands, but we will do this in a particular way. On the count of three we will ask that you throw your right hand open and just allow your left hand to do what it does.

Ready...1...2...3... Now throw your right hand open and just allow you left hand to do what it does.

What do you notice?

Most people find that throwing their right hand open involves a relatively brief flash of discomfort followed almost immediately by a sense of relief. The right hand begins to tingle, the color starts to return, and very soon you have full use of it again.

But what about your left hand? If you have not forcibly opened your left hand, but merely stopped clenching it, you will probably find that the fingers are still curled, some of the numbness is still present, and the energy has not yet begun to flow fully into it.

Okay, now open your left hand as well. Clap your hands together and rub them until they are both feeling normal again.

Whatever You Hold on to You Are Stuck with

A few things you may want to take away from this exercise:

- Holding on to anything produces pain because life is a constant flow and holding on stops or limits the flow.

- Holding on to something, even if it is only your own hand, prevents you from being able to reach out to other things — that includes objects, experiences, and people.

- The pain you feel when you let go of something you are holding on to is generally momentary and nowhere near as great or as incapacitating as the pain you feel if you keep holding on — especially if you are holding on tightly.

- Unless you do something intentional to open, after a while your being, your heart, your hope — like your left hand — remain closed and stuck in place.

- It is not possible to do things that are constructive and helpful when your mind and your heart are closed.

- There is relief in letting go. Openness allows new energy to flow.

As you take your next steps on this road to exploring your past, allow yourself to keep these lessons in mind. Give yourself the gift of being a genuine explorer. Examine your past with the curious mind of an investigative reporter. Do not be afraid of whatever is in your past. It is past so all you need to do to be free is to examine your past — forgive yourself and others — and then come back into the present.

All you need to do to heal yourself and prepare for a marvelous new world full of hope, energy, and possibility is to let go of whatever you are holding on to and open your heart and your mind. And remember, this opening will be much less difficult or painful than you imagine. In fact, once on the other side of holding on, you will look back with genuine amazement on the fact that you allowed some of your memories and fears to dominate and limit you.

You may also discover that these experiences — the betrayals, the regrets, the failures, the losses, and much more — are actually things that, once you have opened your heart and your mind, you will come to treasure. For they are just as valuable and important to living the life you were born to live as what you call your good experiences. The victories and the defeats, the successes and failures, the stumbles and the breakthroughs are, after all, the distinct and unique gold of your life.

Life Rule

"If you want to go forward, walking backward is obviously not the most effective or intelligent way to proceed."

~ George and Sedena Cappannelli

Life Achievement

Buckminster Fuller, philosopher, inventor, and innovator, was still exploring breakthrough concepts and innovations in design at age 80.

Life Tool

As you take this portion of your journey, we invite you to become an observer. Notice that events that occurred long ago have no ability to hurt you in the present moment unless you attempt to hold on to them and stay closed (like your fist). By comparison the only hurt you will experience when you consider these past events is the brief release of trapped energy when you open your heart and your mind, similar to what you felt when you threw open your clenched fist. New energy will flood in. Any other hurt that you experience is the result of your thoughts, and you are free to release or change these any time you want.

Dealing with Incompletes

"Security is mostly superstition. It does not occur in nature
nor do the children of man, as a whole, experience it. Avoiding
danger is not safer in the long run than outright exposure.
Life is either a daring adventure or nothing."

~ Helen Keller ~

If You Only

Stephen Levine, author and healer, asks a fundamental question at the beginning of one of his books. "What would you do if you only had one year to live?"

A powerful question! A life-altering question — especially if you stop, even if only for a few moments, and let it lead you to that place where your truth resides. And that is precisely what we hope you will do in this chapter — explore this and other life-altering, life-enhancing, life-affirming questions.

We also hope that working with these questions will impact the way you view and experience the life you have been living; the life you are living; and, of particular consequence, the life that you can create for yourself going forward.

When and Why

Unlike the scenario that Stephen Levine suggests — an artificial limit of one year to live — some of us who are in the second half of life may live another 10, 20, or even 50 years or more. If this is true, why are we suggesting that you take time now to look back at your life? Why set aside hours from this active period and spend them sorting and sifting through what may be somewhat challenging and difficult subjects? Isn't this the work we are supposed to do at the end of our lives?

Well, it is true. You can put off this work of harvesting wisdom from the past for some other time — if you are sure there will be enough "gas" of will and clarity left in your tank when that time arrives. You can also wait and do this work later if you don't mind spending the time between today and that future moment repeating some of the same mistakes and living a life that may be less expansive and expressive, less energetic and passionate, less healthy and engaged, less conscious and grace-filled than it could be.

Plus, we all know how those "I'll do it someday" kinds of things go. Many of us have closets, drawers, file cabinets, and garages full of them. And this is precisely our point. Many of us have areas of our lives that are full of incomplete actions, unfinished personal promises, unlived hopes, and unfulfilled dreams that we tell ourselves we will attend to — someday.

And yet the truth is that life cannot be lived "someday." It can only be lived in the here and now! That is why we suggest that reflecting on and processing the experiences of our lives (what Zalman Schachter-Shalomi and Ronald Miller have defined as "harvesting") is one of the most valuable things any of us can do, not someday, but today and every day. In this way we get to squeeze the juice from the fruit of our experience and apply this wisdom to everything we do going forward.

Here are some other benefits that we and others have gotten from doing this work:

- ❀ Greater appreciation and gratitude

- ❀ More energy and vitality

- ❀ More passion and engagement

- ❀ More freedom

- ❀ Better health

- ❀ More love

- ❀ More joy

- ❀ More contentment and peace

Not a bad list is it? So if you could use a little or a lot more of any of these experiences, we invite and encourage you to jump in and do these suggested exercises.

A Small Price for Greater Freedom

Of course, like all worthwhile things, better health and more passion, energy, joy, and love requires an investment on your part. For even though there are a number of infomercials and self-help programs that claim you can make money with no risk and lose weight with no exercise or major changes in your diet, as we said earlier, most of us know that there are no free rides. In fact, to get the most out of the recommendations in this section of the book, these are a few things you will have to do:

⚜ Identify some of your limiting beliefs and habits.

⚜ Revisit some memories that you normally avoid.

⚜ Experiment with some new ideas, beliefs, and behaviors.

⚜ Accept aging and make peace with your mortality.

⚜ Commit to your spiritual development.

⚜ Allow yourself to have some fun doing these and other things.

If you are willing to do at least some of these things then we can promise you that by the time you finish this book, you will have put down some of the emotional and physical toxins you may be carrying. You will have moved past some of the habits that may be limiting you, and you will have begun to experiment with some simple but powerful new strategies that can make a significant difference in the way you live the rest of your life.

If this sounds worthwhile then we encourage you to participate in this next process. And remember, our job is to present this information and guide you through these experiences, and your job is to get involved — for as you know, no one can live your life for you.

Clearing the Decks

Taking our clue from the closed fist exercise — *whatever we hold on to we are stuck with* — we invite you now to look at some of the things you may be holding on to that may be getting in the way of experiencing a more joyful, engaged, passionate, and satisfying life. And please note that although there are a number of reasons for holding onto things, there are two that seem to be the most common.

The first we call the "just in case we need it" strategy. An example of this can be found in the way some of us pack for trips. We lay out far more clothing or equipment than we need — telling ourselves that this will allow us to sort through all of the possibilities and select the things we really need to take. Good concept, except that in executing it we generally find ourselves putting much more stuff in our suitcases than we actually require for our trip — just in case we need it. While this approach may seem like a good idea in our bedroom prior to our departure, it often leads to a number of less-than-satisfying moments when we find ourselves lugging those heavy bags around airports, lifting them onto shuttle buses and into cabs, and packing and unpacking them in hotel rooms.

We tend to use this same strategy in other areas of our lives — especially when it comes to memories, upsets, angers, frustrations, petty grievances, old beliefs, habituated ways of doing things, and more. Why do we do this? "Just in case we need them." At least this is what we tell ourselves.

There is another strategy we employ for holding onto things. This is the one we mentioned earlier — the "I'll do it someday" strategy. The best example of this is the approach many of us take when it comes to cleaning out closets, office file cabinets, attics, garages, etc. We apply it as well to exercise programs and hundreds of other well-intentioned promises we make to ourselves to learn new skills and do things better.

Indeed, if you are like most us you probably encounter a number of these "I'll do it someday" things in your life. And each time you pass by that closet or garage, that gym or learning opportunity; every time you retrieve something or put something else in that drawer or storage space; each time you find your body not as limber or light as you'd like it or you bump up against one of those old limitations — you renew that promise that you are going to learn, fix, clean, or begin working on it "someday soon."

So in this chapter we invite you to go through some of the closets, garages, promises, and memories in your life to see if you can discover a better, more effective strategy for packing and cleaning than either the "just in case I need it" or the "I'll do it someday" approaches.

The Incomplete Exercise

Please take out a journal or a blank notepad and start by making a list of some of the incompletes in your life. As you do this, remember we are only asking you to make a list. We are not asking you to jump up and start completing everything on your list. So just let your eyes drift over the categories on the following list and write down whatever comes to mind. Incompletes can include:

Step One

- Projects at home that you have started and have not yet completed.

- Projects at home that you want to start.

Just let your mind drift over each of these categories of projects and make your list.

Step Two

- Projects at work that you have started and have not yet completed.

- Projects at work that you want to start.

Again, just let your mind drift over these categories and make your list of incompletes.

Step Three

Make a list of these kinds of incompletes, as well.

- Promises you made to yourself about things you want to learn and do that you have not yet fulfilled.

- Places you want to go that you have not visited.

- Skills you want to develop that remain undeveloped.

- People you want to meet who you have not yet approached.

Step Four

Now let's look at other things that may be incomplete and may be weighing you down and clogging your energy field.

- Things that occurred between you and your parents or siblings that are incomplete.

- Betrayals, broken promises — by others to you.

- Betrayals, broken promises — by you with others.

- Experiences that hurt you.

- People you have not forgiven — including yourself.

Please remember, you are just making lists here. So let your pen move without censorship. For now you do not have to give a lot of detail, explanation, or justification. Also remember as you make your list to pause periodically and take a few, slow, deep breaths.

Step Five

Let's take this a little deeper.

- Choices you made that did not work out the way you wanted.

- Shortcuts you took that led to longer and more arduous paths.

- Things you knew you should do but failed to do earlier in your career.

- Relationships you left or in which you were left that feel incomplete.

- Times you let yourself down or violated your own values.

Step Six

Please pause again here and go back over your list and be sure you have included:

- Things that still trouble or limit you emotionally.

- Major commitments and important personal dreams that are unfinished.

- Anything else not on the list that is incomplete and still troubles you.

We know this is not an easy exercise. But please keep in mind how good you are going to feel when you have sifted through and reduced some of this internal baggage and clutter that you may have been dragging around from moment to moment, relationship to relationship.

Clearing the Decks — Part Two

We suggest you take a break at this point. Get up, take some deep belly breaths (expand your stomach on the in-breath and collapse it on the out-breath), and walk around a little. In short, allow some of the stuff that might have come to the surface to integrate a little.

Then, when you are ready, go back over the list and identify those things that are no longer relevant or that you no longer have the desire or need to complete.

These you can simply cross off. Those that remain on the list, especially those that have a particular heat or emotional charge associated with them, are the things you may want to pay some additional attention to. And remember, the idea is not to try to complete each and every one of them in the next 20 minutes. The idea is simply to begin the process of clearing the decks so you can free up all of that energy you currently have tied up in these incompletes so you can live more consciously and age more wisely.

Life Rule
"If not now, when? If not me, who?"

~ Hillel the Elder

Life Achievement
Peter Drucker, author and management guru, wrote *The Changing World of the Executive* at 73.

Life Tool
If there is someone in your life with whom you have unfinished business, identify them and then call or write that person today. If there is someone you have harmed in some way, take the time to write, call, or visit them and ask their forgiveness. If that person is no longer in your life, you can go inside yourself where that memory is still alive, call them to mind, and forgive them or ask their forgiveness.

Please don't let this opportunity pass. Give yourself a timeline in which to complete this. It is a terrific opportunity to put down some baggage you may be carrying and to check off this incomplete. As you know, traveling light is a wonderful, liberating experience.

Unloading Additional Baggage

"No one can do anything to us. No one can do anything for us. Someday you will see this."

~ Lester Levenson ~

Incompletes at a Deeper Level

Many of us often invest a lot more energy and attention in avoiding our incompletes than in identifying them and turning them into finished pieces of our lives. Unfortunately, avoiding them is akin to trying to keep an inflated ball underwater. Not only does it require a substantial physical effort, but every time our attention shifts the ball pops to the surface.

So if you have been using your valuable energy to avoid dealing with the incompletes in your life, not only will you exhaust yourself, but over time you will also end up experiencing a slow draining of your passion and a significant reduction in your effectiveness. In short, the energy you may currently be using to avoid your incompletes is the very energy you could be using to fulfill your dreams. We repeat this sentence because we believe it is so important — *the energy you may currently be using to avoid your incompletes is the very energy you could be using to fulfill your dreams.*

So at this time we invite you to revisit the list of incompletes you made in the last chapter. Give yourself the opportunity to make a few additional notes about specific actions you can take to start clearing the decks. We believe you will notice that just the act of making a decision to complete something has a positive impact on your self-esteem and the level of energy you reinherit.

Then, when you are ready, we ask you to take a look at a special category of incompletes. In our experience, this particular category often contains a significant amount of trapped energy and so is particularly worth our attention.

As with many of the exercises in this book, you can do this exercise alone in your journal or with a partner. Doing these and other processes with someone you trust can prove to be a very rewarding and bonding experience.

If you elect to do this with a partner, please decide which of you will ask the questions first (Partner A) and which is the partner who will answer first (Partner B). If you select the partnership route, in addition to asking the questions, the asking partner should do their best to remain quiet and neutral and hold the space into which the answering partner can speak.

After cycling through the questions a few times, the partners can switch roles. Once both partners have worked with the topic, turn your attention to the next set of questions and do the same thing.

If you elect to do this process alone, we recommend you treat your journal as your partner and record your answers there. If you do it with a partner, take turns recording each other's answers in your respective journals so that you can review them later on.

Guilt and Resentment

Guilt and resentment are two experiences most of us are, unfortunately, already very familiar with. Guilt, of course, is what we feel about something that we have or think we have done to ourselves or others. Resentment is what we feel as a result of what we believe someone has done to us.

In this exercise we ask you to return to the list of incompletes you made during your last exercise and pay particular attention again to those that continue to contain what we describe as some kind of "heat" or "charge" for you.

You will probably find that these items on your incomplete list have some degree of either guilt or resentment associated with them. So take a moment now and put a "G" or an "R" next to each of the items on your list that involve either guilt or resentment or both.

The Guilt Experience:
Cycle through these questions alone or with your partner

- ✦ What is something you feel guilty about?
- ✦ When did this occur?
- ✦ Can you identify a way in which feeling guilty about this has served you?
- ✦ Is there something you can do to resolve your guilt?

Once you have answered these questions about one event or experience, please select another event or experience that may involve some guilt and cycle through the questions again.

If you are working with a partner, you can alternate turns with Partner A cycling through the questions a few times and Partner B answering, and then reversing the process. If you are working in your journal, just keep cycling until you have covered at least several items. Then pause and note how you are feeling. You may even want to make some notes in your journal about how you feel and what you have learned.

Now, turn your attention to an item on your list that has an R (for resentment) beside it.

The Resentment Exercise:

🌼 Who do you resent?

🌼 What do you believe they did to you?

🌼 Can you identify a way in which holding on to the resentment has served you?

🌼 What can you do to resolve this resentment?

As was the case with guilt, once you have dealt with one event or experience, select another item on your list or a new memory that may come up that has some level of resentment associated with it. Keep cycling through the list until you and your partner feel complete.

Things I Learned

If you participated in this exercise, you have, no doubt, stirred the pot and brought a number of feelings and emotions up to the surface. So take a few moments to write down some of the things you learned and some of the things you are feeling.

Pay special attention to any patterns that might become apparent. Also pay close attention to any actions that you feel you may want to take in order to further release any remaining guilt or resentment you may be feeling associated with any of these incompletes.

You can also download the "Forgiveness Meditation" at our website: www.donotgoquietlythebook.com. We know you'll find it valuable at this time.

Secrets

Another area of your psyche that can benefit enormously from a little spring cleaning is the place in which you store your secrets. Everyone has them, of course: large ones, small ones, long-standing, and more recent ones. We categorize some secrets as major, others we consider relatively insignificant. But we tend to hold them close and protect them from the light of day nonetheless. And this protection, like that which we accord to things we feel guilty or resentful about, ties up our precious life energy.

Some secrets are a part of that dream you may have turned away from which we talked about in the earlier chapter entitled, "It's Never Too Late or Too Soon." Perhaps you were embarrassed to share the dream or some aspect of it. Perhaps you did not want to share it with those who called your dream foolish or romantic.

On the other hand, some secrets may involve things we have done or had others do to us that we are ashamed of — perhaps things that are considered immoral, unethical, or even criminal. For obvious reasons we rarely if ever talk about these.

Major secrets are those that most of us believe, if disclosed, would disrupt our relationships; change people's opinions of us; and, in short, disturb our world. When disclosed, however, some of these end up being far less disruptive than we imagine. On the other hand, secrets to which we assign relatively low levels of importance can sometimes prove to be major in their impact on ourselves and others.

No matter what the projected or actual consequences of the secrets we are holding, they are burdens that we carry around with us every day. And these burdens separate us from others and from ourselves. They also require that we expend a significant amount of energy guarding them. Indeed, in order to continue guarding these secrets, we have to create other secrets that, in turn, require even more of this same protective energy. In some cases, the secrets we are holding also require that we invent or employ very complex strategies to keep them from seeing the light of day.

In short, some secrets constitute parts of us — past and present — that we consider unacceptable. For this and a host of other reasons, these secrets end up getting in the way of our ability to freely and positively move forward in our lives. They are part of the baggage that we carry on our journey that prohibits us from advancing at the pace that many of us would like to move.

There are other kinds of secrets, of course. These are more positive, but also more personal and special. In some instances we do not communicate them because we sense that they are still too fragile or delicate to be exposed to the harsh light of other people's judgment or criticism. Some of these fall under the wise advice to protect vulnerable beginnings, and we do so because we sense that too early exposure can undercut our ability to execute them. Other secrets — still in the positive domain — are fragile for other reasons. They come to us in unusual ways — through flashes of intuition, flights of fancy, or even our night dreams — and we sense that they are too special or too different. Carl Jung once reported that he had discovered that among his patients were those who were motivated by a secret that they could not or would not share and that often these individuals were able to accomplish levels of change and transformation that others were not.

So our advice to you at this point on your journey is to find a way to differentiate between these two groups of secrets. Let's leave the second category alone for now and focus on the first. Let's articulate these secrets that may be encumbering you; and in this way, let us begin the process of releasing the energy that is associated with them.

Step One — Identify Your Secrets

Small, medium, or large, it does not matter. Just take some time and make a private list of them. This may, of course, not be easy for there may be secrets that you have been holding for so long or holding so tightly that they are not immediately accessible. If you have patience and courage, however, they will begin to come into focus.

Step Two — Accept Your Secret and Honor Your Reason for Keeping It Secret

For example, the secret may be something you believe is a sign of a weakness or a character flaw or an addiction. It may be something that you believe violates your own or someone else's values. It may be something that gave you an unfair advantage or allowed you to profit or gain in some way that you did not believe you were entitled to. It may be something that brought something into your possession that did not belong to you. It may be something that hurt someone or brought them blame; something you believe might damage a close personal or professional relationship or your reputation.

Whatever it is, acknowledge it, accept it, and then begin the process of forgiving yourself for anything that may be a part of the secret; anything that is still prompting you to keep it secret. And while you may not feel an immediate release of the energy associated with this secret, if you are patient and stick with the process — if you keep forgiving yourself — in the end, you will find that you can make peace with your secret.

Step Three — Bring Your Secret(s) To Light

When and if you feel it is appropriate, the next step in this process can be to share the secrets you've identified with others — professional counselors, religious guides, mentors, loved ones, and/or friends you trust. Or you can just write some things about your secret down in your journal. Bring your secret into the light of day and discover what happens. In short, we suggest you do whatever is appropriate, necessary, and constructive in significantly reducing and eliminating any guilt-inducing secrets you may be carrying that are preventing you from living the quality of life you desire.

Once again, this may be a very good place to listen to the "Forgiveness Exercise" at our website: www.donotgoquietlythebook.com

Life Rule

"The whole object on the path is to let go of the ego. What remains is yourself."

~ Lester Levenson

Live Achievement

Jack LaLanne, considered by many to be the godfather of fitness in the U.S., did a two-hour workout each day, even in the 95th year of his life.

Life Tool

One way to learn how to lighten the baggage you carry into the future is to make it a point today to pause before you speak or act. Ask yourself if what you are about to say or do will result in something that you will have to keep secret from others. If this "something" is negative or you know you will be ashamed about it later, then you may want to consider *not* doing it.

At the same time, if you discover that whatever you are about to do or say is not negative — but may be perceived to be so by people you are associated with — then you may want to reconsider what you are about to say or do. Or you may find other people to associate with who will appreciate what you have to share.

The Poet

T.S. Eliot's Story

T.S. Eliot is considered by many to be one of the most, if not the most, influential poets in the English language. He is also one of our favorite poets and someone who has had a profound impact on our lives. In fact, Eliot's words and images have, from our earliest encounters with them, helped to inform and open us to new levels of understanding and experiences of some of the mysteries that lie beneath the surface of our lives. In many cases, his words and images have also given us new insights into the way contemporary religions have emerged from earlier practices and rituals. And his work has introduced us to the path taken by so many in pursuit of the mystical traditions.

Eliot was born in September of 1888 in Saint Louis to an upper-middle-class family. He was the youngest child of seven. It has been said that from the beginning he seemed to exist on the border between different cultures.

Although his family had founded the Unitarian Church, he was raised by a Catholic nurse and hence spent time in both worlds. Although his family was well off, they lived in that section of Saint Louis that was in decline. Therefore he experienced the inside of Saint Louis society as well as life on the streets.

He attended Milton Academy and Harvard University and then spent time in Paris. This year would dramatically change his life. Later during his time in Paris he wrote many of the poems that would catapult him into the limelight: "The Love Song of J. Alfred Prufrock," "Portrait of a Lady," "La Figlia Che Piange," "Preludes," and "Rhapsody on a Windy Night."

Eliot had a very tumultuous marriage to an emotionally challenged woman. It was a relationship that we believe enormously deepened his sensitivity to life and challenged him greatly. He was deeply involved with the intellectual and artistic elite of Paris and London, and yet his daily work — the work that allowed him to earn his living and that underwrote the writing of his poetry, plays, literary criticism, and a lot more — was that of a bank clerk.

"Four Quartets" is not only one of our favorite sets of poems in our language, it is also, in our opinion, one of the greatest poetic works that has ever been written. From the first line through the last, one is drawn deeply into his mythical universe, so much so that to this day his words and images inspire and assist us and so many others we know to unlock doors to some of life's deeper mysteries. T.S. Eliot was still writing remarkable plays and poetry at the time of his death at the age of 77.

Whose Beliefs Are You Living?

"We often refuse to accept an idea merely because the tone of voice
in which it is expressed is unsympathetic to us."

~ Nietzsche ~

Believing vs. Knowing

Have you ever stopped to consider where your beliefs come from? As part of your process of making peace with your past, we invite you to do this very thing. We invite you take a look at some of the beliefs you are currently holding, especially some of your beliefs about aging, about the options and possibilities this time of life holds for you, about your fears and worries, about your victories and celebrations, and even some of your confusions and regrets. In short, we invite you look at some of the beliefs you hold that have shaped your life to date and will, if they are left unexamined and unchanged, most certainly shape and perhaps limit your life in the years ahead.

Carl Jung, one of the fathers of the science of psychology, took great pains to point out that believing is very different than knowing. Beliefs most often depend on what other people say, think, or claim to have experienced. In short, belief rests primarily on the opinions held by others and, in many cases, a majority of others who make up our world — people in our families, churches, schools, businesses, ethnic and religious group, nations, etc.

Alan Watts, author and spiritual teacher, had this to say on the subject: "Beliefs are what we wish to (or think ought to) be true."

Knowing, by comparison, is based on one's own personal experience. And while it is true that our experience is sometimes the result of faulty assumptions or misguided beliefs, in the end — at least in our opinion — there is a form of knowing that aligns with an inner yardstick that each of us possesses and is far more accurate and consequential than anyone else's beliefs.

Knowing also sometimes comes from an intuitive flash or insight that may or may not be immediately verifiable to others or traceable to something that has happened in our present lifetime. But it still has certainty and undeniability to it. Finally, there is a form of knowing that sometimes manifests at first in the form of a flight of fancy or imagination. For example, it is said that as a boy, Albert Einstein dreamt of riding a beam of light through space. Later, when his skill in mathematics allowed him to do so, he verified this dream through the theory of relativity.

Although knowing is much more powerful than believing, in this age of philosophical materialism when science and technology are worshipped as the primary means of determining what is real and what is not, beliefs shape our experience of the modern world. This is, of course, not a new path for humanity — history is full of examples. At one point in history the prevailing belief was that the world was flat. Earlier many believed the Earth was the center of the universe and the sun and the stars revolved around it.

When one adds an understanding of the impact that the information age now has on this human tendency to build the world upon a foundation of beliefs, then our contention that unfounded beliefs too often shape the modern world becomes much more plausible.

Yes, in the information age when media trumpets the same message and perspectives over and over — as if repetition were the basis of truth — it unfortunately often becomes so. We say unfortunately because from our perspective, our world could be much richer, truer, more balanced and aligned with nature and with the rhythms and harmonies of the universe if each of us only used our assumptions (beliefs) like crutches — temporary supports on the road to actual knowing. Instead, in our world where unsubstantiated beliefs are often accepted as justifiable substitutes for knowing, we all become the poorer for it.

We could, of course, spend a lot of time exploring numerous examples of this phenomenon, but we hope that one example will suffice. Consider the topic of weapons of mass destruction, the blatant manipulation of unfounded beliefs that surrounded it and the fact that we actually went to war and put the lives of our own youth in jeopardy while at the same time slaughtering countless numbers of innocents. We hope it will serve as proof enough of the particularly egregious and errant power of beliefs in the information age.

Another reason for paying close attention to where our beliefs come from is the Law of Manifestation that holds that energy follows thought and manifestation follows energy. While the validity of this law is becoming more obvious to more of us, it may not be as obvious that if thought equals knowing then the energy that results is powerful and aligned. If, however, thought equals believing, the energy that results is less stable and requires the participation of others to interpret and translate. What's wrong with this?

A great deal! Beliefs require interpreters and translators (those who support, defend, and promote the beliefs) — what today we refer to as spin doctors. As a result, in this age of beliefs we are always at the mercy of the frailties and the imperfections that are often present in the character of these translators, and that eventually show up and shape their interpretations and in their intentions.

There is something else worth considering here. Although there is a significant confusion in our time between believing and knowing, so much so that there are some who believe they know when they are in fact simply under the sway of an unexamined assumption — the truth is that once one experiences something sufficiently to be able to say "I know this to be true!" then one no longer questions the difference between knowing and believing.

Paracelsus, the 16th century physician and alchemist who served as a guide for some of Carl Jung's most transformative work (work explored in his book *Psychology and Religion*), had his own way of saying this. Paracelsus believed that if one was willing to fully explore (come to know) any one aspect of the universe, one would come to know the universe itself. A single leaf, for example, examined and understood, could, according to Paracelsus, assist one in understanding the primary foundations underlying the physical universe.

So if our actions and choices are based on a strong sense of inner knowing rather than on a set of inherited, learned, and too often untested beliefs, it is far less likely that others will be able to lead us down errant paths or encourage us to pursue fraudulent or faulty goals that do not benefit our lives. It is also far less likely that we will lead others astray.

Conversely, basing our actions and choices on inner knowing (or direct experience), allows us to move more directly toward being able to manifest our own destinies. And in a world like ours — a world that moves at such an astounding pace and is driven by such group think and group behavior — being able to manifest our own destinies could well be the key to creating a much more sane and sustainable world.

So we invite you to explore this difference between knowing and believing in your daily life. We know it will be one of the most valuable things you will ever do. And remember, to arrive at knowing we must be willing to let go of the beliefs we may be holding and to use curiosity and as much objectivity as we can as the instruments of our search. We would also be wise to adopt what in Zen is called the beginner's mind. Through these tools one can be a little more certain to enter the path of truth with the best of intentions.

Tracing the Source

Since Jung and a number of other wise beings have invited us to remember that believing is nowhere near as valuable or powerful as knowing, it would seem that a next and very significant step on this path of exploring the difference between the two would be to identify the source of the beliefs we hold. And one of the easiest ways of doing this is to begin by making a list of some of these primary beliefs.

To help you, we have identified some of the categories of belief you might want to consider. You can use this as a starting point or you can create your own list from scratch.

We recommend you do this exercise quickly and without censoring your responses. Just write down any and all beliefs that come to mind as you read each of these categories. Here are a few examples of beliefs that come up for us in the first category:

Beliefs I Hold about Being Young

- A time without care
- Young people have few of the responsibilities that burden adults
- A time when you have to do what other people want you to do
- A great time of life
- A lonely and frustrating time

Now make your own list in this category and in each of the following categories:

- Beliefs I Hold about Youth
- Beliefs I Hold about Success
- Beliefs I Hold about Health
- Beliefs I Hold about Money
- Beliefs I Hold about Meaning and Purpose
- Beliefs I Hold about Aging
- Beliefs I Hold about Death
- Beliefs I Hold about What Happens After Death
- Beliefs I Hold about God, Spirit, Oneness…

Yours or Theirs

As you look over this list of some of the primary beliefs you hold, consider the following questions:

⚙ How many of these beliefs are your own — that is, how many of these beliefs are based on your own experience versus the experiences of others that you have decided to adopt?

⚙ How many of these beliefs have your revisited or re-examined in the last few years?

Please put an "M" for mine and an "O" for others beside each of the beliefs on your list.

For example, is the belief you hold about the political party you support your own belief or did it come from someone else — a parent or relative, a teacher, minister, or friend? What about your belief about what is possible for you? Does it come from personal experience, trial and error, or was the path you followed determined largely by beliefs that were shared or even imposed upon you when you were young?

Do you see what we mean about the difference between believing and knowing? While we can't speak for you, a number of the beliefs we held before starting on this path to more conscious living and wise aging did not originate with us. In fact, for a number of years many of our beliefs were automatic and very few of them were original and authentic.

What about you? What about the beliefs you hold about life, about death, about God, about right and wrong, about whom to trust, about who to love and how to love? What about the beliefs you hold about what you should or could spend your time doing, about what rewards are important and valuable, and about the means by which you judge something you do to be successful? What about the beliefs you hold about aging, and about what happens after you die? Are these beliefs that you adopted from someone else — or have you observed, experimented, and experienced things relating to aging and dying for yourself?

Yes, beliefs...beliefs... a steady stream of beliefs most often coming from others and adopted by us automatically — and too often with an enormous amount of innocence, confidence, and gullibility. Amazing, isn't it? And yet many of us think we are in control of our own lives and the pursuit of our own destinies. Many of us think we are running our own lives. Well, look at your list and then think again.

And please do not take our comment as a judgment about you. This topic involves all of us. This is why, from our perspective, we think it is time to examine our beliefs, identify which of our beliefs actually belong to us, and finally which beliefs actually advance the cause of our waking up and which keep us dozing on the sidelines in our own lives.

A few additional questions you may want to consider:

 Where did the beliefs that others hold and those that you have adopted come from?

 How long has this practice of believing versus knowing been going on in your world and what results has it produced?

Life Rule

"O God, help me to know the truth about myself, no matter how beautiful it is."

~ Macrina Wiederkehr

Life Achievement

Toni Morrison, author and activist, received the Nobel Prize For Literature at 62.

Life Tool

Now that you remember how much more valuable knowing is than believing, we invite you to continue to experiment with how powerful, joyful, inviting, and successful your life can be when you base your thoughts, words, and actions on your own deep inner knowing.

This is not to say you should not or cannot utilize other people's beliefs as starting points until you have the time or expertise to arrive at your own conclusions. However, it is our recommendation that from this day on you differentiate between what you know and what you merely believe.

A few other things you may want to experiment with: Stop arguing over beliefs. Notice how many people around you punish, shun, try to dominate, and in some instances even go to war and kill others simply because their beliefs are different than yours.

Then ask yourself: "What would happen if I act each day on what I know rather than what I believe? And what will my life be like when I learn to think, speak, and act based on my knowing?"

Limiting Beliefs — A Limited Life

"No longer needing to compete and to be acceptable, likeable and all those other things considered respectable in society, people are finally uncaged in their elder years, free to release energies and capacities that the culture restrained in them when they were younger."

~ Jean Houston ~

The Limiting Power of Limiting Beliefs

Let us now turn our attention to a particular category of beliefs — limiting beliefs — and about how they not only impact but literally shape our lives. Consider 1,200 words a minute and 50,000 separate thoughts a day — that's the estimated speed at which we think and the average number of separate, discrete thoughts we have each day. Clearly that adds up to a whole lot of thinking, a whole lot of thoughts and images and a whole lot of beliefs that impact our lives — especially if they are negative.

In the language of computers there is a phrase that was current not very long ago — garbage in, garbage out. The meaning, of course, is that the quality of the output we can expect from our computers depends primarily on the quality of the data we input. Since computers are, in some important ways, modeled after the functioning of the human brain, it certainly follows that some of the same rules that apply to computers also apply to our brains.

So depending on information (accurate or inaccurate) that we store in our minds in the form of thoughts, images, and beliefs (positive or negative), our experience of the world (and of our lives) will be significantly affected.

To continue this comparison between brains and computers, there are software programs that have been designed to keep the hard drives of our computers free of viruses and functioning optimally. Some of these defrag (order and compress) information and others eliminate unnecessary or duplicate files; some of them empty caches and others protect us from unwanted viruses. In short, these programs are designed to keep our desktops, laptops, tablets, and smartphones running efficiently and smoothly. But what about our "Headtops"? What do we do to keep them clean?

If we are smart, we can — at least occasionally — do the same things with our brains that we do with our computers and smart devices — we can review the contents, delete old unnecessary files (unneeded memories and thoughts), and check for viruses (limited and negative beliefs). In short we would be wise to keep the basic operating system of our minds running efficiently and successfully.

Warm-Ware Revisited

There are several ways we can keep our brains in relatively good working order: perform mind-expanding exercises; limit our exposure to toxic people, information, and media messages; and pay close attention to the thoughts, images, and beliefs that continuously circulate through us. We can also benefit by eliminating or reducing some of the viruses (negative emotions) these beliefs stimulate or attract. Yes, curiosity and experimentation with new concepts and practices can go a long way toward keeping our brains sharp and our lives on track.

It is also valuable to pay attention to our beliefs. As with the kinds of software we mentioned, some of our beliefs are empowering and others are limiting. Some speed up our lives and allow life to move more effortlessly and effectively, and others slow us down and encumber us.

As to limiting beliefs — especially those that have been passed on to us by others who in turn unconsciously accepted them from others — they are like pirated software that does not arrive in a package checked by the manufacturer and scanned for viruses. As a result, many of the beliefs we hold individually and collectively are simply unevaluated and unauthenticated opinions that over time and through sheer force of repetition and habit have been widely mistaken for reality. As just mentioned, two obvious examples that stand out in history are the "scientific certainty" that the Earth was flat and that the sun revolved around the Earth.

Once people held the belief that beyond the borders of the known world was the realm of dragons — hence the phrase written on maps made by ancient cartographers, "Here There Be Dragons!" Clearly if our ancient explorers had not sailed right through that commonly held belief much of the modern world would have never been discovered.

A more contemporary example is that for a very long time many athletes and a number of scientists strongly believed that the human body was physiologically incapable of moving fast enough to break the four-minute-mile barrier. And that belief held sway until one day a man named Roger Bannister simply tied on his running shoes and ran right through that limit.

Michael Murphy, one of the two founders of the world-renowned Esalen Institute in Big Sur, wrote *The Future of the Body: Explorations into the Further Evolution of Human Nature* based on his enormous collection of verified reports of people who exceeded what is generally believed to be humanly possible in a dozen areas of life. By so doing, he helped gather the evidence that makes it clear that we are living our lives based on mutually agreed upon limitations while believing that these limitations are true.

Fortunately, not all of the beliefs we hold are negative or as transitory. For example, if we believe that we can accomplish something; if we believe we are competent, worthy, decent, effective, productive, etc., then we have a very real shot at coming to experience our competence, effectiveness, etc., and consequently living more satisfying and successful lives. Conversely, if we hold the belief that we cannot do something, that we are not competent, deserving, or worthy enough, this limiting belief, like a corrupt software program, will most likely prevent us from achieving our goals and living the life we were born to live.

As Henry Ford said, "Whether you believe you can or you can't — you are right." Napoleon Hill, the author of *Think and Grow Rich*, said it another way: "Whatever the mind can conceive of and believe in, it can achieve." But no matter how you say it, what you believe largely impacts the quality and content of your life.

Doing Does It

Here's a short experiment you can do to test this theory for yourself. All you have to do is take an ordinary paper clip — larger sizes are better — and run a piece of sewing thread or string about 20 inches long through the single end of the clip. The thicker the thread or string the better, but any thickness will do. Then tie the two ends of the thread together into a knot so that the paper clip hangs down on the thread like a pendulum that is about 10 inches long.

The Pendulum Exercise

- Hold this pendulum at the knot in the thread or string so that the paper clip hangs down.

- Hold the pendulum out in front of you so that your elbow is neither resting against a surface nor held tightly against your side.

- ✹ If the paper clip pendulum is swinging, bring it to a stop.

- ✹ Focus all of your attention on it.

- ✹ Take a few slow, deep breaths and do your best to quiet your mind.

- ✹ Give the paper clip a clear instruction to swing toward and away from your body. Do your best not to swing your arm or move your hand. Just keep focusing on the paper clip and giving it the same instruction.

- ✹ Give the paper clip time to respond to your instruction.

- ✹ Pay close attention to keeping your mind neutral and focusing only on the intention of having the pendulum move toward and away from your body.

- ✹ Once the clip is moving toward and away from you, give it a new set of instructions to move side to side.

- ✹ Give it time to make the adjustment.

- ✹ Then ask the paper clip to move in a clockwise direction.

- ✹ Finally, ask the paper clip to move in a counterclockwise direction.

What did you notice? What did you learn?

Take a few moments to reflect on your experience. If you did your best not to move your arm or your hand, what do you think caused the pendulum to move? Our answer, of course, is that energy follows thought and manifestation follows energy. But we invite you to consider these two questions that make up the title to this section: What did you notice? And what did you learn? In fact, we invite you to use these questions whenever you want to learn something from any interaction with another, any activity or experience.

Part Two — Testing the Power of Your Beliefs

If you want to have some additional fun and further test the impact your beliefs have on what you do each moment of your life, once you have the paper clip moving in any direction you wish, start telling yourself, "This whole exercise is ridiculous and I could not possibly be making the clip move simply with my intention."

What do you notice? What did you learn?

A Second Doing

For those of you who did not stop long enough to construct this homemade paper clip pendulum or who want to take this further, there is another exercise involving reflexology that you can use to learn about the power your beliefs have on the quality of your life.

Reflexology utilizes muscle testing as a way of determining your alignment with given concepts, ideas, foods, medicines, environments, and much more. You can use it in hundreds of ways each day to assist you in taking better care of yourself. And you can certainly use reflexology to test Napoleon Hill's premise that whatever the mind conceives of and believes in can be achieved.

Here is one simple way to do this:

Press the thumb and first finger of both hands together to make two small circles; then open one of these circles and interconnect it with the other. Once you have this basic equipment ready, follow along as directed:

⊛ Tug on them to feel the strength of the connection.

⊛ Repeat the following sentence, "My name is_____," (fill in the blank with your real name) and test the strength of the connection between the two circles.

⊛ Now repeat the process, only this time fill in the blank after "My name is" with a name that is not your own.

⊛ Test the strength of this connection.

Many people find that it is not easy to pull their fingers apart when they say their own name, but it is relatively easy to do so when they use a name that is not their own.

⊛ Now test this simple yet valuable tool in other ways: Put a piece of fruit or some other food that you like on your lap and test the strength of the connection. Then do the same with a food item that you do not like. Do the same with a remedy or medicine you take. The next time you go to a restaurant, test the choices on the menu in this way. You can use reflexology to measure your reactions to hundreds of possibilities you choose from each day. Literally, use the natural intelligence of your body and heart as well as your mind to act as your guides. Let them help you find your way to greater alignment.

And remember, whatever the mind can conceive of and believe in it can achieve.

What Have You Learned?

So what do these two experiments have to do with learning to live the lives we were born to live? From our perspectives they can help us become more aware that the beliefs we hold either support us in living more engaged, empowered, passionate, healthy, and involved lives — or more limited, restricted, and less conscious ones. Constructive, authentic beliefs that lead to inner knowing assist us to do what is important, to make the kinds of contributions we want to make, and to fulfill our roles as stewards of this planet and mentors to future generations. In short, positive, constructive beliefs assist us in leaving behind a worthwhile legacy.

So if these are some of the results you want to produce, you might want to start asking yourself: "Which of my beliefs help me to ensure that the rest of my life is indeed the best of my life?"

Greed, Fear & Other Negative Beliefs

If we keep this awareness about beliefs in mind and couple it with a concept we discussed earlier — that energy follows thought and manifestation follows energy — then it becomes particularly clear that the kind of life experiences we manifest are a direct result of the kind of thoughts and beliefs we hold. This reality becomes particularly important when we stop to consider some of the negative beliefs that sometimes come up in our lives.

Let us use greed, fear, or hatred as our example. What states of mind, experiences, behaviors, etc., do we manifest when we are under the influence of the limiting beliefs that promote these negative emotions? By comparison what states of mind, experiences, and behaviors do we manifest when our thoughts, words, and actions issue from positive beliefs and the emotions and mental states they generate — including gratitude, courage, compassion, and joy?

And please note — these are not hypothetical questions. Most of us have known this to be true most of our lives. We have heard it explored in classrooms and from the pulpits and lecterns of our churches, temples, and mosques. We have read about it in the great books and have had direct experiences of what happens in our daily lives when we either fail to remember or practice this knowing. But in the second half of life, when we have less time to manifest what we know, this truth about beliefs becomes even more essential.

Dr. David Hawkins has spent decades studying the phenomenon of energy and its impact on the physical universe and physical manifestation. In his book *Power vs. Force*, he explores how applied kinesiology (muscle testing) can help us identify a corresponding frequency associated with each emotional state (and each positive or negative belief associated with it).

The more positive the emotional state, the higher and more powerful the frequency and hence the more powerful the resulting physical manifestation. The less positive and more destructive the emotional state the lower the associated frequency and the resulting physical manifestation.

Here is a brief excerpt from the section of Dr. Hawkins's book where he describes this "Map of Consciousness." When he is speaking about going weak or strong he is referring to what happens when reflexology is used to test strength or weakness in the body.

> The critical response point in the scale of consciousness calibrates at 200, which is the level associated with integrity and courage. All attitudes, thoughts, feelings, associations, entities, or historical figures below that level of calibration [pride, anger, desire, fear, grief, apathy, guilt, and shame] make a person go weak — those that calibrate higher [neutrality, willingness, acceptance, reason, love, joy, peace and enlightenment] make subjects go strong.

As if this is not already enough to encourage those of us in the second half of life to pay close attention to our thoughts and beliefs, and to their corresponding emotional states, Dr. Hawkins has also used his calibrations to draw the following conclusions:

> One individual [who calibrates] at 300 [the level of willingness] counterbalances 90,000 individuals [who calibrate] below level 200. One individual at level 400 [reason] counterbalances 400,000 individuals below level 200. One individual at level 600 [love] counterbalances 10 million individuals below level 200.

Please take a moment to reread this last paragraph and consider the implications of these calibrations. Even if Dr. Hawkins is only partially correct in his calculations about our emotions and the frequencies they calibrate at, imagine the impact you can have on your own consciousness and on the world around you simply by changing a few of your negative, limiting thoughts and substituting more positive thoughts and elevated behaviors.

Life Rule
"What makes greatness is starting something of value that lives after you."

~ Ralph Stockman

Life Achievement
Lionel Hampton, American jazz great, was still performing at 80.

Life Tool
Identifying limited beliefs and replacing them with positive ones may be one of the most important things you can do. Remember that energy follows thought and manifestation follows energy; so what you think and how you think shapes your world.

Over the course of the next several days, we invite you to pay attention to what you think and how these thoughts arise from underlying beliefs. For example, when you find yourself in a particularly challenging interaction, ask yourself, "What belief am I holding at this moment, and is this belief producing a positive or negative result?"

Once you identify the underlying belief, you do not have to change it. Just observe what is going on and discover if your belief is contributing to the kind of life you want to be living. If it is not, you might want to assess its validity, identify another more accurate and empowering belief, and focus on that instead.

Squeezing the Juice
from the Fruit

*"All things are individual instruments through which Spirit thinks,
speaks, acts and reveals Itself... We are members of a vast, cosmic orchestra
in which each living instrument is essential to the complimentary and
harmonious playing of the whole.*

~ J. Allen Boone ~

Dealing Constructively With Your Past

In *From Age-ing To Sage-ing*, the book that helped to launch the conscious aging movement in the U.S., Zalman Schachter-Shalomi and Ronald Miller explore one of the most essential and critical steps any of us can take in turning the grist of our past into the gold of the present and future. It is a step they call "harvesting."

What is "harvesting?" As the name implies, it is the process of reaping the fruits from seeds we have sown or failed to sow earlier in our lives. It is a life review in which we take time to identify and turn the grist of our strengths and frailties; challenges and opportunities; our defeats, victories, and achievements; our incompletes and undones; and our contributions into the gold of processed experience and wisdom.

Harvesting is also a form of cleansing, a sifting through, and, if we allow it to be, a valuable healing and life repair. Yes, harvesting, as we have explored in our chapters on incompletes, gives us a chance to make sense of our past; heal old wounds; let go of old baggage; and regain our emotional, physical, mental, and spiritual balance so that the lives we lead today and tomorrow will be richer, more rewarding, and fulfilling.

Schachter-Shalomi and Miller suggest that during harvesting:

We also appreciate the friendships we have nurtured, the young people we have mentored, and our wider involvements on behalf of the community, the nation, and ultimately the Earth. Harvesting can be experienced from within as quiet self-appreciation or from without through the honor, respect, and recognition received from family members, relatives, colleagues at work, and mentees.

Harvesting

We invite you to turn your attention to this valuable life review process and discover for yourself some of the wonderful benefits it has to offer.

Harvesting will allow you to:

1. Explore the events of your life from an emotional and psychological standpoint.

2. Clear away some of the clutter and excess baggage and make sense of your experience.

3. Answer important spiritual and philosophic questions: What does life mean to you? Why are you here? What does death mean? Is there a Next or is this all there is?

4. Get your personal affairs in order — wills, power of attorney, medical directives, funeral arrangements, etc.

Step One — You have already begun the harvesting process in the work you have done on reclaiming your dreams, on dealing with your incompletes, and especially in your work on guilt and resentment. In fact, you have already done a reasonable amount of the heavy lifting.

So in this section we invite you to continue that process of exploring the life you have lived up until now so you can turn more of the straw of your experience into the gold of learning and higher consciousness. This means looking at the good stuff as well, the achievements and accomplishments, and the lessons well learned.

To do this effectively you may, as Zalman Schachter-Shalomi suggests, "try to suspend the normal ways in which you evaluate success or failure...and search for the deeper, sometimes more elusive patterns that may be operating beneath the surface."

Getting Specific

In other words, viewed on the surface and from a short-term perspective, a specific event or relationship you experienced earlier in your life might seem to be negative — the end of a friendship, the loss of a job or career opportunity, a financial hardship, an accident or illness, a divorce, etc. As a result you may have pushed it down into the storehouse of your unconscious or you may have done your best to minimize its importance or try to forget it entirely.

As you know from our beach ball analogy, however, no matter how hard we sometimes try to suppress past events — whether they involve failures or successes, pains or pleasures — pushing down requires a significant amount of energy. And ultimately, as soon as we turn our attention elsewhere, our unresolved or incomplete issues pop up to the surface of our awareness.

When viewed or reviewed from the higher or longer-term perspective presented in the harvesting process, however, you may discover that the job you lost or that opportunity you believe you missed actually opened the way for a new career direction or proved to be the impetus to start a new business. That accident or financial setback may have led you to a shift in values or priorities or to a different way of life and to the development of new skills. The end of a relationship or the loss of a loved one may have opened the door to a new love and a greater sense of strength and freedom within yourself.

So as you take this next step on this journey, we invite you to remember the Marcel Proust quote we used earlier, "the real journey of discovery is not about new destinations, but about having new eyes."

We also invite you to engage in your life review with the curiosity and neutral observation of a reporter attempting to uncover the truth, and above all with the enthusiasm of one who is about to make new discoveries.

In doing your harvesting we suggest you take to heart what author Stephen Levine has to say about the life review process:

> We look back at our life, not as if we still owned it but as though we were about to give it up. A recollection of the past as though this might be the last sip of that old wine, the last kiss from that departed lover, the last time to appreciate a life so full of our very human experience.

Step Two — Another important piece of advice you may find of value in doing the harvesting/life review process is to be sure to take good care of yourself. For some this might mean diving right in to the depths and distant corners of the past, while for others it might mean wading in more slowly. The truth is — there is no right way to do your life review. There is also no hurry. Indeed, unlike those old beliefs about performance and perfection that may have pushed and plagued you during the first half of your life, there is no reason to gauge your success here based on the speed of accomplishment. In fact, in your harvesting, slow and sure will probably serve you better; the only thing that really matters is the yield of your crop, i.e., the wisdom and experience you gain that you can apply in your life going forward.

So no matter what method you choose, no matter what speed you work at, the most important thing you can do is to bring care, compassion, and appropriate pacing to your harvesting. And above all, do not do yourself the disservice of hanging on to feelings of guilt, resentment, or regret that may come up in the process. Just acknowledge and then release them. Indeed, you might find it valuable to visualize your different memories as balloons. Let them come up, observe them, acknowledge them, and then let go of the string you may be holding on to so they can drift away. And do not be discouraged if this takes longer than you expect or you feel the need for some additional support in the form of a coach, therapist, or a support group. At the same time do not be surprised if letting go of some of these feelings happens more quickly than you expect. For in the end, releasing can happen immediately if you continue to stay focused on the present moment.

In short, trust your process. Trust your pacing. Also trust the fact that like a corkscrew entering a bottle, you can go down one level at a time into the past until you have done the primary work you want to do. And the wonderful thing about the harvesting and life review process is that you can come back again and again to areas of your life until you eventually process all of the grist of your past into the gold of understanding and wisdom. And remember, harvesting is about gathering all the fruits of your life and all of the good and noble parts of you as well.

At this point, you may also find it helpful to go back and review the questions we recommended in the section on guilt and resentment in the chapter entitled, "Unloading Additional Baggage."

Life Envisioning — The River of Time

As the next step in harvesting, we suggest you first take a short guided-imagery journey. If you go to www.donotgoquietlythebook.com, under the envisioning section you will find the "River of Time Guided Imagery Journey."

As you listen, please remember that although the language we use involves the word *sight*, there are a lot of different ways to "see." Some people see through their feelings. Some see through sound. For still others it is smell or touch or thought that gives one access to images. Finally, there are those who, when they close their eyes, actually see full color images. No right. No wrong. Just do whatever works for you and allows you to follow along and benefit from the experience.

Life Rule
"If you only expect the best, that's what you will get."

~ W. Somerset Maugham

Life Achievement
Martha Graham, who some regard as the grand dame of American dance, was still choreographing new work in her 90s.

Life Tool
As part of your harvesting process, we ask you to identify several of your most outstanding life achievements: either those you recalled during your "River of Time" visualization or those you call to mind at this moment. Then take a few moments to feel the feelings associated with these images. Savor them and anchor them inside you. You may find there are times in the years ahead when these strong, positive feelings will provide you with just the right amount of energy and joy you need to overcome an obstacle, deal with an adversity, or regain your sense of balance.

The Thinker

Auguste's Story

Auguste Rodin, considered by many to be one of the greatest figures in Western sculpture since Michelangelo, was born in Paris in 1840. His life was as full of turbulence and conflict with authority as it was with the creation of remarkable works of art. He was known as both "the last of the great romantic sculptors" and the "first of the great modern sculptors." To us Rodin demonstrates the power of commitment and passion. When we are willing to live out our destiny (the life we were born to live) and deal with the obstacles fate presents, it is a path not only worth walking — it is the remarkable and essential journey we all must take if we are to fulfill our reason for being.

At 14 Rodin went to what is still called the Petite École to learn to draw and to launch his artistic career. At 23 he completed the bust of Father Eymard, and in 1864 he completed his first bronze bust of Father Pierre-Julien and <u>Mask of the Man with the Broken Nose.</u> For those, like us, who love sculpture, this portrait truly captures both the agony and ecstasy of life.

In 1865 he finished his famous <u>Portrait of a Young Woman.</u> The model, Rose Beuret, was to be his mistress until a few days before she died in 1917 when she became Mme. Rodin. Over the course of his life, Rodin pushed the boundary of classical sculpture until he broke with the academic tradition of his day and produced a body of work that marks the beginning of modern sculpture.

In 1880 he began work on the <u>Gates of Hell,</u> a double set of doors originally intended for the Museum of Decorative Arts, which was never built. Many of his now famous works however, came from this piece: <u>The Thinker, The Fates, The Martyr,</u> and many more. From 1884 to 1886 he created <u>The Burghers of Calais,</u> the profound group of larger-than-life-size figures that some believe to be his crowning accomplishment.

If one has been privileged to see Rodin's work in person, to feel the power of The Thinker, to stand close to a bust of The Man with the Broken Nose, to look up at the figure of Balzac, and to stand in awe before The Gates of Hell, one understands the power of his work and why he continues to motivate and inspire all who experience it.

What many people do not know is that Rodin did not have an easy path. His talent was questioned. Many of his early submissions to competitions were dismissed. Some even suggested that he was an artist of questionable skills. But like other artists who the world today honors, Rodin persisted through all of the disappointments and rejections to develop and refine the skills he needed to produce works of genuine power and relevance.

Rodin was working on several portraits when he died in November of 1917 at the age of 77.

The Gift that Keeps on Giving

*"Forgiveness does not change the past,
but it does enlarge the future."*

~ Paul Boese ~

More than just Another Step

So far in Part Three we have worked with some of our incompletes and taken some important steps in examining and in putting down additional baggage — in the form of guilt and resentment — that we may have been carrying. We have also explored the process of harvesting the fruits of our wisdom and experiences through a life review process.

We are now ready for a next and particularly valuable step: exploring the concept of forgiveness more deeply.

Most of us have, of course, heard about and practiced various forms of forgiveness most of our lives. In fact, in our experience the concept of forgiveness is so familiar that we tend to take it for granted and practice it rather superficially. Recently, however, we were introduced to an ancient Hawaiian practice called ho'oponopono and, as a result, discovered that we had, in fact, only been gliding along the surface of the real grace and power of forgiveness.

It is reported that at one stage of his career, Dr. Hew Len was a health practitioner associated with one of the most difficult wards in a psychiatric facility in Hawaii. This ward was reserved for those who were considered the most dangerous and who were unlikely to be released — ever. During his tenure there, however, Dr. Hew Len is reputed to have demonstrated an unusually high success rate that not only assisted many of these psychiatric inmates to experience improvements in their conditions, but to be rehabilitated.

You may be shaking your head and dismissing this claim as unbelievable — as we did at first. And yet, according to those involved, Dr. Hew

Len's unorthodox methods produced miraculous results that were beyond those achieved by traditional forms of psychotherapy.

His approach mirrors the Buddhist concept of the unity of all life, and the inseparability of the individual from the environment. According to this principle, what we see outside ourselves is a mirror for what exists inside us.

Given that he was surrounded by people who were classified as seriously troubled, Dr. Len had to accept that these same potentialities were within him — though, fortunately, in a dormant state. Taking responsibility for the existence of these tendencies in the human psyche, he then turned within and asked for forgiveness from his higher power. When he felt this forgiveness well up from deep inside him — not only for himself but for the inmates and all of us who possess the potential for aberrant behavior — he expressed deep appreciation and love to Source. Over time, this approach bore remarkable fruit.

A Unique Forgiveness Process

What we have learned from our use of ho'oponopono is that it provides us with the opportunity to:

- Open our hearts;

- Put down long held burdens of anger, fear, disappointment, and resentment;

- Assist in the healing of past and current relationships;

- Experience greater compassion and understanding for ourselves and others;

- Return from being held captive by the past or preoccupied by the future to the present moment where all things are possible.

The bottom line is that forgiveness is a remarkably powerful tool and we believe each of us — and the world at large — benefit enormously from its application.

We know, of course, that to do this it might be necessary to set aside (even if only temporarily) some beliefs you might have about forgiveness. One of these beliefs, for example, may be that forgiving this or that person lets them off the hook for what you believe is the harm they have committed against you. And you may not want to give them what may seem like a free pass.

On the other hand, you might believe that in forgiving yourself for what you define as some bad or unkind act you have committed against another, you will be letting yourself off the hook. And you don't believe you are entitled to such relief. Or maybe you believe that only God can forgive you or others for some of the insensitive, mean, hateful things we human beings are capable of doing to one another.

No matter what beliefs you may hold about forgiveness, however, the truth is that although it may not seem logical or rational, as Lewis Smedes once said, "to forgive is to set a prisoner free and to discover that the prisoner was you."

Bishop Desmond Tutu, who along with Nelson Mandela helped establish the Restorative Justice Movement in South Africa, said, "Without forgiveness, there is no future." And that, indeed, is our personal experience. Without our willingness to truly forgive ourselves and others for our apparent sins and transgressions, we walk through life looking backward, always a prisoner of the past. In addition, when we move through our lives without forgiveness, we carry within us toxins of anger, vengeance, and violence that not only distort our view of life, they can literally lead to illness and disease in our relationships with others and ourselves and within our own bodies. Indeed, without forgiveness we live in a world where at least some portions of our hearts are closed to others, to life, and to the life we were born to live.

Four Simple Steps on the Road to Deeper Forgiveness

So we invite you to participate in one of Dr. Hew Len's ho'oponopono forgiveness processes. This practice may appear simple, and indeed it is, but that does not mean it is not powerful and restorative.

Step One — Find a quiet place where you will not be interrupted. Take a few deep, slow breaths and then read these simple phrases over a few times and then start repeating them in your mind or out loud until you are familiar with them:

> I'm sorry.
> Please forgive me.
> Thank you.
> I love you.

Just four simple statements:

> I'm sorry.
>
> Please forgive me.
>
> Thank you.
>
> I love you.

Now, when you are ready, close your eyes and call to mind the image of someone you believe may have caused you some harm or discomfort. We suggest you begin with the image of someone you believe has caused you relatively minor harm or discomfort — like a disagreement you had with your significant other earlier in the day or a small amount of impatience or criticism you believe someone exhibited toward you.

Do this until you get the hang of this exercise and then gradually you may want to progress to other individuals and instances where you believe more harm or discomfort are involved, like a lie someone told you that caused you deeper pain or a greater sense of betrayal. No matter, just hold the image of this person in your mind's eye, feel some of the discomfort or pain the image of this person brings up, and say these four statements.

> I'm sorry.
>
> Please forgive me.
>
> Thank you.
>
> I love you.

Now repeat them again and, this time, go deeper into your willingness, into your acceptance, into your authenticity. How will you know that you are finished with this event or issue? You will begin to feel that whatever has been in the way between you and this other person has lightened and dissipated, and you will feel freer and more complete. You may even find that when you call up an image of that person, all or most of the heat you once felt will have cooled substantially.

So from here, you can go as far and as deep as you chose. Keep calling to mind other people or instances. These events or actions may be at the same level of intensity as the first or even stronger. Hold the image of each person in your mind and then keep repeating the four statements, once, twice, or however many times it takes.

Notice how once you feel a clearing with this person — the next person or event will simply pop up like a plate on one of those automatic servers in your local salad bar. And so just surrender to the process. And, when you are ready, you can also switch over to the other side of the equation, start calling to mind people who you believe have injured you, in minor and then in more and more major ways. Although this may, at first, seem to be an attempt to shift responsibility away from yourself, we find that it eventually leads us back to the awareness that we are all one.

So with each one, hold their image in your mind and keep repeating the four statements. Keep allowing their images to come to mind and keep saying the four lines over and over again at deeper and deeper levels of commitment. And please remember this process — as indeed any forgiveness process — works best when your heart as well as your head is fully engaged.

I'm sorry.

Please forgive me.

Thank you.

I love you.

Lewis Smedes gives us another very important clue:

"You will know that forgiveness has begun when you recall those who have hurt you and feel the power to wish them well."

Cycles Within Cycles

You may discover from your first experience with this forgiveness process that it can be both powerful and freeing. Or it may take a while before you are convinced of its effectiveness. If the latter is the case, we encourage you to keep experimenting with it.

Ho'oponopono can be applied to every corner of your life. And if you allow it to, it can assist you in cleansing your inner landscape of the weight of encumbrances that may have littered it for a long time.

These four simple statements can act like a gentle Roto-Rooter that goes deeper and deeper into the past. You can also make these four statements a song that you sing, a song of cleansing and healing, a song that can lead you to better understand what is meant when someone says that they are 100% responsible for the world.

Life Rule
"Forgive or Relive."

~ Anonymous

Life Achievement
Country music legend Willie Nelson tours and creates new albums with his distinctive voice in his 70s.

Life Tool
Your road to conscious living and wise aging will certainly pass directly through the territory of forgiveness. So as we close out this chapter we invite you to consider participating in a 30-Day Forgiveness Process.

To begin with, please make a two-part list of people who have offended you in some way and things you have done that have either offended others or yourself.

Once you have done this we invite you to order the list from the lightest to the most serious according to the scope of the offence and the degree of charge that you feel around it.

Then starting at the top of the list with the lightest issue, work your way down using Dr. Len's ho'oponopono statements or whatever forgiveness method you might prefer.

We suggest you work each item on your list until you feel more confident with the method you have selected and more comfortable with the result.

You might also want to record your experiences in a journal. Do you notice a lessening of intensity in your feelings about the other person, about yourself, etc.? Do you feel lighter and freer and is your heart more open?

Little Deaths

"The territory of little death is where simple knowledge can give way to a deeper revelation."

~ Michael Meade ~

In his rich and thought-provoking book, *Fate and Destiny*, Michael Meade reminds us of the role "little deaths" play in our lives. And so before we shift our attention from harvesting the wisdom and experience of our past to learning to focus more fully in the present, we think it might be helpful to take a brief look at this subject.

What are "little deaths"? As Michael Meade reminds us, and as our personal experience validates, they are moments in our lives when the illusion that we are invincible and that death is someplace well off in the future is pierced by a wake-up call from fate. A serious financial setback, a major accident or illnesses, the loss of a loved one, and even those odd occurrences when the veil of what we call reality is lifted and we experience one of those "between the worlds" moments. These are moments in which we remember that there is a lot more to the mystery of life than our usual focus allows us to see.

These experiences can, and most often do, bring us up short, even when we do not want to be brought up short. They also remind us that we are not immortal and that we are not, contrary to the constant rumblings of our egos, masters of the universe either.

But why, after spending time encouraging you to stop waiting and start living the life we were born to live, do we visit this subject? Why at this juncture — when we are about to turn our attention to the present moment and explore the remarkable and unique possibilities that each moment offers us — do we invite you to pause and consider the topic of little death?

We actually believe it is a most appropriate time to do precisely this. Indeed, as we get ready to explore how we can live more mindfully in the present moment, we know that remembering the fragileness and impermanence of life can be of great value. We also know that we can all be a little stubborn and resistant to change and that sometimes we require an occasional interruption to the normal flow of things in order to help us get back on the path of our true destiny. We also know that in order to remember the value and wonder of life, the life we were born to live, we all need a little prompting; and this prompting often occurs in the form of little deaths.

In our experience when we are in touch with life's fragility and impermanence we are open, aware, sensitive, and available to others and to the ebb and flow of life. This is another of the reasons why — we are fairly certain — these little deaths suddenly show up. Indeed, without them we might be inclined to believe our own reviews and forget that all things in the physical realm have a beginning and an end, an entry and an exit point.

Unfortunately, in the modern world — especially the world of virtual reality and collective thinking where we have become spectators rather than proactive participants; where we are becoming more divorced from the rhythms of the natural world — we can sometimes get caught believing that death need not concern us, or at the very least, death is something that will only concern us sometime in the future. This assumption allows us to spend our time and energies on the self-directed pursuits of consumption and accumulation that pass as meaningful activities in the 21st century.

So in this moment we invite you to try on a different point of view. We ask you to remember one or more of the little deaths you may have experienced already in this life. Let them inform you of the truth and purpose of your life and redirect you back onto the primary path you have come here to walk. Let these little deaths become your allies and encourage you to take better advantage of the substantial challenges and remarkable opportunities this path involves.

Yes, little deaths are allies that bring the gifts of wisdom and redirection. They provide us with glimpses, even if only for a short period of time, into the profound mysteries that lie beneath, between, around, and within the ordinary business of life.

In our personal lives we have experienced at least a few little deaths. We offer them here in the hope they may encourage you to remember and explore some of your own.

A car accident during George's freshman year in college comes to mind. A rear tire blow-out on a narrow mountain road late at night resulted in the car being thrown, tossed, and tumbled until its crumbled form came to rest under the dangling remains of a telephone pole and close to a rock ledge. Not only were there no major injuries, there were no minor ones. Standing there looking at this crumbled wreck, the only thought George and his passenger had was one of utter disbelief — not only that the accident had occurred but that they were alive. And not only that they were alive — but that they had escaped without a scratch.

George and his passenger realized in that moment that the old cliché about "not dying before your time" was absolutely true. Nothing could have made this truth more evident to them than the sight of that totaled vehicle. This realization led to another, one that would come up again and again in the days following and for many months to come. Why had they been spared? Was there something of significance they were meant to discover and accomplish?

A fall through a ceiling occurred in an almost surreal moment for Sedena. She had thought that the floor of the attic *might not* be strong enough to hold her weight. But being an inquisitive teenager, she chose to stand on it anyway. That decision was followed almost immediately by the shattering of the plasterboard and her rapid descent to the floor of the room below. An awareness of something predetermined came to her during her sudden yet slow-motion descent.

A back broken in several places. Immobility, interruption of a young life, a long period of recuperation. A major life lesson. Pay attention to one's first instinct — the one that in this case had cautioned her that the next step was not safe. But something larger as well, the understanding that interruptions in the normal flow of things occur when there is something one is required or being given a chance to look at. After weeks of recovery and relative isolation, Sedena came to look for the gold in everything — no matter how trivial or seemingly out of sequence it might at first appear to be.

Later in life, there were painful ends to relationships in both of our lives that literally caused us to feel the world had ended. Lost, disinterested in life, and the actual sensation of being unable to breathe led ultimately to redirection in our lives.

Other little deaths on the other side of the coin: Moments of remarkable insight for both of us brought about by experiences with breathing techniques and hallucinogenic drugs, through long periods of fasting, silent retreats, and deep meditations when the normal boundaries of the physical world became less rigid and much more permeable.

These are some of the little deaths we have experienced. Each in a different way a reminder of life's fragility and impermanence, each an opportunity to reflect on our direction and on the kind of life we were living and on our commitment to find and fulfill life we were born to live.

These experiences are, when we choose to reflect on them, as indelible today as they were undeniable at the time. Indeed, each of these experiences and interruptions in the flow of our lives offered us rich opportunities to turn the dross of the everyday into the gold of greater consciousness.

What about you? As we stand on this border between an exploration of the past and a deeper, richer involvement in the present will you take a few moments now to let your little deaths inform you? Who are you? What do you want? And what are you doing here?

Life Rule

"Those who would live a bigger life and become conscious of their purpose and destiny in this world must somehow face a 'little death' in order to grow, in order to know where their soul would have them go."

~ Michael Meade

Live Achievement

Jimmy Carter, 39th President of the United States, founder of the Carter Center, winner of the Nobel Peace Prize, and best-selling author, is still a major force in world politics in his 80s.

Life Tool

If you are willing to stay in touch with the natural world and observe the flow of the seasons, the patterns and rhythms that underlie the life cycles of the various species as well as the flora and fauna, we believe you will always remember the true meaning of life. So make the observation of the natural world a daily practice and you will never be far from the wisdom that will inform and enrich your life. You will know intimately the cycles of life, death, and rebirth.

PART FOUR

Here and Now —
Your Next Step on the Road
to Living the Life
You Were Born to Live

"I wasted a lot of my life attempting to be like everyone else.
Elderhood gives me permission to delight in my uniqueness.
I've discovered that as we age, we don't become more like others,
we become more like ourselves."

~ Pam, A Hospice Counselor ~
Excerpt from *From Age-ing To Sage-ing*
by Zalman Schachter-Shalomi & Ronald S. Miller

The Trotter

Leo's Story

According to a report by Jim Suhr of The Associated Press, Leo Burns drove his horse, Winsome Wyoming, to five wins in as many races in the first half of 2006. Apparently this was not such an unusual feat for this resident of Albion, IL, and member of the United States Trotting Association, who has a record of more than 450 wins and career earnings of over $400,000.

On July 25th he put on his colors and his helmet and goggles and drove Winsome Wyoming to a win against six horses in a mile-long race. At the quarter pole he had a six-length lead and by the time he and the horse crossed the finish line his lead was 15 lengths and he had broken the track record for 2-year-olds with a time of 2:05.4.

The victory gave Leo Burns and Winsome Wyoming winnings of $5,009 for the first part of 2006. This is a rather impressive record for anyone in any sport, but Leo Burns, who was born when Woodrow Wilson was President of the United States, is continuing to break records at 91. According to Suhr, "no record shows anyone older having taken part in such a race in North America, much less winning." As for Leo, "he seems to take it all pretty much in stride and says, 'As long as I feel good, I'll keep going and I'll be OK.'"

Living in the Now

"Friend, hope for the truth while you are alive…
If you find nothing now, you will simply end up with
An empty apartment in the City of Death."

~ Kabir ~

Present Moment Awareness

Let us turn our attention to a most important step on the road to living consciously and aging wisely: learning to live more fully in this moment.

In *The Power of Now* and *The New Earth,* author and spiritual teacher Eckhart Tolle explores the value of living in the now as few before him have. Ram Dass in *Be Here Now* and *Still Here* illuminates this as essential as well. If you have not read these books, we strongly recommend that you give yourself the gift of doing so.

So let us follow their lead and explore the importance of placing our attention in this one, unique, and unduplicatable instant — this point of power, this choice point that has never occurred for us in quite the same way before and never will again. As we do, we invite you to re-read the lines above by Kabir, the Indian mystic and poet.

Pay careful attention not only to the irrefutable logic of his words, but also to the flow of your breath, the beating of your heart, the sounds that are happening around you, the smells, the temperature of the air, and the quality of the light around you as you read them. Remember that although your mind may appear to be occupied with the words and their meaning, your senses are constantly tuning in to all that is going on around and within you, which in so many instances is an extension and demonstration of that meaning. In short, the universe is constantly giving us opportunities to learn and grow in countless ways and sometimes the smallest expansion of focus between head and heart, between the object you are focused on and the magic that is happening between, around, and within can be of inestimable value.

It follows then that if you want to have a fuller, more remarkable, and rewarding life you may want to expand your focus beyond your thoughts. You may want to pay attention to all that is occurring simultaneously in each instant within and around you. In this way you can deepen your experience of life by a hundredfold, by a thousandfold, perhaps by a thousand-thousand fold.

This is what we can discover when we open our hearts and hence our awareness, even just a little, and let in more of what is happening in each moment. Jack Kornfield, noted teacher of mindfulness and meditation, says it this way, "The power of loving-kindness, the power of those living from the heart, makes the power of armies and technology seem like child's play. For it is the heart force that brings all life, that creates all life, that moves through us."

Even if we only add one new awareness, one new sensory experience at a time to our experience in each moment the benefit can be enormous. We become most alive, to each other and to the most ordinary and yet remarkable experiences of our lives. This is what happens when we follow the good advice of the Zen Master who Mark Nepo reports said, "The greedy one wanted to taste all of the cherries, the wise one tasted all of the cherries in one."

So let us remember the wisdom that Kabir, Eckhart Tolle, Ram Dass, Nepo, and many other teachers and mystics have shared — that the present moment is truly the only real moment we have, the only moment we can count on, and the only moment in which anything actually happens. Let us remember that our failure to be aware of what is happening within and around us in each moment deprives us of enjoying much of the richness of what is set before us. One can liken the common state of distraction — in which we miss the moment because we are captured in the past or are trying to project into a future — to taking a few hurried bites at a huge feast. We may momentarily satiate a small degree of our hunger, but in the end we deprive ourselves of much that is present that can truly nourish and enrich our lives.

Eckhart Tolle describes this "is" in *The Power of Now*, "*Have you ever experienced, done, thought, or felt anything outside the Now? [...] Nothing ever happens in the past. It happens in the Now. Nothing will ever happen in the future. It will happen in the Now.*"

If this is true, and in our experience it most certainly is, why do so many of us spend so much of our time focusing on the past or the future? This is an important question. In many ways, this may very well be *the* most important question. So we invite you to go to the one and only place where you will be able to find your own answer, which is in each and every present moment of your life. Indeed, it is not unlike that game of hide-and-seek that some of us used to play. If you remember, when someone got close to their goal of finding the person or object that was hidden, clues would be given as to whether they were "hot" or "cold." So if you are looking for that which is hidden, go to the place where what you are looking for is hidden. Everywhere else is "cold" because it doesn't actually exist — except in our memory or our projected imagination.

What May Be in the Way

In the end, the actual journey of living in the present moment is ours and ours alone to take. And in our experience, unless we are willing to take this journey; unless we are willing to have a direct experience of our unique and individual life, which awaits us in each Now; unless we allow it to unfold moment by moment and in its unfolding disclose itself to us, life will remain an intellectual exercise, a kind of passive virtual experience rather than a passionate actual experience. It will only serve to raise additional hypothetical and theoretical questions and keep us forever trapped in the realm of "words and notions."

This has certainly been true for us. Even with all of the wisdom many teachers have imparted to us, we often find ourselves struggling to stay awake, struggling to come to terms with the idea that life can be as simple as "eat when eating, sit when sitting, stand when standing."

Years of training and traditional education — what Don Miguel Ruiz calls "domestication" — have certainly increased our challenge. Yes, in the world we were born into we were taught to focus on the past and project ahead into the future. Carrots and sticks, goals, objectives, fears, threats of punishment, promises of approval and of rewards, acceptance, and acknowledgment, these are the tools that have been employed to induct us into a way of living that is, we are discovering, as unhealthy as it is unnatural.

Is it any wonder then that our experience in the present moment is often uncomfortable? We fidget. We experience anxiety. We wonder what we are supposed to do because we have been taught that "being" is not enough. That "doing" and "becoming" rather than "surrendering and allowing" are the reasons for living. As a result, "being" is unknown territory. And when faced with the suggestion that we just "be," discomfort shows up. So we go back to a time when — at least according to our memory — our lives weren't as uncomfortable. Or we try to journey ahead in the hope that some future moment we can imagine will have greater success, more joy, achievement, approval, or whatever we think will be better than whatever is going on in this moment.

But if we want to live the life we were born to live, we will have to get beyond these "ruts of ordinary perception." We will have to get outside the limits of our minds and our focus on "being" rather than "doing." This is the key. Yes, learning to live in the present moment requires — like the lessons we discovered in the "closed fist" exercise we did in the last section — that we be willing to pass through a little bit of discomfort. Then we can find legitimate and more permanent relief — the relief that comes from opening up, from trusting, from surrendering, from allowing rather than holding on, staying closed, clinging to the past, or hoping for the future.

And what about Kabir's contention that salvation is what occurs before death? If this is true then it also holds that if we are not living in each present moment, if we are spending (or wasting) most of our time in our thoughts hoping that we will magically find something of value by reliving the past or anticipating the future, we will surely miss the nourishment of the meal before us.

Powerful thought! Powerful and perhaps a little uncomfortable! But we invite you, to the best of your ability, to stay with both the power and the discomfort moment by moment. We invite you to explore this — not just intellectually, but viscerally. Yes, here in this chapter and as often as you can in your life, practice keeping your focus on this now and on how you are showing up within it. And when you forget — a thing we all do on a regular basis — acknowledge it and then do your best to simply return your attention to this moment by focusing on your breath and on whatever you are seeing, hearing, tasting, smelling, and feeling. Just now! Just here! Just you!

Gratitude is another way to practice being in the moment. Gratitude for whatever is happening within and around you in the present moment — even if your mind wants to call it unpleasant, boring, or even painful. When you honor whatever you are doing — reading these words, standing in the shower, feeling the coolness or warmth of the Earth, experiencing sadness, taking a walk, exercising, talking to a friend or loved one, playing catch with a grandchild, watching a child laugh or cry. Whenever you honor whatever you are feeling — the wind on your face, the intimacy you are sharing with someone you love or the coolness that occurs when a cloud covers the sun, then you are being present.

The same is true when you honor and acknowledge the remarkable assemblage of qualities, characteristics, experiences, talents, and skills (both developed and latent) that you are. When you allow yourself to experience the sheer and indescribable wonder of the millions of cells and processes that conspire to allow you to take this next breath, and then this one, you come into the present. In these moments of awareness, these "nows," these expressions of gratitude for what is, you will be one with the divine, for how else could the divine manifest but in this moment, and in this one.

Yes, with a slight shift in awareness away from what you have done (past) or might do (future), away from doubt and worry and to a focus on what is currently going on, you will step through a doorway into the realm of new opportunities, new experiences, and new levels of interaction with yourself and others. Through this doorway, everything is possible! Through this doorway, you will be able to sense and even merge with the presence of God, Oneness, Source, Divinity, or whatever you call the organizing force of the Universe.

Some say this is the reason living in the present is so challenging. For to live in the present is to live in the Light, is to experience the mysterious unfolding of the Oneness. And after living so long in previous or future nows — in virtual rather than in actual existence — living in the Mystery and the Light takes a little getting used to. It is similar, in many ways, to the experience of walking out into the bright, warming sunshine after spending time in a darkened theater watching images being projected on a screen. It's like stepping out of a dream that felt so real — into the Greater Reality.

Life Envisioning — A Journey into the Present

With this information in mind, we invite you to join us on a short journey. All you have to do is go to "Life Envisioning — A Journey into the Present," which you will find in the guided imagery section of www.donotgoquietlythebook.com. We wish you a joyous journey.

Life Rule
"We can do noble acts without ruling Earth and Sea."

~ Aristotle

Life Achievement
Frank Lloyd Wright, one of America's preeminent architects, designed some of his most imaginative and celebrated buildings in his 70s.

Life Tool
"Sit when sitting, stand when standing, eat when eating." This piece of extraordinary and practical wisdom from the Zen tradition is one we were exposed to many years ago. Simple. Seemingly obvious. Of course, we say. One sits when sitting, stands when standing, etc.! Not true. At least not in our experience! And if you doubt it, ask yourself when the last time was that you just sat without doing anything else. When was the last time that you stood just for the sheer pleasure and joy of standing — with nowhere to go and nothing to do except experience standing. And as for eating, we all know the answer to that question don't we? When did you last just eat — paying attention to the scents and flavors of the food and focusing on chewing, swallowing, and digesting? When did you just eat and not read, talk to someone, watch television, surf the Internet, or think about where you were previously or where you are going to be later. You see what we mean — *Sit when sitting, stand when standing, eat when eating.* Simple — but not so easy. You could even call it a spiritual practice. And that's what's required to really "accomplish" it: practice as well as patience, compassion toward yourself as well as the desire to connect to the Divine.

Learning in the Now

"Keep the gold and keep the silver,
give us wisdom."

~ Arabian Proverb ~

All We Have to Learn Is Here and Now

So we have talked about the fact that the majority of us spend a lot time thinking about, reevaluating, and revisiting the past as well as projecting ahead and wondering and worrying about the future. In short, we have discussed that life doesn't happen in the past and it has yet to happen in the future.

What we haven't talked as much about is that a lot of us also spend a lot of our time thinking and talking about what we think we know, what we once did, who we are, what we own, what we'd like to do someday, and all of that. Unfortunately the time or energy most of us invest in this practice is not very valuable.

Indeed, if we are honest with ourselves, our tendency to dwell on what we know, what we once did, and what we are going to do someday is often an attempt advanced by our sometimes fragile egos to justify an existence that may not be as stellar or even as acceptable to us as we would like it to be.

So as we move further along on this path toward living more consciously and aging wisely, let us try on the possibility, at least for the time being, that if we stop defending what we know and who we think we are, our hands, heads, and hearts will be a lot freer to focus on whatever is right in front of us. And in case you haven't noticed — what is right in front of us contains hundreds of clues as to what we still have to learn and what we can celebrate and enjoy. And while some of these clues may be subtle, some are pretty obvious and all are part of the remarkable conspiracy between our destiny and fate to provide us with a script that we can follow to live the life we were born to live.

So if you are willing to step out of the "ruts of ordinary perception" and experiment with living more fully in each precious moment, join us as we take a deeper look.

This School Called Life

Health issues? Then this is where your next great present moment learning can be found. Relationship challenges with your spouse or partner, one of your children, or a friend? This is where your next lesson awaits. Obstacles at work, staff or client disharmony, challenges in the organization you volunteer for, or the club you support — you guessed it, this is where your next best lesson is. Internal questions and confusions about what to do with your energy and talent? You guessed it!

We are not exaggerating. You do not have to enroll in a graduate level program or even sign up for classes at your local community college to discover what you have to learn in order to inherit more of who you are and live a more conscious existence. Not that traditional academic courses are not valuable. Nor do you necessarily have to take an online correspondence course, participate in a weekend seminar, do years of personal therapy, or spend weeks at the library doing research in order to discover what the essential lessons are that are available to you in this moment. Simply look at the syllabus called your daily existence and you will find more than enough material to focus on. Then that graduate program or community college class, online course, weekend seminar, or research can be a gold mine. For you will understand how and where to put your new knowledge to work.

On the subject of when to start your next class, the answer to that question is also simple. Now! Now is the best time! Now is the most appropriate time! *Sit when sitting, stand when standing, eat when eating.*

You can put it off, of course. You can try to figure out where on your calendar you have the time to learn to be more caring, more insightful, or more generous. You can look for a few periods to become a better friend, partner, mentor, volunteer, or someone better equipped for that journey into the "inscape" — your interior consciousness. Or you can just roll up your sleeves and take a work/study program in this and every other moment in your life.

And the good news is that you do not need to apply, wait for admission, save your money, or take out a student or home equity loan in order to do any of this. All you have to do is realize that this is a live-as-you-go, study-where-you-are, moment-by-moment process. Indeed, your best learning opportunities are right here at the check-out counter of your local market or at the dry cleaners; in your next conversation with one of your children, your spouse, or a friend; in your next personal interaction, email, phone call, or meeting at work; in the next quiet moment you take sitting on the deck, or when you are out walking. Your next and most important learning opportunity happens on an airplane, sitting in a conference room, waiting at the doctor's office, or in your car in traffic.

Yes, each present moment holds enormous opportunities for each of us to become better students in our next and most important subjects in the school called life. Literally, each thought, word, and action — each and every moment of our lives — holds our next lesson; and each person we meet is our teacher. In short, each present moment is both our next and our best opportunity to learn whatever is next on the life syllabus that will allow us to live the life we were born to live.

Life Rule
"The road to success is usually off the beaten path."

~ Frank Tyger

Life Achievement
Ethel Barrymore, member of one of the country's leading theatrical families, appeared in 20 films from age 67 to 78.

Life Tool
Your express ticket to the Land of Now is your willingness to pay attention to what is happening in this moment, and in this moment, and in this moment. You may be in a room full of other people or you may be by yourself; you may be at work or at home or somewhere out in the world. No matter where you are or what is happening around you, this moment is your doorway to your next truth, your next unfolding, and your next discovery. This moment is not a place to pass through on the way to someplace or something else. This moment is an end and a beginning unto itself. Nothing you have to do. Nowhere you have to go. Just this moment, just your moment to be your authentic and original self.

Living No Faster than Feelings Can Follow

"As we approach the October, November, and December of our lives, the time for harvesting arrives. This involves reflecting on our achievements, feeling pride in our contributions to family and society, and ultimately finding our place in the cosmos."

~ Zalman Schachter-Shalomi & Ronald Miller ~

Searching for Sanity

A good friend introduced us to the expression that serves as the title of this chapter. It is one of the premises in a spiritual study she has pursued for many years called "thinking and destiny." It is, in our opinion, a very important key to living in the now.

Indeed, remembering to live no faster than feelings can follow seems to us to be of relevance to people at any age, but of particular value to those of us who are in or are approaching the second half of our lives. Why? Because in this complex time, a number of us continue to spend a lot of our time still trying to propitiate the same Gods of Approval and Security that we worshipped in the first half of life. In fact, contrary to the natural laws of life which would have us change both our pace and our focus as we age, many of us find ourselves doing more, pushing harder and faster in lives that are more challenging and oftentimes less satisfying.

Yes, many of us continue to attempt to deal with life's opportunities and challenges by thinking, analyzing, worrying, and doing more. With so much thinking, worrying, and doing, however, it is no wonder that an increasing number of us sometimes get out of touch with our feelings.

The God of Productivity and those who fervently champion its dogma encourage these strategies and another that suggests that it is important to become proficient at multi-tasking. "Faster, More, and Cheaper" has become the mantra of the day in business and so it is no wonder that this same message has bled through into our personal worlds where our so-called free time has become almost as pressurized as our work worlds.

Crowded social calendars and a seemingly endless array of recreational activities that we often pursue with a mind-numbing and body-exhausting frenzy seem to have become the rule of the day. And then, of course, there are the many forms of entertainment and the increasing social media engagement that preoccupy our minds and distract us from living in the present moment.

Yes, it has become a fast-food, do-it-on-the-run, media-mad, 24/7 activity-obsessed world where our bodies and our minds are constantly on the go. But in this fever-pitched, instant-gratification world, what happens to the true language of the heart and the soul? What happens to our feelings?

The World of NLP

Several decades ago, two social scientists, Richard Bandler and John Grinder, conducted a study on communication styles. Their original objective was to discover what made some people highly effective at communicating ideas and information while others were less effective. As a first step they identified some well-known individuals — the renowned psychiatrist and hypnotherapist Milton H. Erickson most notably among them — who were known for being highly effective communicators. They studied their patterns and practices, the order or sequence in which they said or did particular things, and then compared this with data collected in studies of other people who were not as effective in their communications. Slowly a number of interesting implications began to emerge and after more research they evolved what has come to be known as the study of Neurolinguistic Programming (NLP).

Without burdening you with more detail than is necessary at this juncture, suffice it to say that one of the primary things Bandler and Grinder discovered was that the majority of us tend to fall into one of three primary communication groups — visual, auditory, and kinesthetic. That is, we tend to think, process information, and talk using visual, auditory, and kinesthetic predicates — look at this, see this, picture that; hear this, listen; or feel this, get a handle on that, etc. Yes, sight, sound, and feeling are the three primary modalities by which the majority of us access information and interact with the world around us.

Another interesting thing that Bandler and Grinder discovered is that each of these communication groups tend to process and deliver information at different rates of speed. Visual types speak the fastest of the three types. Auditory types process information and communicate slower, and kinesthetic types (feeling-based communicators) are appreciably slower than the other two types in their communications style. It's important to note here that the speed of processing or communicating information does not equate with levels of intelligence — only with the natural style an individual exhibits in taking in and communicating information. A second point of relevance is that individuals often possess more than one communication style, but one style seems to dominate.

What do these findings have to do with living the lives we were born to live and "going no faster than feelings can follow"? Well, since those who communicate in a feeling-based style (kinesthetics) speak slower than either visual or auditory types, in order for visual and auditory types to be able to communicate effectively with kinesthetics they would be wise to slow down their rate of communication.

Of course, we do not want to oversimplify the work of Bandler and Grinder or suggest that it can be fully appreciated in just a few paragraphs. But it is clear that one of the essential lessons of their study is that if one communication type wants to talk to another, they are more effective when they adjust the speed of their communication and their use of predicates (sight, sound, feeling) to match that of the other type. Bandler and Grinder's work also suggests to us that since feeling is the dominant language of people who communicate slower, it would be wise for those of us who want to get in touch with our feelings to learn to talk no faster than feelings can follow.

Vibration and the Art of Stone Carving

Similar lessons can be found in other disciplines. The art of stone carving is an excellent example. In today's fast-paced world, supply and demand are driving a lot of sculptors to use power tools in order to produce works faster and thus remain economically competitive. While these power tools do allow sculptors to produce more work in shorter time periods, there are some who believe that the pieces produced lack the same level of emotional depth and feeling that pieces carved by hand have.

And here's one possible reason why! Our scientists tell us that all of the elements in the universe are comprised of the same basic ingredient — electromagnetic energy. They also tell us that the only difference between a form that appears dense, like rock, and one that appears light, like air, is the rate at which the energy that comprises it is vibrating. Air, for example, vibrates relatively fast. Rock vibrates relatively slow. The human body, which is neither as dense as rock nor as light as air, vibrates at a level that is somewhere between these two substances.

So when a sculptor works on a stone that is vibrating appreciably slower than he himself is (because of the molecular density of the stone) and this sculptor works with a power tool that vibrates at a rate that is even faster than the rate at which he is vibrating, instead of narrowing the frequency gap between himself and the stone, the use of the power tool increases this gap. Under these conditions the sculptor, working with power tools, dramatically impacts the outer skin of the stone, finding shape and texture relatively quickly, but the inner essence (or heart) of the stone is not necessarily ever touched.

A comparison to the tendency young people have today of meeting, experiencing physical attraction, and almost immediately sharing sexual experience may be helpful here. While this kind of interaction (what today is called "hooking up") may produce a sense of connection, it does not often result in true relationships and genuine intimacy. Intimacy and relationships take time, patience, investment of attention, and willingness to understand and appreciate. Hence in both relationships and in carving, speed often results in experiences that are sometimes aesthetically or sensually satisfying, but may lack true inner essence — what we take the liberty to call "soul experiences," which are accessed using the language of feeling.

If we return again to the Bandler and Grinder study and remember the lesson found in the study of various communication types, we can draw the conclusion that in order for the sculptor to communicate with the heart of his stone he must — contrary to the laws of economics — slow his process down and find a frequency of communication that is somewhere between his own and that of the stone. Hence the caution by some of the great masters of the art to carve stone using hand tools. And while the dealers and collectors who control much of the art world today might disagree, the fact is that pieces carved by hand end up enduring over time because they have a certain essence that is lacking in the machine-tooled pieces. So perhaps we — as sculptors, lovers, and individuals who want to live the lives we were born to live — would be wise to remember to go no faster than feelings will follow, at least on those occasions when it is important to include this vital language of the soul in life's equation.

Of course some would argue that unlike the example of one human being attempting to communicate with another, trying to draw a similar parallel between the stone and the artist does not hold up because the artist is human and the stone is, well, at least in some belief systems, just unconscious rock.

But, if all of the stuff in the universe is made up of the same basic electromagnetic energy and the only difference between one physical form and another is the rate at which that energy is vibrating, then it must also hold that there is life in all physical forms — even those we think of as inanimate.

What If

So if we are willing, even if only for a few moments, to accept this premise that the only difference between human beings and the ground we walk on and the trees and rocks around us is the rate at which each of these elements vibrates — then our sometimes casual indifference to the way we use or abuse countless numbers of other physical forms, the way we muscle them and do our best to bend them to our will, and at times destroy them indiscriminately, might have to be reconsidered.

Indeed, the implications become truly astounding. For if we are living in a universe in which each physical object, each substance, each element is alive, then we would be wise to treat each object, substance, and element with a new level of respect. We would be wise to stop acting as if we were masters of the universe and start remembering that we are only one aspect of a very complex whole system and that we need to go no faster than feelings can follow.

Other Implications

What other implications does this concept hold for us? If we think at a frequency of approximately 1,200 words a minute, if sound travels at a speed of 800 miles per hour, if our sight operates at the speed of light — 186,000 miles per second — and our feelings operate at a much slower rate of vibration, then to stay in alignment with life, to be able to process and integrate our experience, we would be wise to slow down the speed at which we live.

So as you take your next steps on the road to living the life you were born to live, we invite you to remember to experiment with going only as fast as your feelings can follow. Indeed, if you take only one piece of advice from this entire book, please remember that your life happens in each present moment and your feelings are a primary key to this precious moment and to this one and to this one.

Life Rule
"A little Integrity is more valuable than any career."

~ Ralph Waldo Emerson

Life Achievement
Michelangelo, master painter and carver of the Renaissance, painted the Sistine Chapel at 77.

Life Tool
For the next few days, we invite you to conduct a simple experiment. Before you speak, before you act, slow things down enough to ask one question — "How do I feel about this?" That's all! You don't have to put your life on hold or stop that headlong rush toward whatever goal you are chasing. Just pause long enough to find out how you feel about what you are about to say or do. In short, practice going no faster than feelings can follow!

The Difference Between
Believing & Knowing

"Where is your self found? Always in the
deepest enchantment you experience."

~ Hugo von Hofmannsthal ~

Beyond Believing

arl Jung, one of the founding fathers of modern psychology, went to great lengths to make a distinction between believing and knowing. He pointed out, in fact, that many of us live lives based almost entirely on believing rather than knowing.

From our perspective, this fact has become even truer in this age when the Gods of Opinion and Belief exercise such relentless control over our lives. In fact, Jung's critical distinction seems to have almost been forgotten. This condition has been reinforced by an educational system that rewards mimicry over inquiry and some media companies that often seem to find it entirely acceptable to literally make up information and trumpet them as real.

It is no wonder then that our world is in such trouble; for what we have is not just "a failure to communicate," it is a failure to be able to differentiate. Yes, a failure to differentiate between fact and fiction, between ordinary and authentic, between virtual and actual, and between believing and knowing. And this, in turn, appears to be leading to a further strengthening of the position held by the God of Opinion. This "God," of rather questionable values and virtues, as well as the God of Belief have, indeed, become the dominant Gods of our time while the Gods of Intuition, Imagination, Curiosity, Insight, Creativity, Perception, Revelation, and Discernment have been reduced to a small "g" status.

Indeed, one of the prevailing beliefs seems to be that if these small gods had their way, we would waste all of our time in the pursuit of idle pleasures and non-productive practices — things like daydreaming, reflection, meditation, and imagination — practices that are not considered of genuine value in the mechanistic world where the God of Economics is also faithfully worshipped.

Present Moment Distraction

We exaggerate this somewhat troubling state of the state, of course, but unfortunately not all that much. One need only walk down the street of one of our towns or cities or enter one of our public places to experience some of the madness we accept as part of our daily lives. Like armies of somnambulists many of us spend the majority of our present moments preoccupied by our thoughts about where we have been or where we think we are going and facilitated in this by technological toys that re-enforce these practices. We walk and talk, but to people who are not present. In fact many times we are talking to their answering machines while they talk to someone else who is not present with them. When we are not doing this we are watching videos, reading our email, or texting. Rarely do we just walk and breathe, walk and observe, walk and feel into the world and relate to other human beings who are actually occupying the same physical space we are.

We are, in fact, so seduced by this glut of mind noise and so tumbled and tossed about by the sirens trumpeted by the media that we avoid eye contact and interaction with our fellow walkers and instead settle for our relationships with iPods, tablets, and our smartphones. In fact, these toys seem to have literally become extensions of our ears, hands, and brains.

Even if you happen to be among the relative few who do not spend the majority of your precious nows in this manner, you probably have children or grandchildren, co-workers, or friends who are seduced by the speed and glitter of this contemporary communications madness. If so, you may have trouble encouraging them to spend time interacting with other real people rather than with virtual friends who are not physically present with them.

You may also have trouble getting across the point that turning strangers into new acquaintances and friends, interacting with and learning from the world of nature — and learning to be alone and comfortable in the silence — are not just options, but essential practices that allow us all to connect with our sanity, humanity, and individuality in the midst of the rush of accelerated change and manic preoccupation with being someplace other than where we are.

These are, after all, essential steps on the road to living consciously and aging wisely. These are essential steps and practices that lead to other essential doorways and to dimensions that lie within and beyond the physical boundaries — dimensions that can, if we take the good council of some of the world's great mystics and visionaries, actually allow us to do all of the things these technologies promise without our having to be wired up, plugged in, and connected.

So if you are one who remembers that life is not just about video games and text messaging, game consoles, and tracking the minutia of other people's lives via social media; if you are someone who recognizes that these technologies that have become the nannies and babysitters of the 21st century may bring us some benefits, but they also cast very long and significant shadows, then we encourage you to stay connected to the world around you.

What's the Big Deal?

Are we being unnecessarily harsh on the modern world? Is it simply that we have grown old and crusty and are out of touch and out of step with what's happening? We don't think so! If anything, we think those of us who are in or approaching the second half of life have an important job to do. We who still remember what life was like before it became fully digitized and largely unconscious — when we, as human beings, were not so easily seduced into accepting this gargantuan denial of our knowing and of the now — can act as translators, way-showers and truth-tellers. We can, without obstructing the great rush of progress, actually contribute discernment that can lead to a more sane, sustainable, and humane world.

In fact, we may be among the last of our species to actually remember how valuable it is to be engaged in real rather than virtual lives. We may be among the last to know that unless we wake up and change some things by injecting genuine connectivity, intimacy, and compassion back into the Game of Life, our seemingly harsh judgments about life in these times will not be nearly as harsh as the life we will all face in a world in which we blindly accept and follow the manufactured opinions of others and call that truth.

If you are not sure what this has to do with living the life you were born to live, let us ask you a few questions:

- When was the last time you frittered away an afternoon reading your favorite poet or listening to Bach or Adele?

- When was the last time you allowed yourself to daydream without feeling guilty about the "real stuff" you were not getting done?

⊛   When was the last time you simply posed a question or identified a problem and then let it go, knowing that in its proper
time and under the right conditions, the solution would appear
intuitively? Yes, the solution, all at once and without any doubt.

If your answer to some of these questions, like ours, is "not often
enough," then perhaps we've made our point! Yes, fortunately, those of us
in the second half of life still remember when life was not pre-packaged,
shrink-wrapped, and delivered digitally to our overactive, noise-filled
minds. We still remember a time when being introduced to an idea or
concept and then creating a direct experience of it — exploring our own
knowing — had more relevance than watching or listening to a celebrity
or authority on a talk show, reality show, movie, or article tell us what life
is like.

This, you see, is one of the great advantages of having arrived in or
at the threshold of this stage of life. We remember what knowing feels,
sounds, and looks like — at least those of us who have continued to pursue our dreams, weathered enough of our own storms, and continue to
listen to that still small inner voice.

Alternate Lifestyles

So what choices do we have? How do we get from being conscripts
in the Army of the Preoccupied Believers to Champions of Knowing and
Present Moment Awareness? How do we as individuals demonstrate the
value of living lives of greater purpose and meaning?

As you know we favor a primary and important step — remembering that our lives happen in this moment, and in this one. A second step
involves becoming a fervent champion of the difference between believing
and knowing.

Pay more attention to being rather than doing or, at the very least, follow Frank Sinatra's good advice and "Do-Be, Do-Be, Do." Here are some
suggestions you may find helpful:

⊛   Re-learn to fritter and putter.

⊛   Simply sit, listen, and watch in the silence — in nature and in
your home or apartment.

⊛   Reactivate your imagination.

⊛   Daydream.

⊛   Wonder.

- Surrender as completely as you can to what is happening around you.

- Communicate more in person.

- Talk less and listen more.

- Get out in the world — spend more time living actually rather than vicariously.

- Simplify.

- Share and cooperate more.

- Substitute making your own news for listening to news about others.

- Learn to be comfortable with discomfort.

- Feel your feelings.

- Laugh more.

- Be grateful for all that you are rather than all that you have.

- Be very curious.

- Listen to your inner truth and trust it.

- Celebrate what makes you unique nor similar.

- Look for the hundreds of miracles that make your life possible each day.

Yes, if you are willing to explore some of these practices more often we can guarantee that you will actually enjoy your life more. If you are willing to deal with the discomfort of not doing and not even knowing how to "be" for a while, you will redefine your priorities and learn to acknowledge and value new goals, objectives, and abilities.

If you are willing to sacrifice some of what you call your material abundance, your addiction to self-medication, and your preoccupation with the past and the future and the technologies that encourage these practices you will discover that your life will change for the better.

So if you still remember a pre-digital, pre-automated, pre–belief-and opinion-driven world and you are willing to start doing some of the things listed above; if you use your time and energy to be more present and at ease in this moment and in the next one, the time ahead will be a great ride.

In short, you have the choice to spend your precious time doing more of the authentic, original work you have come here to this planet to do. And if this sounds a little overwhelming at first, we suggest that you simply begin taking some small steps in the direction of what really gives you lasting pleasure. "Follow your bliss," as Joseph Campbell famously said.

Life Happens

Knowing comes from living in the present moment where life happens! Where we happen! Where truth happens! And with this direct experience, everything becomes possible. Without this direct experience, we are like rudderless boats, adrift on the sea of believing and subject to the manipulation of others who want us to believe what they believe so that we can continue to kneel to the God of Economics and to the other less-than-laudable political, social, and religious gods they worship.

Without direct experience, we lack a touchstone, a watermark, a unique and original guidance system. Yes, without being able to tell the difference between believing and knowing, we have no direct access to the doorway that leads us to our purpose for being here on the Earth and to discerning what we are here to contribute to life.

So what do you say? Don't you think it is time those of us who are in the second half of life, and who still remember other choices and other alternative paths, demonstrate what we know? Don't you think it is time for us to remind those in younger generations — before it is too late — that delegating our sovereignty to this wired, overstimulated, unconscious, belief-driven world is not in our best interests?

Don't you think it is time to declare early retirement from the Great Army of Believers and enroll or re-enroll in the vulnerable, uncertain, but miraculously alive and alert and incredibly vital assemblage of beings who know?

And remember, no matter how overwhelming the task of reclaiming our world from the grasp of the techno-addicts may seem, one never knows when one individual action can become the final grain of sand that initiates a sea change to sanity.

Life Rule

"One's real life is often the life that one does not lead."

~ Oscar Wilde

Life Achievement

Sir Isaac Newton, one of the leading minds of the 19th century, revised his version of *Principia,* considered to be one of the most important works in the history of science, at 84.

Life Tool

One easy way to get beyond the "ruts of ordinary perception" and all of our obsessive thinking and addiction to believing is just to focus on our breath. Follow it in and out. Yes, just follow this breath in and out. In and out. Notice that it is impossible to focus on your breath and to think at the same time. So whenever you find yourself getting caught up in that endless conversation with that committee in your top office, just breathe and allow. Breathe and be present. Even if you are in the middle of an important "doing," remember to breathe and pay attention to the doer — You. How do you feel? What do you see? And in the silence of no-thought, begin to know again.

The Extraordinary Gift of Being Curious

"Nobody grows old by merely living a number of years; people grow old when they desert their ideals."

~ Samuel Ullman ~

Stop Pretending, Start Expanding

It's been said that curiosity is the cure for boredom and that, fortunately, there is no cure for curiosity. So the next step we recommend on the road to living more mindfully is to stop pretending you know it all or have done it all and start expanding into what you do not yet know and have not yet done. In this way life can become more of a real-time adventure and each "now" an opportunity for richness and wonder.

Yes, in order to discover more effective solutions to old problems — in order to explore new alternatives to habitual patterns and poorly functioning systems — we would be wise to stop pretending that we have it all together and start being curious about life again. Curiosity, you see, is a key to living in the now. And as most of us know, now is the only time and place we can experience the magical, the marvelous, and the unknown.

After all, if it were not for the fact that we were once curious about the things we did not know and could not yet do, we would not have learned all of the things we now know and can do. At the same time, the things we now know tend to be about how the physical universe works and how we can relate to and navigate within it. The things we know are mostly about doing; and while this knowledge is important and has served us fairly well in the first half of our lives, it may be less valuable in the second half. Indeed, most of us do not know as much about the worlds within us and beyond form and physical action as we do the world around us. And yet as Ralph Waldo Emerson once said, "What lies behind us and what lies before us are tiny matters compared to what lies within us."

This is why we devote this entire chapter to being curious. And if you doubt the value of this recommendation, spend an hour with your or with a friend's child or grandchild. Take an afternoon off and volunteer at the local boys or girls club or just sit in your local park and watch children at play, especially young children.

Notice how curious they are. See how involved they are in their moment-to-moment experiences. Pay attention to how open most of them are to life, to learning, to experimenting, to making things up and acting things out, and to making friends — sometimes immediately — with other children. See how unafraid they are to be silly, in fact, see how much they love being wild and silly — and calling it that. Even if you are only looking at these children in your mind's eye, experience what we are talking about — the freedom to do and be whatever they want in the moment without fear of being judged or ridiculed is a precious gift we can reinherit.

Yes, children are curious. They have to be. It's the only way they get to learn and do things they do not know and cannot yet do. It's the only way they get to understand how the world works. Unfortunately, as we grow older, we often assume when school is over that we already know a lot about how things in the world work. Or if we don't know, then we pretend that we do. We get smug, certain, and habitual and that's how we sometimes end up being so damn dull. Yes, habitual, automatic, and of course arrogant. "Don't tell me! I already know! After all, I did that back in my day!" Isn't that what we say?

Kind of ridiculous, don't you think? Ridiculous to go through the second half of life clinging so tenaciously to what we think we know and, in the process, miss the opportunity to learn about all of the things we will need to learn for this next stage of our journey.

So we invite you to set aside what you think you know about the world and have some fun seeing it with new, more compassionate, connected, and receptive eyes. Set aside those habitual patterns and familiar ways you have of doing things and start exploring the landscape of your life as if you were young, innocent, and courageous again. To paraphrase that oft-used biblical quote — lest you be as children you will not enter the kingdom of heaven.

There are other advantages to this recommendation about being curious besides getting into heaven, and these advantages can serve you during your remaining time here on Earth. Do you remember how much time you seemed to have when you were a child? Do you remember how an afternoon or a day sometimes seemed to last forever? Do you remember getting up in the morning and feeling all of that energy and enthusiasm? Some of it issued from your physical well-being, of course, but a lot of it also came from your curiosity about life and your willingness to live in the present moment, to learn, to explore, and to be adventurous.

Steps to Being Curious

So we offer you a few suggestions to assist you to be more curious and to start having more fun in your life.

Experiment — Experiment with the way you look, the way you wear your hair, the kind of clothes you wear; what you do each day, the route you drive to your home, store, or office; what you do for entertainment; what kinds of books you read; and what kind of food you eat. Literally change your interactions with physical form and some of your habits, and you will change a number of your perspectives. And be sure to keep track of what you experience in a journal. You will find that it helps you to anchor your new experience.

Change your perspectives — Literally try seeing life from someone else's point of view. Imagine what the things you do every day look, sound, and feel like to others — younger people, peers who are more or less fortunate than you, people who don't speak your language, and those who are older than you. Try on the perspectives of someone who may not have the ability to see or hear or walk. In short, become a student of life again. Experience the familiar with fresh eyes and you will find your experiences change and life no longer feels as regular, habitual, and automatic.

Change your physical environment and habits — Change the color of the room and the layout of the furniture in your home or office. Travel to other parts of the country or the world. Join a club that offers new interests. Take up a new hobby or a different sport, something you've never been good at and then experience the fun of not knowing and not giving a damn about knowing. And above all, do whatever you do with a kind of abandon — and if your inner critic should arise, tell it to sit back down, for this is your life and the goal is enjoyment not perfection.

Be curious about the way things work — Take courses, take things apart, and learn how to put them together — watch, observe, understand! And we are not just talking about physical objects — pay attention to the less tangible phenomena. Notice what happens between the notes in a musical composition. Pay attention to what happens in the space between breaths, between laughter and tears, between this moment, and this one.

Remember, in order for life to be different we have to experiment, explore, imagine, and find ways to be curious. We have to think, talk, and act differently or at the very least we need to take Marcel Proust's advice about experiencing these things with new eyes.

Of course, changing externals alone will, in the long run, not provide us with a permanent fix. It is, however, a terrific start! To permanently alter our life circumstances, however, we will also have to keep eliminating our limiting beliefs, and releasing the emotional baggage of regret, guilt, shame, and resentment we keep accumulating. We will also have to examine and experiment with our core values and constantly re-examine our priorities.

Again, let us stress that changing externals does have genuine merit. Often working on externals starts the pump and gets flow and momentum going. It allows us to build up the speed to move past our internal barriers and into the new and the marvelous. Remember what old Mr. Newton had to say about an object at rest remaining at rest. So get the ball rolling again and allow momentum to be your ally.

Life Rule
"Each of us needs to withdraw from the cares that will not withdraw from us."

~ Maya Angelou

Life Achievement
Romana Kryzanowska has been teaching Pilates since she learned it from Joseph Pilates 60 years ago. Romana is 84.

Life Tool
We invite you to experiment with creating a daily intention. We believe you will find that this practice can help you to keep your focus during the day and that can provide you with a touchstone or through-line that you can return to at the end of the day. Your daily intention might be just to be present. Setting this and other clear intentions may be one of the most important things you do today. And don't forget, at the end of today, reflect back on the day and ask yourself, "How true was I to my intention and what did I learn?"

Here are a few other intentions you might experiment with: "Today, I am going to focus on being a better listener." "Tonight I am going to practice giving — my time, my attention, my acknowledgments..." "Today I am going to do my best to make each of the things I do as good as I can." "Today I am going to look for the very best in everyone I meet and acknowledge that to them."

Staying Awake

"Most of us abdicate the management of our dying and delegate it to doctors, scientists, gerontologists and others. ....We put our faith in the intensive care unit, presided over by the priest/doctor who prolongs our lives as long as possible through medical technology....in this way we surrender the right to die our own deaths. When, despite all medical interventions, we succumb to death, we usually sleep through the event, drugged, sedated, and unconscious of this great transformative moment."

~ Zalman Schachter-Shalomi & Ronald Miller ~

Dulling Our Senses, Dimming Our Lights

In our book *Authenticity*, we suggest that our culture has, in our opinion, become "The Aspirin Culture." And indeed, from our perspective this trend continues.

Of course, in some ways, it is an understandable trend. We live in complex and challenging times and many of us — especially those of us who are dealing with the challenges of aging — are often overwhelmed by some of these challenges and complexities. As a result, at the first sign of physical, emotional, intellectual, or spiritual discomfort, we look for something to either dull down our feelings or satiate our senses. And we certainly have plenty of help and encouragement in following this trend toward self-medication, don't we?

Our media, many of our institutions, and our leading companies advance and promote an almost unlimited number of beliefs, images, products, and services that overload our senses, numb our feelings, and dumb down our intellects.

In fact, while heart disease, cancer, diabetes, AIDS, and new forms of pandemics may rank as the leading causes of physical death on this planet, we believe that our growing addiction to the many forms of self-medication is rapidly becoming the primary cause of spiritual death.

We say "spiritual death" because, as a result of many of the practices that now permeate our culture, many of us are not only turning down and away from our feelings, we are also turning down and away from the wisdom that issues from that "still small voice" within. In doing this, we miss many of the hints and clues that life is constantly giving us about choices we can make and things we can do to inherit more of the light of our consciousness. In short, when we turn away from our feelings we also turn down our passion, dim the light of our intellect, depress our energies, and in the process prevent ourselves from achieving the very thing we came here to this earth to accomplish — mastering the lessons of this lifetime. In this way and only in this way will we be able to take our next steps on the road to what Carl Jung called "individuation" and others have called "wholeness" and "enlightenment."

As we have already discussed, many of us are also out of touch with our feelings. This is a crime because our feelings are one of our truest allies. They are also one of the essential ways life communicates to us. Feeling out of sorts, feeling anxious, awkward, afraid, confused — these are just some of the ways that life lets us know when there is something out of balance or something we would be wise to learn or to experience. And unfortunately, when we self-medicate and turn away from these so-called negative feelings we also turn down and away from other feelings as well, even feelings we call positive and joyful.

The underlying belief that motivates this avoidance behavior appears to be that if we dull our feelings we will not have to deal with them. We seem to apply the same reasoning when we self-medicate to avoid the physical discomforts that arise from minor injuries, head and body aches, and especially awkward transitional states.

We accomplish this dulling by taking a plethora of non-prescription dulling agents. We also pump ourselves up with caffeine and energy drinks, dull ourselves down with liquor, and preoccupy ourselves with thought and overwork. We fill ourselves up with food, wear ourselves out with exercise, preoccupy ourselves with sex, or lull ourselves into a stupor with television, video games, and endless hours on the Internet. And when all else fails we seek out the brave new world of wild and whacky prescription drugs — many of which have side effects far more harmful than the conditions they are designed to remedy. And they are, of course, provided rather willingly by a medical establishment whose ethics are sometimes as questionable as their level of knowledge about being human.

This growing inclination to self-medicate to ease our discomfort and help us avoid life's ambiguities and the intense feelings associated with these states robs us of our will, courage, and our ability to stay awake.

As if this were not already enough to cause all of us serious concern, this growing tendency to normalize and sanitize existence denies us the ability to pay enough attention to life to be able to change some of the things that would eliminate not just the symptoms of our distress but the cause.

In dulling and dimming down we also lose touch with our feelings, which are, as we mentioned earlier, our best allies. They are the warning buzzers and red lights on the dashboard of life. Feelings let us know when something is out of alignment and needs our attention. They are also the signals that let us know if we are moving in the right direction.

Finally, the practice of self-medicating prevents us from turning toward rather than away from the only place in which we can do something to truly address the underlying conditions of which these feelings are but effects. In short, self-medication in all of its forms keeps us from being present in our lives.

Aging Is not a Time for Dulling

We are spending this time talking about The Aspirin Culture because, as the old Chinese proverb suggests, it is easy for an act to become a habit and a habit to become one's destiny. And the destiny we create through self-medication is definitely not one that most of us want to create. For a self-medicated being is not capable of living as consciously and aging as wisely as one who is awake to life.

So we invite you, at the next sign of discomfort, to experiment with turning toward the flashing red light, toward the discomfort and away from drugs, coffee, food, sex, work, alcohol, entertainment, exercise, other people, or doctors — many of whom are all too willing to prescribe drugs rather than offer real treatment. In fact as Reverend Michael Bernard Beckwith recently shared with his congregation, when these signs of discomfort and imbalance occur — "SYBD: Sit Your Butt Down and meditate! Sit Your Butt Down and get back in balance and in touch with who you are."

So we invite you to experiment with this alternative behavior because it is simply not possible to lead the life you were born to live if you are numb and dull. And numb and dull are certainly not what we need, particularly in the second half of life. Instead we need to be wide awake and up on the balls of our feet and looking life in the eye.

We also encourage you to stop self-medicating because those of us who are aging need to have our faculties firing on all cylinders, especially if we want to explore the inner dimensions of consciousness. To do this we have to learn to live with and ultimately befriend uncomfortable emotions, unpleasant thoughts, confusing choices, awkward and unfamiliar states, ambiguity, and a lot more. Yes, as strange as it may sound, our salvation lies not in avoiding or trying to suppress these things, not in trying to normalize and sanitize life, but instead in having the courage and the willingness to explore the mystery that is natural, unadulterated, and undulled life.

So experiment with not using things that dull you down. Stop participating in activities and associating with people who dumb you down, prompt indifference, and take the edge off your life. In fact, we invite you to do all that you can to stay wide awake to the real meaning and purpose of life. And to do this you may want to experiment with more edge, more discernment, more engagement, and even more discomfort to whatever degree is possible and appropriate for you.

None of this is meant to imply that there are not times when taking some kind of relief or muting agent for physical or emotional pain or trauma is not both necessary and desirable. Clearly, there are times postsurgery, postaccident, post–emotional trauma, when some seriously debilitating illnesses occurs — and occasionally when the world simply overwhelms us — when the relief gained by pain medication or some kind of self-medication can be a life-saver. There are also times — perhaps far more than we allow — when some recreational and consciousness-altering drugs can provide us with unique insights and glimpses into alternate realities that can greatly expand our capacities.

So please start saying *enough* to dimming your lights! Enough to nodding off in the padded chairs in soundproof rooms of denial! Enough to limited attention and highly managed, normalized states.

Instead, start saying an enthusiastic *yes* to being wide awake and ready. Start stepping right into the thick of life, because in order to live the life you were born to live you are going to have to make some major decisions about how you want to use the precious years you have remaining in this life and, equally important, how you want to die.

Life Rule

"It is a great art to saunter."

~ Henry David Thoreau

Life Achievements

Mel Brooks, comedic genius whose films and recordings continue to make us laugh, is in his 80s.

Life Tools

Today and for the next few days ask yourself: "Am I willing to stop turning down the volume of my feelings? Am I willing to pay more attention to the many clues that life offers me? Am I willing to stay more awake to remarkable discoveries I can make in this 'now,' in this unique and unduplicatable moment of my life?"

The Producer

Ted's Story

Theodore Jones "Ted" Flicker was born in New Jersey in 1930. He attended a local school in Tom's River and then went on to study at The Royal Academy of Dramatic Arts in London along with a few other people who would make their mark in the world of entertainment, Joan Collins and Larry Hagman.

In 1954, he became a member of Chicago's Compass Theater, America's first theater of improvisational comedy, a subgenre he and fellow comedian Elaine May are credited with founding. Together, they established the official rules for improvisation, which are still followed today. Eventually, he worked as producer, director, and performer with the Compass Players in St. Louis. The company was such a success that he was able to raise money to establish the Crystal Palace Theater, then the only monthly repertory stage in the country.

In 1959 he wrote the book and directed <u>The Nervous Set</u> on Broadway; and in 1960, he established The Premise, an improvisational theater in a basement venue on Bleecker Street in New York, with casts that included Buck Henry, Joan Darling, Gene Hackman, and George Segal.

Ted Flicker went on to direct and co-write the screenplay for a number of films, including <u>The President's Analyst</u> with James Coburn.

As the writer of the pilot for the television series <u>Barney Miller,</u> he became the show's co-owner, and also wrote and/or directed episodes of a number of well-known television series including <u>The Andy Griffith Show,</u> <u>The Man From Uncle,</u> and <u>The Dick Van Dyke Show.</u>

At 65 Ted left the world of theater, film, and television behind and moved to Santa Fe, NM, with his wife, Barbara. Even though he had had a lot of success, Ted was obviously not finished. The creative drive was still strong and when he took a sculpting lesson from a friend a doorway opened into a totally new world.

With the same passion that had marked his early career, Ted began to sculpt — he not only created works that celebrate the beauty of physical form, but also developed new forms of photography that assist sculptors in better understanding their subject and experimenting with new kinds of sculpting materials.

Today, in his 80s, Ted Flicker continues to explore the world of form, having created an entire sculpture garden filled with his own remarkable pieces.

Been There, Done That

"Whatever you can do or dream you can do, begin it.
Boldness has genius, power, and magic in it."

~ Goethe ~

Moving Past Old Habits, Taking New Paths

One of the terrific things about getting older is that we've done a lot of stuff; and if we are smart, we will look back on these things, harvest them, and recognize that to a large extent, especially when it comes to many of the things that occupied and preoccupied us when we were younger, we have been there, done that, and in a number of instances do not need to do that again.

For example, most of us have been a part of the army of the employed for 20, 30, 40 years or more and so we understand the ups and downs of that process. We remember the annual goals and the corporate visions and mission statements. We remember our annual performance reviews, the promised rewards and bonuses as well as the cutbacks, the layoffs and letdowns, the betrayals, breakdowns, and occasional breakthroughs.

Most of us have also spent a reasonable portion of our lives and a great deal of our time, energy, and effort in pursuit of money. The goal, of course, has been to ensure our financial security so we can buy what we need and want and do things we want to do. But many of us now know that the pursuit of money for its own sake offers less reward than we imagined. In fact we know that the accumulation of a lot of the stuff we have may have inflated our egos and our sense of self-importance at the time and contributed to a fleeting sense of safety, but it certainly has not advanced the cause of our hearts, guaranteed our health, improved the quality of our personal relationships, or elevated our consciousness.

Most of us have also spent a lot of our time during the first half of life working to get credentials and establish reputations, and a part of this process has involved our focus on what other people think. And we certainly now know how flimsy, illusive, and transient this latter pursuit is. And in the end, of course, no matter how many certificates and plaques we have on our walls or trophies on our bookcases, no matter how many other people praise us, we and we alone know the real truth about ourselves and about the way we show up every day as human beings.

So the point is that a lot of what we have done and the reasons for doing these things may have been fine for the first phase of our lives, fine for learning the lessons they are designed to teach us. But unless we want to keep running that fast and chasing those same worldly carrots, there are probably a number of other things we will want to focus on in the second half of life.

Indeed, if we keep focusing on form — on accumulating material possessions, on pursuing money for its own sake and on what other people think of us — we are not going to have much time to focus on some really important stuff for which the second half of life is designed, like living in the present moment, sharing our wisdom with others, and exploring the remarkable dimensions that lie within us as well as around us.

Inward Bound

So the first part of our journey is primarily outward bound. We move away from the womb and in search of our place and stance in the world. This place might be a particular geographic location, a ranking in a career, a position in our community, or all of this and more. No matter what it is, however, our search during the first half of our lives generally involves striving, desiring, and working to achieve things outside ourselves. Yes, this first part of our journey is often about the movement away from the moment of our inception and toward a set of goals that are perceived as being important, part of the purpose of our lives. And even if these goals are not consciously articulated, they are often informed and motivated by the trends, needs, or demands of the particular historical period in which we find ourselves.

Our study of various cultures as well as our work with thousands of individuals in various organizations, seminars, and programs in both the private and public sectors confirms the reality of this outward-bound, first-half-of-life focus. These same studies, however, also indicate that if we continue this outward-bound focus in the second half of life, we often misuse our resources and talents and end up missing our true mark. And so this is where the "been there, done that" adage comes home to roost.

The second half of life is about creating a different set of goals and focusing on a different set of values. It is about turning inward and toward home, and about surrendering. To what? To God, Spirit, the Divine, Self with a capital S, Soul, our Higher Power — or to whatever one calls the central and organizing Force we turn to for wisdom and guidance.

It is about making peace with the Earth, making sense of our time here, our role, the legacy we will leave behind us, and especially with the state of our spiritual evolution. And, of course, this is a direction we head in and not necessarily something we achieve easily or quickly.

In short, the second half of life is a time for a new kind of journey and a preparation for the experiences that lie beyond the territory of physical life.

Our Choice

If those of us in the second half of life understand that this change of direction and focus is as natural a part of the journey as the outward bound focus is in the first half — if we admit that all physical objects in the physical universe follow this same path of expansion and then return — we can stop struggling, stop posturing, and pretending that we are immune to this natural order, and start surrendering to it.

Indeed, if we use our time in the second half of life for that which it is intended, we can have the opportunity to not only complete our individual journeys, but to share with those who come after us alternative life choices and valuable lessons. Yes, we can avoid being seduced by the siren's song of youth that does not contain any notes to describe that which is a part of the end-of-life journey and that which lies beyond the boundaries of the physical world.

When we surrender to this natural cycle of life, we come to understand and even appreciate some of the limitations we experience as we age — changes in mobility and physical flexibility, changes in our level of energy and stamina, changes in our access to the world of commerce and career, changes in our attachment to sexuality, etc. We come to discover that these are not limitations as much as they are redirections that lead us to new doorways we can walk through.

This does not mean that with a good diet, appropriate exercise, the continued expansion of skills, and appropriate financial resources we cannot and will not extend some of the previous boundaries associated with aging. Nor does it mean that we cannot experience an engaged, energetic level of physical and sexual intimacy in the second half of life. However, if we choose to do any or all of these things, we believe the primary reason for doing them is not to prolong the illusion of youth, but instead to allow us to be the best we can be on every level so we can better accomplish the new and different goals the second half of life offers. So experiment and expand the limits until the cows come home, but not out of anxiety and fear and not in an effort to deny aging and defeat death.

Not an Easy Adjustment

We are not suggesting that this redirection of our energies and attention from outward to inward is always easy to accomplish. Nor are we suggesting that this inward focus should be exclusive. For as long as we are a part of the physical world, we have the opportunity and, at least from our perspective, the responsibility to remain involved in what happens in the world around us, especially in regard to those policies, procedures, and laws that directly impact our lives and those we love. We also have the opportunity to share our gifts, talents and our love with the world.

So we encourage you to listen to the wisdom of poet, Guillaume Apollinaire, captured in the lines of his poem, "Come to the Edge."

Come to the edge, Life said,

They said: We are afraid.

Come to the edge, Life said,

They came. It pushed them…

And they flew.

Life Rule

"Real unselfishness consists in sharing the interests of others."

~ George Santayana

Life Achievement

Morgan Freeman, one of Hollywood's most sought-after actors, is involved in civic projects, is a political activist, and is a lover and promoter of music. He is in his 70s.

Life Tool

If you are in the mood to experiment, find a comfortable chair, close your eyes for a few moments, and pretend that you are slowly passing out of your body and rising higher and higher, leaving the physical world and all of its cares and concern behind. Yes, just envision yourself slowly floating up and out through the crown of your head, then up through the ceiling of the room you are in, through the roof of the building you occupy in the same way you would float up from below the surface of a pool of water. Just float up and out and allow yourself to experience the feeling of freedom and boundlessness, the feeling of being present instant by instant with nothing to do except experience and observe. As you rise higher and higher, just enjoy the increasing perspective you gain of the world you live in.

Mastering the Three
Great Illusions

"The beginning of wisdom is a firm grip on the obvious."

~ Anonymous ~

Valuable Keys to Present Moment Awareness

There are three illusions that significantly impact our lives and often prevent us from living in the present moment. These three great illusions are control, safety, and security. And learning to master them is, we believe, the next important step you can take on the road to living more consciously and aging wisely.

Control

In the modern world, where the Gods of Science and Technology are worshipped so ardently, many of us spend a great deal of our time living under the illusion that we can control things — our physical environment, our financial future, our careers, and in some instances, even the people around us. And yet, if we look closely at the most important and impactful events in our lives, we will probably admit that for all intents and purposes, life has been pretty much outside of our control from the start. We did not control our birth and the majority of us will not control our death.

In addition, even the basic physical functions that allow us to stay alive — respiration, digestion, elimination, and circulation — are automatic. Some have even suggested that this is a very good thing for if we were required to remember to breathe, digest our food, eliminate waste, and circulate our blood, the majority of us would have died a long time ago.

Regarding other aspects of control, if you look closely and without ego at your life, we think you will also admit that many of the really meaningful and consequential events you have experienced fall into the category of surprises, unexpected events, and what Carl Jung called synchronicity — chance exceeding probability. For example: the moment the love of your life showed up in your world or the day your career took one of its most surprising and beneficial turns (a turn which might have begun as a negative); changes in your health that prompted you to adopt new practices and consequently led to new discoveries and sometimes even a new way of life; chance encounters with people who later became your close friends; unanticipated intersections with allies and mentors; and dreams that delivered sudden flashes of insight and inspiration.

You see, this control thing is pretty much a fabrication, a hoping against hope on the part of a species for which this complex universe — and our reason for being — still remains pretty much beyond comprehension.

Of course, we sense at times deeper levels of connection with the natural flow and rhythm of life that give us the opportunity for greater collaboration and cooperation with our destiny. But this is very different from our awkward, exhausting, and ultimately futile attempts to muscle and force life to fit some preconceived and false notion that we are the primary masters of the universe.

Safety and Security

So much for control! What about safety and security? How do these things impact our ability to live in the present moment?

Well, we certainly spend as much if not more of our lives in search of safety and security as we do trying to exercise control. In fact, if we are honest with ourselves, we think we will have to admit that this holy triumvirate of control, safety, and security is not only greatly valued, but worshipped and clung to with tenacity that ranges from the compulsive to the obsessive.

On the surface, of course, some of us appear to succeed in our relationship with safety and security. We accumulate a certain amount of wealth — small, medium, or giant size — and use whatever we have accumulated to erect buffers between us and the world: gated communities, 401(k) plans and other investment accounts, special insurance policies, offshore accounts, special health coverage plans, investment properties, and in some cases even security personnel. With all those buffers in place we appear on the surface to be safe and secure.

If you look a little closer at these conditions, however, we think you will also admit that just like control, safety and security are temporary illusions. For no matter how much money we have, no matter how many private clubs we belong to or protective gates we build around our communities, and no matter how many extra health plans or insurance policies we own, in the end, we are all subject to the same laws of life that govern longevity, health, chance, and fate.

And while some of these elements sometimes make our lives more comfortable, at least for a while, in the end none of them truly protect us from aging, illness, loss of loved ones, intersections with unhappiness, and ultimately our own deaths. None of them protect us from the underlying terrors that Paulo Coelho describes so brilliantly in his novel, *The Devil and Miss Prym*.

> *There was terror in each and every one of the people on that beautiful beach and on that breathtakingly beautiful evening. Terror of being alone, terror of the darkness filling their imagination with devils, terror of doing anything not in the manuals of good behavior, terror of God's judgment, of what other people would say, of the law punishing any mistake, terror of trying and failing, terror of succeeding and having to live with the envy of other people, terror of loving and being rejected, terror of asking for a raise in salary, of accepting an invitation, of going somewhere new, of not being able to speak the language, of growing old, of dying, of being pointed out because of one's defects, of not being pointed out for one's merits, of not being noticed either for one's defects or one's merits.*
>
> *Terror, terror, terror. Life was a reign of terror....*

While this is a passage from a work of fiction, from our perspective it unfortunately rings true in real life as well. So as we make our way through this and the next chapters we suggest that instead of focusing so much of your time, effort, and energy on trying to exercise control and gain security and safety; instead of huffing and puffing against the tide of inevitability that is physical existence, it might be both interesting and ultimately far more effective to begin exploring the value of surrender, acceptance, and trust.

Surrender

When we say surrender, acceptance, and trust, we are not talking about throwing in the towel and rolling over on life. Nor are we suggesting that you stop paying attention to the upkeep of your home, the payment of your bills, the monitoring of your investments, the care of your health, the nurturing of your relationships, or the ordering of your affairs. Surrender, acceptance, and trust are not synonymous with indifference, inattention, and disinterest.

As many wise beings before us have said, we do the best we can do, we hold the highest thoughts possible, we live life according to our truest set of values, and then we ultimately have to trust in the flow of life and to the higher order of things.

Indeed, a very wise old man, a master sculpture from Spain named Jose DeCreft who was still carving and modeling remarkable pieces well into his 90s, used to say, "It is not our job to worry about the music. It is our job to become the best instrument we can so that the music of God can play through us."

So as we continue taking our next, important steps toward learning to live more fully in each present moment, we invite you to keep asking yourself what the three great illusions — control, safety, and security — contribute to your life and what other practices and qualities you could devote your time, effort, and attention to that would bring you a much more valuable return.

Life Rule
"Everyone seems to want to be somebody, fewer people want to do what it takes to grow."

~ Goethe

Life Achievement
Pablo Casals, considered by many to be one of the world's greatest cellists, played his last concert in Israel at 93.

Life Tool
Before moving on, we invite you to take a few moments and reflect on some of the major achievements and events of your life. Pay close attention to the part you played in the outcome and then, with humility, pay equal homage to the part fate, chance, good fortune, other people, remarkable synchronicities, and unexpected surprises played as well.

Notice how these other elements, things outside your seeming control, contributed in ways that ultimately served you and that you would not have thought of or executed on your own.

Turning Toward Things
that Scare Us

*"I rejoice in life for its own sake… It is a sort of splendid torch, which I
have got hold of for the moment; and I want to make it burn
as brightly as possible before handing it on to future generations."*

~ George Bernard Shaw ~

Facing Our Fears

Most of us agree that we are living in challenging times. Most of us are asked to juggle an incredible number of tasks, competing demands and requests that arise in our personal lives, in our careers, in our relationships, in our interactions within our communities, and from the urges and longings that issue from our hearts.

As if this were not already enough to challenge us, as we have discussed in other places, the pace of our world is speeding up and placing even more demands, choices, challenges, and possibilities in our paths — so many in fact, that a lot of us feel under the gun and more than a little overwhelmed. This is one of the reasons an increasing number of us often find ourselves turning away from the present moment, from other people, and particularly from things we do not understand nor have answers to or that scare us.

Some of the things we avoid or turn away from are practical things — the things we are supposed to do at work or chores that await us at home. Others fall into the relationship category — conversations we need to have, amends we could make, commitments we have promised to fulfill, and time we could spend with those we love. Still others involve the things that confound or trouble us.

In our experience, however, those of us on the path of living more consciously and aging wisely cannot afford to turn away from things that are incomplete or that trouble or frighten us because in doing so we turn away from living in the present moment. And, in truth, we have a diminishing number of these present moments left. In fact, if we want to live effective, healthy, engaged, and satisfying lives, we actually have to learn how to turn toward things that are incomplete and that disturb or frighten us; otherwise, there is a high probability that they will turn toward us and encumber our lives in a number of less-than-convenient ways. For as the old cliché suggests — and as many of us have learned the hard way — important things we do not attend to sometimes find unexpected ways at unanticipated times to get our attention.

We are not using this cliché to scare you, nor are we suggesting that dealing with the things that are incomplete or that scare you will lead to a pain-free existence. But in our experience, when we fail to pay attention to the clues and signals our life presents us with, we sometimes regret it and we almost always miss some of the very important opportunities to explore those higher states of consciousness for which the second half of life is actually designed.

So we invite you to take a little time here to go deeper in exploring a topic we can't control and that challenges our concepts of safety and security. That topic, of course, is aging.

Things that Scare Us

Tibetan Buddhist teacher and author, Pema Chodron says, "Fear is a natural reaction to moving closer to the truth." And our life experiences certainly confirm her statement. How about yours? Do you find that you sometimes get afraid when you realize that your body is changing or that your energy level, strength, or the clarity or sharpness of your mind are not what they used to be? Do you notice changes in your sleep patterns, in the level of your stamina, and in your physical appearance? And when you notice these things and the changes in your lifestyle that they may require, do you sometimes get afraid? Do you sometimes find yourself thinking — even if only for a few seconds — that what lies ahead will be troubling; and does this projection prompt you to pull back from what feels like the edge of an abyss?

These concerns are, of course, exacerbated by the fact that we live in a world where older people are often pushed to the sidelines and where the topics of aging and death have been pretty much banned from polite social conversation. Indeed most of us have thousands, maybe hundreds of thousands, of negative images in our brains about what aging means and how it is going to look, feel, and impact our lives, our dreams, and our hopes.

Betty Friedan, Ram Dass, Jean Houston, Stephen and Andrea Levine, Elisabeth Kubler-Ross, Ernest Becker (author of *The Denial of Death*), Angeles Arrien, Michael Meade, Zalman Schachter-Shalomi, and others address some of these negative images and cultural taboos about aging and the way they impact life for many of us.

In fact, even a brief scan of our culture discloses the fact that older people are represented by the media largely as either incompetent or unattractive. In fact, with a few exceptions, the majority of images of aging that our media projects make many of us feel that getting older is some kind of failure. In fact, if we take modern media at its word, we would have to assume that somehow God made a big mistake when he created the over-50 crowd.

In our opinion, however, the energy we call God does not make mistakes. And so no matter how many images the illusion makers throw at us, the indisputable, undeniable truth of nature is that aging is a natural, valuable, even beautiful and essential stage of life.

Moving Forward

We believe that one of the most essential and effective strategies those of us who are aging can use to eliminate these limiting and distorted beliefs is to have the courage to turn toward rather than away from this subject that scares and frightens us. For when we reduce our own fears, society as a whole will have a whole new set of images of what it means to age.

So we invite you to practice the art of accepting aging as a natural part of life. You can do this first and foremost by acknowledging your own age. Second by befriending it, which means looking at the various stages and aspects of it in the eye, admitting its inevitability, and identifying both the gifts and lessons it has for you. And please pay special attention to the word "gifts" because there are a number of remarkable gifts that growing older offers.

One of the primary methods you can use to accomplish this involves doing precisely what you've been told most of your life not to do — start talking to yourself. Yes, this may sound like an odd suggestion, but in truth, who better to talk to than yourself? Who knows more about you and, in the end, has more of your best interests at heart?

We cover this method of talking to yourself in greater depth in our book, *Authenticity: Simple Strategies for Greater Meaning and Purpose at Work and at Home*. So if you are interested in exploring this subject in greater depth, we invite you to consult that book for more specific information. We also invite you to read any of Pema Chodron's wonderful books, especially *When Things Fall Apart* and *The Places that Scare You*. And you can explore some of the original work in this field done by Carl Jung under the title "active imagination" and in the later work that Fritz Perls, father of Gestalt Psychology, developed.

As a result, we will not go into great detail on these processes here, but we will tell you that dialoguing with the things that scare you is as simple as having a conversation, in person or in writing, with a good friend. And like any of these forms of good conversation, dialoguing with the things that scare you takes a little practice and commitment. But it is no more difficult than this, and much will be revealed to you.

So please take a few minutes to experiment with this valuable process. You can begin by making a list of some of the things that scare you about aging. Next we suggest you open your notebook or journal, select one of the things on your list (sadness, loneliness, pain, etc.), write this topic at the top of the page — Conversation with Sadness — and then write out your conversation with sadness. Literally as if you were recording a conversation between two people — one called "self" and the other called "sadness" — simply begin. You might find it helpful to begin by simply asking sadness if it will talk to you. Write down your question and then the answer that sadness gives, then see where the conversation leads you.

Once you've written for a while you may find the conversation ending naturally or shifting to a new topic — fear, anger, etc. If so just flow with it. Obviously, you do not try to cover the entire list in one sitting. Just write until you get a feel for the process and then make a commitment to come back to this exercise again and again until you have begun to deal with all these fears that limit and restrict your life.

At this point, it might be a pretty good time to remember the words to the serenity prayer.

"God, grant me the serenity

to accept the things I cannot change,

the courage to change the things I can,

and the wisdom to know the difference."

Life Rule
"Every person who refuses to accept the conditions of his life sells his soul!"

~ Charles Baudelaire

Life Achievement
Clara Barton, social activist, continued to serve as president of the Red Cross, the organization she helped to found, at 83.

Life Tool
When fear, worry, doubt, anxiety, or any other so-called negative emotion shows up, rather than turning away please experiment with simply observing it. In the beginning you may only be able to observe it for a short period of time before the habitual reaction to turn away clicks in. But the more you practice staying present and observing, the sooner you will be able to welcome these emotions as allies.

When that begins to happen, talk to them as you would a good friend. Ask them why they are in your life and what lessons they are here to assist you to learn. Sit with them, learn from them, accept them, and be grateful they are a part of your life. Ultimately, as you will see if you continue this practice, acceptance and gratitude will become powerful transformational tools that can liberate you from what used to haunt and sadden you.

The Healer/Physician

Dr. Gladys's Story

Dr. Gladys Taylor McGarey, or Dr. Gladys as she likes to be called, is internationally recognized as the mother of holistic medicine. She has been a family physician for more than 60 years and is board certified in holistic and integrative medicine. Born in India to medical missionaries, she is internationally known for her pioneering work in holistic medicine, natural birthing, and the physician-patient partnership.

Often, especially in the early years of her career, Dr. Gladys experienced staunch opposition from a male-dominated medical establishment. In 1970, she co-founded the A.R.E. Clinic in Phoenix, Arizona, where she and her former husband pioneered the integration of allopathic and holistic medical practices, laying the groundwork for the cultural shift of recent years.

Dr. Gladys helped co-found the American Holistic Medical Association in 1978. Her work through her foundation, The Gladys Taylor McGarey Medical Foundation in Scottsdale, Arizona, has helped expand the knowledge and application of holistic principles through scientific research and education, and is helping bridge the gap between traditional and holistic medicine. Currently, she and her foundation are actively involved in healthcare reform. The Foundation's recently published position papers articulate a new vision for healthcare and have been widely distributed. Dr. Gladys is also the author of three books, <u>The Physician Within You,</u> <u>Born to Live</u>, and <u>Living Medicine.</u> Among her other pioneering accomplishments:

- *Successfully championed fathers in the delivery room.*

- *Co-founded the Academy of Parapsychology and Medicine.*

- *Created the only A.R.E. Clinic based on the work of Edgar Cayce.*

⚜   *First to utilize acupuncture in the U.S. and train other physicians to use it.*

⚜   *The International Academy of Clinical Hypnosis started in her living room.*

⚜   *Taught safer birthing practices to rural women in Afghanistan, resulting in a 47% decrease in infant and young child mortality.*

⚜   *Created a task force comprised of more than 100 holistic physicians and other professional healthcare providers to envision a new medical model in response to the need for healthcare reform, and is working toward implementation of this model.*

We have been fortunate to have interviewed Dr. Gladys, and one of the things our experience demonstrates is that the work she has done, the obstacles she has overcome, and the values she has championed contribute to her vitality and her passion and help all of us remember that it is never too soon and never too late to live our dreams.

As of this writing Dr. Gladys continues to push the boundaries of healing and holistic patient care and to serve as an example to so many.

Getting Over Being Right

"To be joyful in the universe is a brave and reckless act.
The courage springs not from the certainty of human experience,
but the surprise...Therefore, despite the world's sorrows,
we give thanks for the loves, the joys and for the
continued courage to be happily surprised."

~ Molly Fumia ~

The Right/Wrong Game

In our personal experience the "right/wrong game" is one of the greatest impediments to our learning to live in each present moment and hence, living the life we were born to live. And this, in our experience, goes for each of us as individuals and all of us within this collective called humanity.

The right/wrong game is, of course, one of the games most of us learn to play early in life and practice earnestly for the majority, if not all, of our lives. Indeed, it's been said that being wrong is one of the things people fear most. Consequently we learn that being right is not only important, but many of us think it is essential and critical to our survival. In fact, once we begin to experience the sense of acceptance and the rewards that come to us when we or others think we are "right," we do our best to build our entire life around valiantly defending what we think and what we believe is right.

This should, of course, not come as a surprise to any of us. From our earliest moments at home, at school, at church, and in our personal relationships we are taught the value of being right. When we are "right" we are praised, accepted, sought out, admired, and so on. And the older we get the greater these rewards become — better grades; more attention from parents, teachers, and other kids; earlier admission to better schools; more attractive prospective life partners; higher-level jobs; more perks; more rapid career advancement; more attractive stock options and bonuses; and, of course, the continuing illusion that when we are right we are in control of our universe and therefore safe.

In fact, as a result of all of the attention and rewards we get for being right, some of us become so committed to being right that we would rather be considered right than be loved. We would rather appear to be right than find genuine solutions to the problems we face. We would rather be right than collaborate or cooperate. Yes, some of us who lead businesses, run universities, are elected to the highest public offices, serve as priests and ministers and rabbis, practice the healing arts, raise children, and volunteer in our communities get so committed to being right that we sometimes sacrifice our close relationships, our personal dreams, the well-being of those we serve, and even our personal values and integrity in the cause of being right.

While this statement may sound absurd, a closer examination may disclose that it contains more truth than many of us are sometimes willing to admit. And unfortunately, this is particularly true for a number of us who belong to the second-half-of-life crowd. Our commitment to being right, which is learned and then habituated over decades, often prohibits some of us from admitting what we do not know, have not done, and do not yet understand. And this commitment, resistance, stubbornness, or whatever we choose to call it also stands as an impediment to making the changes we need to make to finally come to terms with ourselves and to living more honestly and joyfully.

On the other side of the coin, most of us learn that being wrong means we will probably be criticized, left out, labeled as dumb or awkward or inferior, and even laughed at. Being wrong means running the risk of being demeaned, rejected, and punished. Yes, being wrong also has a number of other uncomfortable feelings associated with it, feelings of anxiety, guilt, and shame, and lack of safety.

So it is not surprising that wherever we look these days — whether in corridors of government or in the plush boardrooms of the corporate world, on the sports pages, on the nightly news, or at the front of our schools and churches and hospitals — we experience a growing divisiveness and contentiousness that comes from people trying to be right. Indeed, because we have become so attached to being right and to the perks associated with it, most of us have a hard time saying, "I don't know," or "I'm wrong." And an even smaller number of us are able to say, "I don't give a damn about being right. I'd rather be happy, relaxed, caring, loving, trusting, authentic, collaborative, cooperative, creative, and connected than be right.

"I'd rather live in peace than go to war over what I believe or what you think. I'd rather pray with you than judge or criticize or condemn you because your beliefs about God or religion or politics or life are different than mine."

Yes, in this push/pull world where different is synonymous with wrong, strange, and threatening, very few of us are able to say:

- ✤ I'd rather spend my time being curious about what you see and know rather than spend my time defending what I think I know.

- ✤ I'd rather admit that I do not know something and finally learn what I've been avoiding all of these years rather than stay stuck in my habitual practice of defending my own turf.

- ✤ I'd rather be adventurous, receptive, and involved in life rather than isolated behind some silly idea or concept that I'm supposed to be this or that.

- ✤ I'd rather make a whole lot of mistakes learning new things than look like I have it all together but ultimately miss the boat.

- ✤ In short, I'd rather be free and happy and at peace than right, rigid, and enslaved.

Setting Standards

Since right and wrong are so important, we thought we'd take just a little time here to talk about who determines what is right or wrong. Some, of course, think "right" came down to us on stone tablets inscribed by fire. Some believe "right" was determined, in the beginning, by a higher power. Others believe "right" is determined by local custom, fad, force of habit, accident, the media, the majority, or some arbitrary quirk of fate. Remember when most people thought the world was flat?

On this journey toward living the life you were born to live, perhaps it is time to take a closer look at this habitual pattern that many of us have of wanting to be right and at where "right" comes from. Perhaps it is time to decide that spending our lives, especially the second half of our lives, defending habituated beliefs and opinions that we accumulated during the first half is a big waste of time, especially if the only thing we have left is a diminishing amount of time. And the only thing we need to do to start living extraordinary, satisfying, connected, and loving lives is to start saying, "I don't know."

So if you are ready to stop worrying about being right; to stop defending your turf or your opinion or your carefully constructed rationale about how life is supposed to be lived, and start experimenting in the marvelous land of the unknown; if you are ready to get over being who you thought you were supposed to be so you can start being the unique, uncensored, original, authentic, and remarkable person that you actually are — then you are on the right page at the right time.

Meet Me in the Field

To paraphrase Rumi, the 13th century Persian philosopher and mystic poet, there is a place beyond ideas of right or wrong. He suggests that it is a field. "I'll meet you there," he says. When he wrote these lines Rumi was not describing strategies that were in place in his time. Nor do these lines describe the strategies that currently are in place in many boardrooms and government chambers of our day. And Rumi certainly was not advocating the practice in which individuals seek to gain advantage over others, often only to their advantage and at any cost, and generally under the banner of being right.

No wonder the world is in such jeopardy. All of this posturing, defending, and distancing ourselves from others and unfortunately, in the process, from ourselves; all of these pompous, arrogant, and self-righteous attempts to be right when with just a simple shift we could relax, accept, and experience so much more peace in a world in which we have so much to learn about different cultures and practices, different ways of thinking, and above all from and about ourselves.

Indeed, in asking us to meet him in the field beyond right and wrong, Rumi was asking us to stop wasting our time and energy defending what we believe. He was inviting us to imagine what could happen if we were open to meeting everyone we come in contact with in that place of understanding and connection. Yes, just a simple shift from a primary focus on personal advantage and gain to interpersonal collaboration and cooperation, a shift that John von Neumann has demonstrated so expertly in game theory, in which win/win trumps win/lose every time.

So as you look more closely at what can contribute to your success in the second half of your life, we invite you to ask yourself a few simple questions.

- Would I rather be right or be happy?

- Would I rather hold on to what I already know or discover a way of living in a new and more positive world?

- Would I rather be right or loving?

- Would I rather be right or open to living more consciously and aging more wisely?

Life Rule
Practice Excellence. Avoid Perfection. Practice Acceptance. Avoid Resistance.

Life Achievement
Arthur Rubinstein, conductor and pianist, was still performing at **88**.

Life Tool
Declare today an "I don't know" day. Experiment with living this day as if you had just come here from some other planet and do not know how anything works or why people do what they do. Observe some of the habits and practices, the differences, the unique way each human being has of looking at and interacting with the world. Notice how not knowing leads to greater curiosity, less tension, and more humor. See the world through new eyes, eyes that are fresh and curious and committed to a life of joy and connection rather than fear and separation! See the world from Rumi's eyes, in the field beyond right and wrong.

Death from a
Different Perspective

*"The human biography is a symphony
which each individual personally composes."*

~ Bernard Lievegoed ~

Death as a Reward

If we are courageous, honest, and willing to be supportive of and faith-ful to ourselves, it is certainly time to admit that one of the ways we can live more of our lives in present moment awareness is to give up the belief that death is a dreaded specter and the enemy of life. Instead we can experiment with viewing it as a genuine release and a relief, a reward for having run the course, a graduation, a well-deserved and well-earned rest or vacation after a long and arduous journey.

Indeed, like the final act of a play or the final note in a symphony, death can be viewed as a fitting conclusion not just to what we have come to value while in the human form, but also to the problems, difficulties, and challenges that come with living life on this physical plane.

Death is, in fact, the doorway through which we move beyond the limitations and boundaries of physical movement, of time, of limited energy, and much more and into the next room. It is the end of having to make a living and to paying our way. Death is the conclusion to physical pain and suffering, to the loneliness we sometimes experience when con-fined in the human body, and to the confinement in what Carl Jung once called "the land of boxes." Yes, death is the conclusion to all the things we believe we have to do and be in order to be accepted as a member of this species and perhaps earn our way into a life after life.

As a way of reminding you of what many believe we have to do and be, we share another list that we have compiled from the contributions of people who have participated in some of our programs. As with the previous lists, we invite you to make your own additions or changes.

Things We Don't Have to Do Anymore

Work

Suffer physical pain

Pay taxes

Answer emails

Respond to our boss

Worry about our children

Take care of others

Stand in line

Go to the dentist

Get annual physicals

Experience exhaustion

Save for retirement

Be afraid

Diet

Experience anxiety

Pay for healthcare

Pay the mortgage

Etc.

Alternate Perspectives

In his book, *A Year To Live*, Stephen Levine talks a lot about death, but rather than discussing it in medical or scientific terms, he calls it "not an emergency but an emergence. Like a flower opening…" This view is quite startling because it differs so dramatically from the views so many of us have on death. He says:

> *Those who know the process directly, from experiences shared with the dying, from decades of meditation, from moments of spontaneous grace, do not speak of death as a single moment before which you are alive and after which you are not. They refer instead to a "point of remembrance" in which the holding to life transforms into a letting go into death. It is,*

just a little way into the process, the moment when something is suddenly remembered that it seems impossible to have forgotten. We "remember" how safe death is, we recall the benefits of being free of the limitations of the body, and ask ourselves somewhat incredulously, "How could I have forgotten something so important and what was it that made me want to stay in a body?"

So just now, here in the quiet and safety of your private space, close your eyes for a moment and give yourself permission to feel what it would be like to be free of the confines of the body — to be without pain, without limitation, without all of the responsibilities that keep you so occupied here. Yes, just for a moment or two, allow yourself to feel what it might be like to exist in the space beyond physical existence. And then after you have given yourself permission to experience this possibility, make a few notes in your journal about your discoveries.

We conclude this chapter with a reminder from the poet, Rainer Maria Rilke. In "The Swan" he likens our task to that of the swan who while on land moves awkwardly, but who, once surrendered to the water, appears to be carried with grace and ease. So we invite you, even if it is only in your imagination, to experiment with surrendering to that which exists beyond the confines of your physical form and allow it to carry you with ease and grace as well.

Life Rule
"There is no exercise better for the heart than reaching down and lifting people up."

~ John Andrews Holmes

Life Achievement
William Shatner of *Star Trek, T.J. Hooker,* and *Boston Legal* is in his 80s and still is acting, showing horses, and enjoying his life.

Life Tool
What would happen in your world if you invited death in as an ally and friend? What can death teach you? If you consider death as your consultant and ally, what advice would it have for you before you say this or that, do this or that? If death is a friend, a valued mentor, then what is life?

PART FIVE

Charting a Remarkable Course for Your Future

"Throughout most of history, elders occupied honored roles in society as sages and seers, leaders and judges, guardians of traditions and instructors of the young. They were revered as gurus, shamans, wise old men and women who helped guide the social order and who initiated spiritual seekers into the mysteries of inner space."

~ Zalman Schachter-Shalomi & Ronald Miller ~

The PhD

Maya's Story

Dr. Maya Angelou is considered by many to be one of the great voices of contemporary literature. Biographies abound that speak to the scope of her achievements — poet, educator, historian, best-selling author, playwright, teacher, civil-rights activist, lecturer, producer-director, and so much more.

So this is all a part of the official story. Remarkable credentials and extraordinary achievements. But there is another side to Maya Angelou's story. In her own words this is what she reports:

"I was a mute from the time I was 7 and a half until I was almost 13. I didn't speak. I had voice, but I refused to use it. My grandmother, who was raising me in a little village in Arkansas, used to tell me, 'Sister, mamma don't care about what these people say: "You must be an idiot, you must be a moron." Mamma don't care, sister. Mamma know, when you and the Good Lord get ready, you're gonna be a preacher.' Well, I used to sit and think to myself, 'Poor, ignorant mamma. She doesn't know. I will never speak.'"

Asked when she finally realized her talents, she said, "I still have not realized my talents. I believe that each of us comes from the Creator trailing wisps of glory. So at this wonderful, young age of 65, I don't know yet what the Lord has for me to do. I try to live up to the energy and to the calling, but I wouldn't dare say I have even scratched the surface yet."

When asked if she'd experienced racial discrimination growing up, she said:

"Yes, I have. Yes. A black person grows up in this country — and in many places — knowing that racism will be as familiar as salt to the tongue. Also, it can be as dangerous as too much salt. I think that you must struggle

for betterment for yourself and for everyone. It is impossible to struggle for civil rights, equal rights for blacks, without including whites. Because equal rights, fair play, justice, are all like the air, we all have it or none of us have it."

At the time of this writing, Maya Angelou is 84 years old. We share her story with you because she continues to be a powerful source of wisdom in our world. To be in her presence, to hear the resonance and alignment in her voice, is to sense the depth and the integrity of her journey.

To read her words is to understand that greatness, her greatness, was not born, but instead it was hewn out of the rock of her existence, day by day, courageous act by courageous act.

Quotes taken from an interview with Maya Angelou from January 1997 entitled "America's Renaissance Woman" for the Academy of Achievement.

Packing for the Future

"Everyone is born a king, and most people die in exile..."

~ Oscar Wilde ~

Know Where You Are Going

Anyone who has ever taken a trip knows that the more information one has about their destination, the more likely one will be to pack the right gear; bring along special personal remedies and medications; and, if one is traveling to an exotic or dangerous destination, get the required inoculations. In addition, the more one knows about where one is going, its culture and traditions, the more easily one can make advance reservations to visit unusual locations, take unique excursions, and experience both the geography and the people. In short, the more we know about our destination the greater the likelihood that we will have a successful trip.

Good travelers also make sure things are in order at home and at work before they depart. It is one of the ways they contribute to having relative peace of mind while they are away and limit the quagmire of issues they encounter when they return.

Although some of us understand these obvious facts and, as a result, make pretty good travelers, some of us do not do nearly as good of a job in preparing for various stages and destinations on the trip of life. So as we start this fifth part of our journey — charting a remarkable course for your future — we invite you to first look at some of the more practical things you would be wise to pay greater attention to in order to make your journey through the next stages of your life more successful and enjoyable.

A Few Words about Destination

Before we talk about what we can do to prepare for our journey, we want to revisit the fundamental question about destination. Your work on those questions that our friend, the British philosopher, asks his callers (plus the third question we added) will pay off here.

Who are you?
What do you want?
What are you doing here?

Yes, knowing where one is going — oblivion, heaven, or one of those in-between places where some believe indecisive people go called limbo — will play a critical role in charting your future course. So are you heading for higher consciousness or just a pine box; a return ticket to the gene pool of reincarnation or existence on some other more elevated realm?

Clearly, if you have not given much thought to this topic, you would be wise to consider it now. And if you have already done this, you might find it helpful to re-evaluate and revisit some of your previous conclusions. After all, your tastes and needs change over time and a destination you thought appropriate at 30 or 40 or even 50, might not feel right at 60 or 80 or beyond. Yes, to paraphrase T.S. Eliot's caution, *fare forward travelers, you who arrive at your terminus are not the same as you who departed.*

Another reason it is so essential to take time here at the outset of Part Five to consider your destination is that once you identify it you will then be able to better prepare for it. For example, if you believe higher consciousness and perhaps another plane of existence is your destination, there are many practices and disciplines that can become a part of your daily routine. There are spiritual philosophies to explore, different teachers or guides you might want to work with, and many other personal choices you will want to make as you experiment with being better at being human.

At the same time, if you are not sure if there is a next destination — but like the idea of leaving your mind and options open and are willing to explore the possibility of something unexpected and amazing — then the time you spend investigating possibilities, the practices and disciplines you experiment with, and the teachers and guides you interview may be helpful in providing you with the opportunity to evaluate the possibilities of a next destination for which you can prepare in a number of ways.

Those Eminently Practical Things

Once you have made a commitment to your destination, we suggest you then turn your attention to some of the eminently practical things you would be wise to pay attention to before you depart. Some of these practical things include drafting financial and living wills, keeping an eye on your financial resources, evaluating your insurance and healthcare coverage, establishing family trusts, and more.

And if you already have most or all of these things in place, you might want to review them to be sure the original plans you set in motion still apply. Stories abound about folks who in the later stages of their lives end up in hospitals undergoing all sorts of medical procedures they do not want simply because they do not have the right documents that outline the scope of the medical care they desire and the list of procedures they do not want performed. Do Not Resuscitate Agreements, for example, let doctors know under what conditions a patient wants to be revived and what measures are acceptable.

Since current studies suggest that most of us will spend between 70% and 90% of all of the money we spend on medical care over our entire lifetime in the final year of our lives, we would be wise to have these documents in place and someone selected as our designated advocate, someone who can and will speak for us and see that our wishes are followed. After all, a lot of these end-of-life healthcare costs result from unnecessary or questionable medical procedures performed either by well-meaning doctors who do not know their patient's wishes, by doctors who are concerned about lawsuits, or by medical facilities driven largely by the need to keep feeding the voracious profit-making structures they have created. And all of this is driven by a society that, for the most part, is unprepared and unwilling to deal with or counsel people on the topic of death.

While we find much about this objectionable, it is not the purpose of this section to explore these topics in greater depth. What we do want to be clear about, however, is that collectively those of us who are in the second half of life would be wise to join forces in changing the consciousness of our time about aging; and we would be equally wise as individuals not to let the economic pressures of a healthcare system that is out of balance — or the values of medical professionals who may have lost touch with reality — determine the quality of our lives at the end of our lives.

On other fronts, most of us are also familiar with stories about people who die and leave estates that are not in order and wishes that are not clearly delineated. As a result, they leave behind a landscape ripe for struggles between their heirs, not to mention legal entanglements and unnecessary expenses. These conditions often lead to interpersonal family breakdowns and a plethora of other unwanted problems, not the least of which is the unnecessary waste of resources the departed had worked long and hard to accumulate.

Our intent here, especially in a book about living in the now and learning to live the life you were born to live — is not to goad you into putting your affairs in order with scare stories. But we do encourage you to be mindful of what you can do to prepare for the final chapters of your life and the many unexpected twists and turns that can happen along the way.

Other Considerations

As part of preparing for the next stages of your life, you may also want to give some additional thought to what kinds of resources you will require. Again, it is not our intention to add fuel to the fire of conventional messaging propagated by a consumer-driven society that measures success almost exclusively by financial standards. And we certainly do not want to align ourselves with the banksters and some of the less-than-scrupulous financial service firms that bombard us with messages embedded with concerns about the amount of money we need in order to retire. This approach, while in some ways grounded in reality, also plays upon our scarcity consciousness and is one of the reasons so many of us stay chained in servitude most of our lives to the great economic machine rather than living the lives we were born to live.

At the same time, it would be foolish not to listen to those who suggest that with increased longevity, declining real estate values, and instability in the financial market, many of us may need to work longer, put aside more in savings, perhaps take some greater risks with some of our investments, and consider alternate second careers.

Others point out that new challenges exist for those of us who are older in finding employment. Together these elements mean that only about 10% of us who today retire have enough money and resources to last us the rest of our lives.

There are other reasons for our inability to support ourselves as we age — even if we have been gainfully employed most of our lives. The so-called experts don't talk much about these factors but here are a few of them:

- The sudden, devastating financial impact that illness can have for the millions who are either still without healthcare coverage or whose coverage is inadequate.
- The absurd cost of pharmaceuticals and other preventative medical practices.
- The growing belief among some segments of our population — primarily those in the top 5% — that it is okay for millions of Americans to exist below the poverty line in the richest country in the world.
- The fact that we live in a world in which many of the needs and requirements of people in the second half of life are considered privileges rather than rights.

We could go on, but the bottom line is that for these and other reasons — particularly during this time of transition when humanity is struggling to get its priorities straight — we suggest you pay attention to your own needs as best you can. For when you couple the information we have just discussed with the fact that the average number of years most of us will live after retirement can be as many as the number of years we spent being a part of the great army of the employed, the future can certainly get tricky. Indeed, the number of us who will have enough money and resources to live on in reasonable dignity and comfort in the second half of life probably will become even lower and that is something we should all pay a lot of attention to.

In short, in a culture like ours, where the free market economy is treated as an invention of the divine, the challenge of living longer will not only come to be more complicated for those of us as we age, but ultimately, the graying of the world's population will put a very substantial burden on everyone. So those of us in the over-50 crowd would be wise to begin to question current thinking, explore new and more innovative life strategies, and above all demand that our governments rethink their policies and the areas on which they are spending our tax dollars before it is too late.

Getting Beyond Getting By

A next and perhaps equally essential consideration regarding our financial well-being includes a reminder that the more we focus on the need for money, the more we will tie ourselves to this system that has so many of us running around like mice on the revolving wheel of economic servitude. And the more we do this, the more we will miss the opportunity to identify new options, explore new priorities and utilize our resources differently.

Indeed, most of us — no matter what our age — currently find ourselves spending the majority of our time working harder than ever before just to get by or we spend a significant amount of time worrying about, tending, investing, and trading time or resources in an effort to protect what is left of a diminishing nest egg.

Instead we invite you to consider what our lives could be like if we — individually and collectively — were willing to re-examine the fundamental values on which our lives are based. Surely it must be clear to you as it is to a growing number of us that all of this huffing and puffing about money and chasing after the illusion of security does not — as the old cliché reminds us — buy happiness, peace of mind, good health, deep personal satisfaction, fulfilling relationships, grace, or fulfillment of our destiny.

If this is true, then two questions come up for us. When are we going to get off the treadmill? And what would our world be like if we lived our lives for life rather than for financial security? And as you reflect on these questions we invite you to remember Matthew's biblical quote about gaining the world and losing our souls.

Alternate Values and Concepts

In a later chapter here in Part Five we will devote time to exploring alternate choices and different life style scenarios. However, since we are on the topic of the challenges we all face in the second half of life — and charting a new course for the future — it may be helpful to consider some of the changes you might want to consider making in your daily life as well as in our collective way of life. Changes that can prevent those of us who are part of the world's aging population from experiencing deplorable and unacceptable conditions at the end of our lives. Making some of these same changes will be necessary for the rest of the population as well, especially if they do not want to experience serious economic hardships and a possible fiscal collapse that may result if we stay on our current course.

Clearly, from our perspective, we know that our healthcare system — even with the recent reforms — is still broken and needs a significant overhaul. Indeed, we believe that until we either reinvent the foundations of private medical care or enact a sensible form of government-sponsored medical care currently known as "a single payer system" — the kind our President, members of Congress, all Federal employees, the members of our armed services, and seniors covered by Medicare currently enjoy — healthcare will remain broken. This is the same highly effective system that is available in every other industrialized country in the world (France, Sweden, Canada, England, Italy, Spain, Germany, to name just a few).

No matter the road we take, however, it is apparent that the healthcare system must change and that profit needs to be either eliminated or significantly reduced as the primary driver of this system if we are to survive economically and be able to receive and deliver the care our citizens require.

On this same topic, it is clear to us that each of us must rethink our responsibility for our own well-being. This means a dramatic shift in our belief system about what causes disease and what constitutes healing. A personal healthcare system that is primarily focused on prevention rather than treatment, a system in which we are the main decision makers and experts from both the allopathic and naturopathic schools of healing serve as our paid coaches and consultants, needs to become the path we walk on.

This system would, of course, dramatically alter the financial balance in the medical and pharmaceutical fields, changing the primary motive for those who enter them from the quest for wealth to a much stronger service ethic. This is particularly true in the pharmaceutical sector. Profit accruing to individuals and absurd amounts of duplication of efforts must cease to be forces driving this industry. Instead, a new system needs to be put in place based primarily on making the retail price of drugs affordable to those who need them. This does not mean that we should not be mindful of the cost of research, development, and distribution, but these factors should be measured against access by the broadest possible population.

In addition, a much stronger focus on the use of natural herbs and preventative and alternative medicines by all of us collectively would dramatically alter the power and influence of drug companies and allow us to focus on prevention rather than treatment.

And please remember, the term non-profit does not mean that jobs would not be created, valued salaries paid, research and development executed, and more. It only means that at the end of the day, the system would be self-organizing and self-replicating and that a few individuals would not extract enormous amounts of wealth (profit) from these industries to the detriment of the system and to the majority it should be designed to serve.

Of particular importance, we believe that those of us who are in the second half of life need to rethink our own priorities. We would be wise to look at how we organize our lives, the kind of environments we live in, and the type and amount of goods and services we actually require. We would also be wise to consider how we acquire, maintain, and replace these goods and services. In short, it is time for those of us in the second half of life to begin exploring new models of collaborative and cooperative living and the real definition of sustainability.

As we said, we will explore this subject in additional detail a little further along in this section. For now, we invite you to simply begin considering both the challenges and opportunities that lie ahead.

Our State of Mind

Another important aspect of packing for the future involves not falling victim to negative thinking. An important part of learning to live in the now is learning to avoid getting more entangled in the world of form, appearance, and acquisition.

So more investigation, greater exploration of alternatives, a lot more compassion for ourselves and others, and attention to detail are some of our recommendations. This does not mean each of us has to become an expert in each area of focus. We do not, for example, have to become day traders or financial portfolio managers to deal effectively with our finances. We do not have to become lawyers in order to have own living wills and trusts created or become world-famous experts on Medicare or Medicaid and alternative- and supplemental-care guidelines to take better care of our health.

There are plenty of experts out there and a lot of sources of information that can assist us in learning enough so that we can separate the chaff from the wheat in dealing with these experts as we put our affairs in order to give ourselves the best advantage possible for this next part of our life's journey.

Allow for the Unexpected

Of course, as most good strategic analysts will tell you, in some ways the whole idea of planning for the future is a bit of a contradiction in terms. The world is changing so rapidly and there are so many new developments in science, technology, and political and economic systems, as well as changes in levels of human consciousness and in the natural world, that our old models of linear growth are now primarily myths of the past. In addition, as those of us who have lived more than a few years know, the future always includes the unexpected.

Finally, of course, when we prepare for the future, we must take into consideration the fact that there are a number of challenges that are arising as a result of our inattention to essential advice we've been given and largely disregarded over the past several decades that can alter the course of human events going forward.

Climate change, for example, a condition that some continue to foolishly and stubbornly deny, is now coming home to roost. So our advice to you is to plan as best you can and then also allow for the unexpected.

In addition, since we have already explored the three great illusions — control, safety, and security — and so can better understand and acknowledge the frailty of clinging too tenaciously to any of the three, we would be wise to acknowledge that surrender plays a very large role in our lives. Indeed, when we stop and truly observe the mystery that is life, we must admit that from the start we each and every one of us has been guided and supported in more ways than any of us can measure.

And while this does not mean that all of us some of the time and some of us a lot of the time do not experience significant challenges and varying degrees of pain and suffering, in the end, these experiences appear to be part of the human journey. Some choose to call these experiences bad.

Others explain them as part of the debt we pay for previous experiences in this and perhaps other incarnations. Some find other answers, justifications, or befuddlements to explain them.

But one thing is apparent to us: life is a mystery, greater and more complicated than anyone we know or have ever met has been able to explain to our satisfaction. So in the end, acceptance of the unknown; a willingness to pay homage to the mystery; and enough humility to do the very best we can to flow with the grace, the goodness, the challenge, and the obstacles that life presents is the best any of us can do.

There are other unexpected elements that may and probably will show up to impact the road ahead. These include other parts of the mystery and the conundrum that is life — natural catastrophes, financial losses, accidents, illness, and the loss of loved ones. Unexpected elements may also come in the form of unanticipated new opportunities and exciting developments that you will want to be able to take advantage of. So learn to go with the flow of things, look for the lessons that are present, get comfortable with ambiguity, and continue to stay present rather than focus on what was or what could have been. These may well prove to be keys to a truly extraordinary life of greater consciousness.

Take Care of Your Instrument

Physical — There is also the subject of your physical body. As we said earlier, there are a number of wise beings like the sculptor, Jose de Creeft, who remind us that, "our primary job is to become the best instrument we can and then to leave the music of life to God." From our perspective this means we would be wise to take the best possible care of our body, for it is the instrument that allows us to experience a quality of life. So paying attention to the right kind of exercise and diet and finding the right balance point for ourselves between activity and rest are all very important.

Sedena's Portable Energy Program (P.E.P.), which can be found at our website, www.donotgoquietlythebook.com, contains a number of easy to-do, valuable, and empowering practices you can adopt to gain greater energy, balance, and renewal as you continue on this journey toward living ever more consciously.

Emotional — In terms of our emotional well-being, we encourage you to take steps at your own pace to do some of the things we have discussed in earlier sections of this book and others that we will cover in this fifth and final part of the book. You do not need to tackle them all at once and you would be best served by paying attention to those areas that your own inner guide brings most strongly to your attention. As to your pace and the level of your commitment, you should also be the determiner of these things, for in the end, it is your life.

Mental — In regard to our mental well-being, exercising the mind with quality stimulation is valuable. Learning new languages, mastering new disciplines, exploring new interests, and ensuring that we know what kinds of supplements and foods can increase our mental acuity. These are all important aspects of taking care of our instrument.

Spiritual — Taking good care of your instrument also involves paying enough attention to the spiritual side of your life. This means that gratitude, reflection, prayer, and meditation are important tools that can keep us in touch with that "still small voice" and allow us entrance into alternative perspectives.

Taken together these practices will assist us to balance our body, mind, emotions, and spirit and keep our instrument tuned up and tuned in to the best of our ability. Again, please remember this is not a competition or a race, and no one other than you should decide what is yours to do or not to do. And, of course, acceptance and surrender apply here as well. The very best you can do is to do your part; if and when the music of life brings you unexpected twists and turns, challenges, and gifts you can flow with them with as much grace and love as possible.

Don't Take Any Wooden Nickels

Finally, when all is said and done, the best any of us can do is to do our part in putting our individual house in order and to contribute to the well-being of others to the best of our ability. Beyond this the quality of our lives will have something to do with the luck of the genetic draw, the architecture of our individual destiny, the often-whimsical nature of fate and the power and clarity of our own intention. One other thing that we can do, however, is pay attention to the two reminders that come to us from traditional folk wisdom — both of which speak to the same caution.

☘ Avoid taking any wooden nickels.

☘ Remember that you can never con an honest man.

The first reminder has, of course, been around a long time and refers to the fact that a nickel is made of copper and nickel and has a basic net worth — no more and no less. So if we come across a coin that looks like a nickel, but is made of some other material, the answer to its value is obvious. Unfortunately, however, when it comes to a lot of other commodities, concepts, opinions, offers, and promises, especially those that are made by some less-than-ethical and self-serving governments, organizations, and people, we can find ourselves being offered coins of the realm that are not worth the material they are stamped upon. So remember those images from the old Hollywood Westerns where one of the characters would literally put a coin in his mouth to test its authenticity. Sometimes you just have to go the extra mile to find your truth.

The second reminder — *one can never con an honest man* — is of particular value, especially in a world where there are so many people who scheme and dream up ways to take advantage of others. Unfortunately, from our perspective, many of them today come dressed in the cloth of religious and political legitimacy. Others, of course, wear more garish plaids and offer financial and investment advice, but still their songs can sometimes be enticing.

No matter what they call themselves, how they are dressed, or what they offer — if you can keep your greed, lust, and fear in check and your honesty, curiosity, and integrity in place; if you are willing to admit what you do not know and keep asking for simple explanations, you can avoid being victimized and throwing away what you have worked so hard to earn in your life.

So whether the promise of a free lunch comes from some Internet criminal in Nigeria, from a seemingly legitimate legal or financial adviser, the pulpit of your church, the front of your temple or mosque, or the halls of your government, don't be afraid to state the obvious, to admit what you don't know, and to point out when necessary that the emperor may not be wearing any clothes.

Life Rule
"There is no cure for birth or death save to enjoy the interval."
~ George Santayana

Life Achievement
James Lipton, host of *Inside the Actors Studio,* one of television's longest-running and most successful programs, is in his 80s.

Life Tool
Make a plan and check it twice. This is our recommendation for you today. Be attentive to details, be thoughtful about your needs, and set aside sufficient time to identify the things you need to do and the specific steps you want to take to ensure that you are packing well for the second half of your life.

You Aren't What You Do

"It would be a good thing if man
concerned himself more with the history
of his nature than with the history of his deeds."

~ Friedrich Hebbel ~

The American Way

A lot of us eventually discover that it is not what we do that makes life truly engaging, interesting, and fulfilling, but the quality, character, and passion that we (the "who") invest in the "how" that gets the "what" done. Our passion is also evident in "why" we do the "what." Of course, the challenging thing about making this discovery is that most of us, especially here in the land of productivity and performance, have spent a significant amount of time thus far in our lives focusing most of our attention on the "what" rather than on the "who," the "how," or the "why." So as we take this next step of charting a new course for the future let's look a little closer at this subject.

The cult of personality and the focus on doing are, as we have discussed, great American pastimes and full-times. In fact, when it comes to making ourselves appear important by doing a lot, we are as good if not better at it than anyone has ever been in the history of the world. In fact, along with fast food, media addiction, technology obsession, and the belief that we are masters of the universe, doing has been one of our leading exports.

Unfortunately, no matter how large our commitment to or our fascination with doing, in the end, doing is not anywhere near as important as being — at least in determining our ability to lead meaningful, satisfying, rewarding, and conscious lives. And so in this chapter we are going to go deeper into this subject of doing versus being and explore why the latter is so essential to living the lives we were born to live.

In our contemporary society, we are encouraged to focus on the primary goals of recognition and reward. And we accomplish this by paying a lot of attention to tasks (the what). Occasionally, those of us who want to avoid repeating mistakes also learn to include some focus on process — (the how). Rarely, however, are we encouraged to focus as much on who is doing the how that gets the what done. Unless, of course, the who is getting a lot of recognition and reward. And even more rarely are we encouraged to focus on why we are doing the what — why in the sense of what is the real purpose, meaning, and contribution to the common good that our what is creating.

At first it may seem like we are just playing with words here, but if you slow down and go no faster than feelings can follow, we believe you will find that exploring this subject can have a very dramatic and positive impact on the course you set for the rest of your life.

Doing Has a Shadow Side

While it is true that our focus on doing has produced some wonderful and positive results, has gotten us out of some tough scrapes when we have been challenged by natural disasters and by foreign enemies, and accounts for much of the economic strength of our consumer economy, doing also has a pretty significant shadow side.

From a global perspective we believe that one of the reasons our world is in such trouble today is that too many of the things we do fail to take the who, the how, and the why into consideration. For example especially in this time of deregulation and in an effort to beat the competition, companies often focus on getting products to market without careful enough evaluation of their long-term impact on the end user and on the environment. As a result a number of products that are on the market today cause significant physical, emotional, and environmental damage.

Governments are also perpetrators of similar folly. They institute policies that may appear practical, logical, and advantageous over the short-term, but in many instances they have not been carefully considered from the standpoint of long-term impact. As a result they often produce unseen and unanticipated implications or negative repercussions. An excellent example of this is the damage that has resulted from the practice of arbitrarily forcing different ethnic and religious groups into common nation states after various wars. This approach has often led to destabilization of the region and the perpetuation of long-term ethnic unrest.

Deregulation of the financial sector is another example. Indeed as a former chairman of the Federal Reserve noted recently, "our desire to stimulate the free market economy did not take into consideration some of the less laudable human characteristics like personal greed that emerged when the regulations were dismantled."

Healthcare reform, bound and gagged by a number of competing and conflicting needs advanced by special interest groups, promises some advancement, but, in the end, has failed to address the primary goal of creating a healthcare system that serves the well-being of the whole population. Draconian budget cuts that focus exclusively on fiscal austerity, without a corresponding understanding of their negative impact on social responsibility, may bring us closer to what appears to be a balanced budget, but much further away from a stable, compassionate, and visionary foundation for the world and its inhabitants.

A second thing of significance we believe you will discover when you examine our addiction to doing the what — especially when it is divorced from the who, the how, and the why — is that the major difference between doing and being is lost. Yes, although most of us have lived a certain number of years getting better at doing a number of things, far too many of us have, unfortunately, not yet put as much time and focus into getting better at being — being better at being human and being better at being our authentic selves. This is of tremendous importance because being better at being human and being who we are — our authentic and original selves — are two of the primary reasons we have come into life in the first place.

Indeed, from our earliest moments, we are taught how to do things. At first, of course, it's all about the essentials: eating, walking, talking, and interacting. After a while we graduate into different skill levels from tying our shoes and getting dressed to learning how to go to the bathroom by ourselves. These doings involve new levels of hand, eye, and body coordination. Again, complex procedures involving significant amounts of expanding gray matter, but still pretty much in the realm of the basics.

Eventually, of course, we graduate to other forms of doing: school, sports, social activities, early-stage relationships, etc. And when we do we discover that when we are successful — success defined under the standards of winning — we are rewarded, recognized, and then given the opportunity to do even harder things.

Having been inducted into this kind of system from birth, it is not at all surprising that we come to believe that doing is what life is all about. We are encouraged to do. We are rewarded for what we do. And we are punished — either by others or by our own opinions and by limited life opportunities — if we do not do enough, or do not do what we do according to the standards set by the Gods of Productivity and Performance. Indeed, doing grants us special rank and privileges in the "great army of doers."

By comparison, this being stuff doesn't get much attention. In fact, if we daydream, if we spend time in quiet reflection, meditation, contemplation, following flights of imagination or merely observing life, we are considered unproductive; and in a world where the great army of doers rules, and consumption and materialism are next to godliness, this being stuff relegates us to the ranks of the unproductive; the impractical, the undisciplined, the lazy, and certainly the ne'er do wells.

And make no mistake these represent deeply engrained beliefs — beliefs that came to great prominence during the Age of Reason and The Industrial Revolution. And unfortunately, these beliefs and values still have an iron hold on our culture. In fact, this grip is so complete that we often are not even aware that we are in their grips until we are sidelined by accident or illness, by some personal loss or tragedy, some unanticipated change in our career status or perhaps simply our age.

It is, however, during these times that some of us take what amounts to our first pass at being. And this is generally when we discover that we do not have very much information about it, experience in practicing it, or many role models to guide us. We also discover that we are not very comfortable and practiced at what was, at one stage of human evolution — prior to the Age of Reason and The Industrial Revolution — as natural as breathing.

Learning to Be

So in this media-mad, overamped, mechanistic, task-oriented, recognition-addicted, production-crazy, and economically obsessed world, how are we supposed to learn to be without completely jettisoning everything we have been taught has value? And even if we can hold on to some of what we value, won't we lose economic footing?

From our perspective the answer to this question is a resounding no! In fact we know there are ways in which we can all turn at least some of this doing energy into a genuine experience of being without jettisoning everything we have been taught; in doing this, we need not lose our economic footing. In fact, we know that if we are willing, we can learn this next and very important step on the path to living consciously; aging wisely; and creating a future that is more meaningful, sane, and elevated than our past.

Some of the concepts we have already discussed in the previous sections of this book will be very useful in accomplishing this transition from doing to being. In experimenting with these concepts, however, we remind you of the caution advanced by Lao Tsu, the Chinese sage who wrote the *Tao Te Ching*, "My words are easy to understand but difficult to put into practice."

So practice is certainly an essential piece and so is patience. To get from this world in which we are too exclusively occupied with doing to a world in which we are at least equally focused on being, we will certainly require a lot of practice and patience.

A short story might prove of value here. For along with practice and patience, humor is always a helpful tool. As the story goes, a couple of tourists were walking along a street in midtown Manhattan. Spotting someone they thought looked like a New Yorker, they approached and asked, "How do we get to Carnegie Hall?" The New Yorker smiled and said, "Practice. A lot of practice."

So being is the foundation for a new way of life. Being doesn't have to go anywhere or accomplish anything. Being doesn't care about what you own, what you have done or accumulated, or what degrees or credentials you have. Being doesn't require any of these things. Being is only interested in what is happening here and now. Being is about harmony, curiosity, peace, surrender, love, collaboration, trust, and grace.

While doing is about activity and accomplishment, being is uncovering what already is. While doing is about trying to bend things to our will, being is about understanding things as they are. While doing is about subjectivity, being is objectivity and effortlessness. Being is about surrender, trust, and grace. Doing is often about desiring, controlling, and efforting.

Unfortunately a lot of doing without as much being is what the first half of life has been about for a lot of us. So now, as we chart a course for the future, as we explore the options that exist that can allow us to get in touch with our dreams and live the life we were born to live, we strongly suggest you experiment with making both being and doing at least equal partners in the second half of your life.

Ways to Practice Being

While we have found no single formula or surefire method — other than practice with patience — that allows us to convert doing into being; and because being appears to be as varied as the number of us who manifest here as individual souls, our best advice is to follow the many clues and many processes a number of wise teachers and guides have shared with humanity over the course of our history.

Here are just a few recommendations that can assist you in remembering and learning how to be. They are offered in no particular order or level of consequence. And as always, please add as many others to this list as you can.

- Sit without having any specific intention in mind.
- Doodle.
- Focus on the place where your in-breath meets your out-breath.
- Sing or chant OM, HU, Nam Myoho Renge Kyo, or another of the hundreds of sacred chants.
- Sit and observe a tree or a flower and let it disclose itself to you.
- Hold someone you love and breathe in and out through your heart.
- Focus on the feeling you experience in each foot as you walk.
- Pay attention to each color in your surroundings.
- Listen to the sounds happening around you.
- Follow a bird in flight with your eyes for as long as you can.
- Watch clouds drift by overhead.
- Pose a question and then wait patiently for an answer.
- Do not pick up the phone until the 3rd ring; instead take a deep breath on each ring and smile.
- Ask yourself how you feel before you speak or act.
- Go inside the music you are listening to.
- Go for a walk without a destination.
- Journal — write your thoughts, observations, and feelings in a private notebook.
- Observe people around you with clarity but without judgment.
- Float in a pool of water.
- Focus on each part of your body one at a time and fill it with light.
- As you walk, keep your eyes on the most distant point on the horizon.
- Stay focused on and aligned with (at one with) whatever task you are doing.
- Observe yourself as you talk to someone.
- Pray often.
- Reflect whenever possible.
- Meditate daily.
- Experiment with yoga, tai chi, and other uplifting practices.
- Be grateful for all that you are and have and the people in your life.

Life Rule
"Let the beauty we love be what we do."

~ Rumi

Life Achievement
Gordon Parks, photographer, continued to work his unique magic with the camera in his late 80s.

Life Tool
Thich Nhat Hahn, the Vietnamese monk who introduced us to what he calls the mindfulness practice, suggests this simple way of being: As you walk, focus on each step. When you step off with the right foot, say to yourself, "I have arrived." And when you step off with your left foot, say, "I am home." It is no more difficult than this. Just with each step — *I have arrived. I am home.* Or: *I am here. I am now.*

This simple practice can bring you in touch with what is happening in each moment you experience. It can slow you down and allow your feelings to catch up with you. It can sharpen your powers of observation. It can bring your heart back into balance with your mind and, as we have discussed in the chapter on "Learning in the Now," it can provide you a direct experience of whatever it is you can learn that can improve the quality of your life.

Marvelous New Possibilities

"For what will it profit a man, if he gains
the whole world and forfeits his life?"

~ Matthew 16:26 ~

As we continue to chart a new course for the future, let's look a little more closely at some of the other life choices we need to make to better prepare for our lives going forward.

One of these involves what we do with our time, our energy, and our talent. Clearly the economy — the one that many of us have spent at least the first half of our lives serving — has now decided that some of us are no longer prime candidates for engagement, let alone advancement.

Indeed, it appears that society, or at least the corporatocracy, has reached the decision that we should either be moved laterally to make room for a younger person whose hunger, energy, and longing for achievement are often mistaken for dynamic leadership; or more commonly we are unceremoniously shown the door.

Indeed, it appears that society and particularly the younger lords and masters who have taken control of it have decided that minds and bodies that are over 50 are pretty much beyond their level of genuine productivity and effectiveness. Of course, that longevity also costs more in salaries and benefits, but few are talking about this form of ageism.

For a while, those of us who are moved laterally or who retire are tolerated by society and exist in a kind of limbo state. Perhaps we work part-time to supplement our income. Perhaps we have sufficient income from buy-outs or retirement accounts to allow us to continue to pay our way and stay below the radar. But for an increasing number of those of us "who weren't born yesterday," the day comes when we realize there is an excellent chance that we will live longer than we expected.

This is when a number of us find ourselves waking up in the middle of the night wondering what to do. This is when many of us realize that we may need to downsize. For most of us it means moving to a much smaller home or apartment, to a retirement community, to an assisted living center, or, if we are even less capable of tending to our own needs, to a nursing home. Yes, we realize we may need to move to one of those places where one either twiddles away their time or where one slowly becomes a hostage within a ridiculously overpriced healthcare system and an overburdened and underequipped life-care system. In short, we become tenants in the medical warehousing model.

Is there another or better answer? From our perspective, if each of us agrees to look with new eyes and to put our individual houses in order — through the inner work for which the second half of life is designed — we can, indeed, begin to design other options and create a more sane, humane, and balanced world.

Yes we believe we can discover a number of alternate choices and lifestyle scenarios that are not only worth exploring, but are, in many ways, better than many of the random, ineffective, and unacceptable choices that are usually presented to those of us in or nearing the end of the second half of life.

Alternate Choices

Career/Employment Options — Since our current system requires a basic access to money and credit as a prerequisite for survival, one of the most important things those of us in the second half of life — who are today being excluded from standard jobs in staggering numbers — can and must do is reinvent strategies by which we can earn money.

Indeed, if we keep standing on the sidelines, waiting and hoping that someone will consider us worthy enough to execute relatively insignificant jobs for equally insignificant wages, then we will probably wait a long time and, in the end, suffer considerably.

A quick look at the world around us clearly shows this to be the case. There now exists an enormous army of people who are 50 and older who have been separated from the workforce and who may, at least under current conditions, never again gain access to it — at least not in the fashion and at the level they are accustomed to.

Instead, many organizations are now sending massive numbers of jobs out of the country; eliminating and/or automating other positions; and hiring younger, lower-paid workers to fill others. Indeed, the era of corporate responsibility and genuine community involvement appears to be a myth of the past, replaced by a level of corporate selfishness and irresponsibility to the common good that would have been considered not only unacceptable but criminal only a few decades ago.

So those of us who are in the second half of life who want to have some say over our destiny will have to make different choices. First and foremost we must take a close, hard look at our skill levels and identify where we need to learn new skills in order to qualify for participation in new industries. But we must go way beyond this necessary but still limited step, because in the end, this approach still puts us at the mercy of others who may or may not want to hire us.

What's beyond the new skills for hire approach? New skills also give us the opportunity to invent new occupations and businesses that we can operate without permission. New skills allow us to organize our experience and convert it into a knowledge base that can be communicated to others. Above all, new skills, especially those that are related to that dream that lives inside of each of us, may be present in far greater measure than we imagine and often point the way to what is next for each of us.

There are also a host of options that are emerging in the form of collective investment scenarios where small groups of people can pool their resources to launch new businesses, buy and operate franchises, start investment pools, launch and participate in microfinance possibilities, and much more. There are also some reputable "network marketing" companies that provide individuals with entrepreneurial skills opportunities. After all, now that many of banks, financial institutions, and investment companies have betrayed our interests in pursuit of their own, it seems time we start taking care of ourselves.

In the years ahead, those of us in the second half of life have it in our power to reinvent an economic system that works for us.

Residential Options — One the most powerful and valuable living models for those of us in the second half of live comes from an area of what used to be called communal living. In short, one choice many of us can make is to utilize our substantial, collective financial clout now, while we still have it, and turn the residential development, social networking, and service industry structures on their ears and to our advantage. In short, rather than allow developers to build environments that we then are required to rent or purchase at substantial profit to the developers and to the bankers who fund them — and with substantial debt and cost to us — we can begin gathering in groups of like-minded people who are willing to build small, sane, and highly efficient communities on land that would be commonly owned by each member of the community and would not bring a profit to any nonmember.

Members of these communities can contribute their services as general contractors and developers, as electricians and plumbers, landscapers, interior designers, etc. Indeed, each resident could trade their services or provide them at below market value in return for their equity participation in the community.

These communities need not require us to sacrifice our desire for privacy and individual living space. Indeed, these communities can take forms we are familiar with such as small apartments, connected patio homes, townhouses, and other known configurations or they might take new forms.

The private living areas of these communities can surround shared common areas where all of the basic services we require can be available. These common areas would house all of the collective clothes laundering, electronics, entertainment centers, and other primary and now-essential services. Following this model would dramatically reduce, and in some cases eliminate, the need for each member of the community to duplicate this equipment and services in each private area. The primary design of all of these spaces — both private and community — would be vastly improved over current models to allow ease of access, mobility, comfort, and harmonious flow.

Clearly, this is not a new concept. Communal dwellers and experimenters have been working this model for centuries. Indeed, long before there were individual dwellings there were communal caves and dwellings. In addition, contemporary builders and developers have been experimenting for years with living complexes with some of these features for people of all ages and especially seniors.

What has come to be called the life-care industry has been doing some of the same. In addition, there are university living experiments in process, and hotels, retreat complexes, and spa centers that incorporate some of these concepts and features; the difference, of course, is that all of these examples are built primarily for profit.

There have also been many experiments — some private and unpublicized and others that have been studied and talked about extensively. The work of Paolo Soleri is an example of the latter. While Arcosanti, the community he built near Prescott, Arizona, has never succeeded to the level Paolo and many of his supporters have wished, his fundamental concepts offer some of the most intelligent, sane, and sustainable choices available.

There are many other alternative living choices worth exploring. Italy, Norway, and Singapore, to mention just a few, are experimenting with new forms of multi-generational housing complexes where some of the values of traditional society are being reinvigorated and explored. In addition, universities are beginning to explore the concept of creating living environments that bring people in the second half of life back to learning environments.

As you consider these options you may want to consider the facts that are emerging in a number of anecdotal as well as more formal studies that greater socialization, engagement in meaningful activities, the contribution of one's talents and abilities to the greater good, the formation of meaningful communities, the expression of care and compassion for others, more laughter and companionship, and other factors play a very significant role in increasing physical, emotional, intellectual, and spiritual well-being. In short, these factors contribute to improving the quality of our lives as well as reducing the costs society must bear for the well-being of a dramatically aging population.

Other Choices — There are also numerous experiments being conducted that explore new economic models where barter, swapping, and new forms of currency are being used. In short, we are not alone in our opinion that we cannot afford to stand by idling while our current economic and political systems head rapidly downhill.

There are unique forms of time banks where members of communities are investing a certain number of hours of their services and, in return, are allowed to access the services of others. Simple in concept but powerful in implication, this system allows an accountant to place five or ten hours of their expertise into the bank and, in return, draw on the services of a plumber or babysitter, a personal coach or a language teacher. Remarkable, the ways in which we can collaborate and benefit.

There are new forms of currency being evolved, new local banking systems that are not based on either greed or gambling, but instead simply use the collective funds of a group for the benefit of the members of that group or constituency. While work needs to be done on ways in which these smaller financial groups can relate to the whole need to be evolved, it is clear that if the intention to serve the greater good is strong, fair and effective methods can be uncovered.

There are also innovative shared public transportation systems emerging, like a public bicycle sharing exchange in Boston where people take bicycles from a central location to a destination where they are made available to others to use and so on.

There are local community gardens where people learn to grow portions of their own food using organic methods and seeds that are free of toxic chemicals and genetic engineering that eliminates nutrition and builds up unwanted toxins in the body.

These and many other innovative concepts are helping people remember they have a lot more control over their own lives than they sometimes think. They are also helping more and more of us to remember that we can experience a great deal of joy and satisfaction from healthy interaction with our neighbors and far more from collaboration and cooperation than from competition; independence; and the old illusions of control, safety, and security.

This is especially true when we experiment with gathering together with people who are dedicated to doing the inner work we've been discussing on these pages. When those of us in the second half of life take responsibility for our own thoughts, words, deeds, and particularly our own feelings; when we dedicate our lives to living more consciously and aging wisely and focus our attention on contributing to the common good rather than to divisions and inequality between people, we truly do begin to chart a course for the future in which we and everyone around us can be healthier, happier, more prosperous, and more engaged in living the lives we were born to live.

So the bottom line is that if we do the individual inner work that each of us must do to reclaim our balance and remember our true purpose in being here on this planet, then those of us in the second half of life can utilize our vast treasure of experience, resources, and energy to create alternative choices that significantly reduce costs, provide sensible ownership possibilities, and substantially increase the quality of the environments we live in and the value of the services that are available to us as we age.

And the good news is that we do not have to wait. There are experiments in alternative lifestyles already underway in all parts of the world. A little investigation will probably disclose some close at hand. And a little conversation with some like-minded friends will probably also disclose that there are a number of people each of us knows that are also seeing the writing on the wall and ready to make a difference.

A Few Additional Alternatives

In addition to the advantages already identified in the previous paragraphs, exploring different alternatives and new choices can provide genuine opportunities to reinvent a number of things that affect or will affect all of us — and one of these is eldercare.

Not only can we as members of various alternative communities begin to care for ourselves in more humane, engaged, and valuable ways, but we can do the same for others.

We can also offer gainful employment to members of our generations who can work as eldercare workers, support staff, and members of the medical and healthcare industries. Our participation in caregiving would also allow all of us to stay active and learn about new forms of healing that could then be shared with others and applied to ourselves.

Designing new alternatives to care for aging members of our community would also give us the opportunity to focus much more on preventive practices and healing concepts. In short, exploring alternative choices will give us much greater control over our individual and collective destinies and allow us to participate much more actively in the destiny of our community — a far cry from the current model.

Taken together, the advantages to those of us in the second half of life of exploring alternative lifestyles are remarkable. Not only will these be a next and valuable step in more conscious living, they will also open up new pathways and beta models for a future spiritually based world.

One More Note

It is also important to understand that we are not suggesting that communal living, barter, time banking, new currencies, collaboration, and cooperation are the only answers or that these experiments and approaches will answer every challenge that lies ahead. But we are certain these and other initiatives will open the floodgates of innovation and imagination and stimulate whole new levels of dialogue.

We are also certain that these and other things will encourage those of us who are in or rapidly approaching the second half of life to take the matter of how we live in the future back into our hands and to use the tremendous power available to us to ensure that whatever happens serves us and this planet well.

So as you explore some of your next steps in creating your future, please keep some of these alternatives in mind. You may just find that your future is much brighter, much more possible, and much different than you currently imagine.

Life Rule

"If the only prayer you say in your whole life is 'thank you,' that will suffice."

~ Meister Eckhart

Life Achievement

Carl Jung, one of the fathers of modern psychology, was actively exploring advances in his work on dreams and mysticism in his 80s.

Life Tool

Take a few moments to identify qualities and characteristics you would utilize to select a like-minded group. Then in your journal or notebook make some notes on the kind of ideal environment you would like to be a part of as you age. How large would it be? Would it be out in the country or closer to an urban center? What kind of private living space would you want and what would the communal spaces be like? Take another few moments to describe the kinds of services you would want to have available and the kinds of things you would like to participate in.

Crazy Wisdom

"To harvest our lives successfully, we must come to terms with our
mortality... In youth-oriented, cosmetically enhanced America,
the subject of one's own death is not only unpopular, but as taboo
as sex was in the Victorian era. A fantastic conspiracy
of silence surrounds the issue of our mortality."

~ Zalman Schachter-Shalomi & Ronald Miller ~

Learning to Live Outside the Lines

Thomas Moore, author of *Care of the Soul,* reminds us that the soul seems to thrive in less-than-perfect places, places where there are no straight and rigid lines and a reasonable amount of uncertainty and ambiguity. If this is the case, and our own life experience certainly supports Moore's contention, it is no wonder that so many of our souls are unhappy and out of sorts. Most of us live in what Carl Jung once described as "the land of boxes."

Indeed, it is a world that prides itself on having orderly square corners and streets bordered by straight sidewalks, marked by solid lines, hardwired for 24/7 digital communication, based primarily on the rational and the logical, and conscribed by limited and restrictive thinking. With this as the platform for life in the modern world, it is no wonder that so many of us are gasping for air.

And most of us have lived the first half of our lives in this world of rules and regulations, of processes and procedures, of bureaucracy, of straight lines and rigid structures. It is a world designed for the collective and not for the individual. It is a practical, so-called productive world ruled by the Gods of Economics and not the whimsy of the Muses and the ambiguous mysteries of the soul.

We also live in a world growing more humorless each day — a world of political and social correctness in which we seem to be losing the ability to laugh at ourselves and to celebrate deviations from the norm. Indeed, deviation and uniqueness, while applauded on our theatrical stages and on our movie and television screens, are getting more and more rare and costly in ordinary life.

This is a world where we like to pretend that we have it all together and strive to stay on the straight and narrow while hiding shadows and irregularities of enormous proportions. This is a world of false piety; inflated and overzealous morality; and what at best can be described as egocentric, inflexible, and divisive belief systems.

Doesn't sound like much fun, does it? Nor does it leave much room for what in so many other societies has been called "crazy wisdom." What is crazy wisdom and what does it have to do with learning to thrive in the second half of life? Crazy wisdom is counterintuitive. It is wisdom that goes against the grain and generally occurs outside the lines of the ordinary. It is wisdom that counsels and compels us not to walk on the straight and narrow with our hair neatly combed and to sit with our knees held closely together and our hands folded in our laps. Crazy wisdom makes sense by not making sense.

Fritz Perls, the father of Gestalt Psychology, used to say, "If you lose your mind you will come to your senses." That's crazy wisdom. An anonymous wit once proclaimed, "kneeling a lot results in good standing." David Ogilvy, founder of Ogilvy and Mather, one of America's leading advertising agencies, shared his own brand of crazy wisdom when he said, "rules are for the guidance of wise men and the obedience of fools."

And we agree and think it's time — no, long past time — for those of us who are in or nearing the second half of our lives to stop paying so much attention to square corners, straight lines, and political correctness. Instead we think it's time to start paying a lot more attention to that crazy wisdom that arises in our hearts and issues from our souls.

We can, after all, well afford to do so. A lot of us are either no longer within or are on the way out of the workforce. Many of us have empty nests, some amount of disposable income, and a reasonable amount of time on our hands. In addition, a large number of us have already served our time between the lines, within the structures and marching to the beat of someone else's drum. As a result we know how boring and tedious all of that can be. So the question we now face is how willing are we to finally get down to the real stuff; to get silly, irreverent, joyful, and above all crazy wisdom that will allow us to start or take our next steps toward living the life we were born to live?

Getting Crazy

How do we get crazy and tap into our own wisdom?

- Doing whatever we do with a lot more spontaneity.
- Breaking a few rules, especially those that the pompous and the pious have turned into absolutes.
- Eliminating the habitual, the regular, and the anticipated.
- Eliminating censorship of what we say.
- Laughing a lot more.
- Crying more often.
- Dancing.
- Being silly.
- Learning to love the silence.

You get the idea. As to how you can tell you are on the right track? Your heart will know and, trust us, you will get plenty of feedback from those living in straight-lined world around you. Some of it in big-eyed stares, gasps, head shaking, disapproval, outright fear, and even on occasion a few winks and some secret smiles of encouragement that will make your heart glad.

Alternative Forms of Life Lunacy

If none of the ways we have described above get you out of the habitual and into the marvelous, you might want to try some of these:

- Take tango lessons.
- Learn to play the tuba.
- Become a circus clown.
- Learn how to tap dance.
- Use only mime to communicate for an hour or a day each week.
- Walk backwards wherever you go.
- Wear red or green sneakers with your suits.
- Shave your head.
- Sing instead of speak your requests.

- Use an umbrella on sunny days.
- Throw a pie at a friend.
- Smile in answer to every question.
- Learn to play a jig.
- Whistle while you work.
- Play with children in a sandbox.
- Make a snowman.
- Learn to whirl like a dervish.
- Play hopscotch.
- Learn to juggle.
- Eat with your hands.
- Roll in the dirt.
- Jump into fountains with your clothes on.

Now go ahead, get a little crazy, and add some things of your own to the list.

Life Rule
"Whoever supermoralizes unmoralizes."

~ Samuel Taylor Coleridge

Life Achievement
John Cheever, well-known American writer, won the Pulitzer Prize at 67.

Life Tool
We suggest that a key to a more remarkable, joyful life is to stop looking for the approval and acceptance of others and start listening to the wisdom of your heart. Approval generally comes with a number of strings and a pretty high price tag. So it may be time for you to stop listening to the noise of the world and to start listening to the wisdom that is available within you. Your heart knows the truth. Your mind relies on other people's information and beliefs.

Learning to Love
Those Empty Spaces

"In the war of ideas it is people who generally get killed."

~ Stanislaw Lec ~

The Gift of Getting Older

One of the real advantages of getting older is that you already know that life is made up of a lot of transitions and changes. You know this whether you have been open and receptive to life and its many shifts and changes or whether you have resisted life and been dragged along yelling and kicking every step of the way.

Openness and receptivity are, of course, at least from our perspective, much better choices, especially if you want your life to be joyful. They also happen to be two of the essential qualities needed by those of us who are committed to living more consciously and charting a successful and satisfying course for the future.

Resistance? Well, that ultimately is both a quality and a strategy best suited to those committed to living out their lives under less than optimal conditions.

Another thing those of us who are in the second half of life know is that the older we get the more life tends to present us with a number of empty spaces. Of course, when we were younger, most of us did not like empty spaces very much, did we? In fact, wherever they showed up we did our best to fill them right away. For example, whenever one of our friends wasn't around or we didn't have an activity planned, we quickly looked to find another companion or activity to occupy us. We literally tried (and perhaps still try) to fill every second of the day with some kind of activity because we thought — and may still think — this is what we are supposed to do.

During the first half of our lives a lot of us also thought that we were the center of the universe, that all other life forms existed primarily for the purpose of preventing us from experiencing boredom, and that we were the masters of our own destiny. As we have gotten older, of course, these beliefs have changed. We have discovered that the universe was not created simply for our entertainment; that the pace of life is not designed to satisfy our every whim; and that many of the sharp turns, changes, and especially the full stops are not determined by us, but instead by the twists and turns of fate and the unfolding of our destiny. Indeed, it seems that the older we get the more pauses, turns, and full stops we experience.

During the first half of our lives, however, many of us still did our best to eliminate as many of the pauses and spaces as possible. We went to school, did our homework, played sports or games, hung out with friends, and joined clubs. We talked for hours on the phone; tried to go to every social event possible; or, if we were shy and more reclusive, filled every spare minute with music or hobbies, and more recently surfing the net, texting, or social networking.

Later, it was work and friends and more social activities, then marriage and children and more social activities. We bought houses or lived in apartments and worked hard so we could fill them up with furniture, art, and electronics. We bought cars, joined clubs, took trips, and maybe became involved in charities or community programs. And, you guessed it, our weekends were full too — of social activities and what are called leisure-time pursuits, like parties, golf, tennis, picnics, biking, boating, winter sports, movies, crafts, antique shows, music, plays, household projects, fairs, and family outings.

Every minute occupied. Every space and gap filled. If we were very lucky there were no major illnesses or accidents, no significant losses of loved ones that, as Eckhart Tolle says, "tear a hole in the fabric of our lives." There were, of course, some wakeup calls! We all have had at least a few minor accidents or illnesses that slowed us down enough for us to notice that we didn't like being slowed down. We also had experiences with aging grandparents or parents who as a result of changes in lifestyle and physical conditions gave us a glimpse into a possible future; but these were things we experienced only vicariously. We spoke about them sadly, but still these things were, for the most part, happening to other people, and so our lives continued right on track and without a lot of space.

The Game Has Changed

Of course, that's not the case anymore, is it? If you are in, approaching, or beyond your 50s, you now know better. Spaces and gaps are beginning to show up more frequently and in more parts of your life. If you are early in your 50s perhaps these spaces and gaps are just a few and only here and there. If you are in your late 50s or early 60s or 70s there are, no doubt, more spaces. Spaces at home that were once occupied by children. Spaces in your calendar that were once occupied by those extra things you had to do to advance your career — stay late at the office, prepare that special report, travel, attend conferences, give presentations, etc. Spaces in your friendships that result because some people you know retired and others have stepped out of your life due to changes in geography, to divorces and illnesses, some even to death. Yes, empty spaces and gaps are no longer things that you experience vicariously. They are very visceral and real now.

Other transitions also are beginning to get our attention. Those early years in which we thought our energy and good health, our physical abilities, sexual appetites, and appearance would last forever are giving way to a new reality. Now there are more inconsistencies and unexpected twists and turns. Our body doesn't recover from excess as quickly or remain as undeterred in the face of exertion. And then of course, there are those other conditions that are essential parts of the second half of life. Loss or reduction in sexual drive and what is called "the change of life." Women, of course, are more familiar with these physical changes. Menopause has been a recognized and treated phenomenon for a number of decades. For men, however, this change of life often remains an unnamed and untreated experience.

In fact, until recently most men have been unwilling and unsupported in naming the unexplained depressions, the rapid mood swings, the awkwardness, the loss of sexual drive, the lack of interest in career goals, and more.

Instead it's been referred to as the midlife crisis. What's the old cliché that talks about fast cars, sudden changes in habits, and affairs with younger women? Yes, all this and, of course, those omnipresent erectile dysfunction drugs. Somehow our society hasn't yet gotten the message that perhaps the reason men stop getting erections is that there is something going on in our world, something that results from too much stress, poor diets, a confusion between sexuality and intimacy, a lack of appropriate marshaling of energy earlier in life, and overly aggressive lifestyles. And maybe something else as well! Maybe some of what is called erectile dysfunction is simply a natural condition that happens to some men who are living longer. Maybe biology is simply allowing men to turn more of their attention inward so they can more fully explore new dimensions in the mystery that is life.

But like it or not, men, like women, are finally acknowledging that they experience a change of life and, unless they are prepared for it, unless they do more than try to white-knuckle it, it tends to grab them by the collar and disrupt their lives.

No Piece of Cake

We do not pretend, of course, that learning to deal with any or all of these spaces, gaps, and transitions is easy, especially when many of us spent the first half of life in a world of tight schedules filled with activity, and a denial of aging, and where we labored under the belief that we were masters of our destiny. And yet, as those of us who have already passed through some of these transitions know, there is a great deal of truth to that old adage that the universe abhors a vacuum.

So if we are awake enough and willing enough to learn and to deal with some of the discomfort these spaces, gaps, and transitions bring up, we believe we will discover that these spaces and transitions do not have to be terrifying — although they can sometimes feel a little scary. If we are patient and courageous enough to look the spaces in the eye and to wait; if we are courageous and patient enough to accept that life is really an endless chain of transitions; we may well discover that transitions provide us with the opportunity to discover new occupations, new experiences, new relationships, and new things about ourselves — about our strengths and challenges, our weaknesses and our opportunities for improvement. Yes, spaces, gaps, and transitions provide us with some very real blessings.

In these spaces that were once occupied with other people and outer-directed focus, we get to experience new states of mind and visit previously unexplored emotional territory. We get to wrestle and make peace with ourselves and explore the miraculous, marvelous, and extraordinary inner landscape. Yes, as a result of the spaces and gaps we can turn inward and discover new spiritual territories, and new multidimensional abilities, and get new glimpses of the mysteries that lie beyond the boundaries of physical existence.

Through meditation, different forms of fasting, chanting, intentional retreats into the silence, through experimentation with mind-altering breathing techniques and the use of MDMA (known as "ecstasy"), hallucinogenic mushrooms, LSD, and a number of other grains and plants long used by indigenous tribes, we can take advantage of this time of life to get beyond the boundaries, to pull back the curtain that is called reality and glimpse, even if briefly, what lies beyond the straight lines and rigid facades we call reality.

Between the Notes

The pianist Artur Schnabel said that, there are any number of people who can learn to play the notes, but that the real music happens between the notes.

In our experience, this is particularly true about the gaps in life. While we often pay a lot of attention to the major events (what we call "the primary notes"), when the pace of our lives slows down a little and we start paying a little more attention, we begin to see that it is often what has happened or not happened between the primary notes that contributes some of the most remarkable and extraordinary music to our lives. These in-between-the-note moments with our children or grandchildren, or in nature; these tender moments with friends and loved ones; these unexpected moments when we make discoveries in gardens and workshops; and quiet moments of reflection are often quite extraordinary.

So as you direct your attention to the time that lies ahead, we invite you to learn how to make peace with and honor the spaces and gaps and celebrate the transitions. We invite you to welcome menopause (female) and andropause (male), changes in career focus, the departure of your children, changes in your health, and other major physical and emotional life changes with greater curiosity and less dread and resistance. And we especially invite you to learn to listen between all of the hustle and bustle, all of the comings and doings. In short, we invite you to practice being, to practice getting familiar with yourself, and to getting to know your God, in the silence.

Life Rule
"Remember: one lie does not cost you one truth, but the truth."

~ Friedrich Hebbel

Life Achievement
Robert Duvall, Oscar-winning actor, has appeared in more than 70 films. At 75 he accepted the role of a poker champion in *Lucky You.*

Life Tool
Identify the spaces, gaps, and transitions in your life. They may be the ones you are most concerned about. Instead of dreading their arrival or denying them, allow the possibility that they may bring with them a gift or unexpected blessing. Identify at least one of these gifts.

Isn't It About Time?

"There is no shortage of good days. It is good lives that are hard to come by. A life of good days lived in the senses is not enough. The life of sensation is the life of greed; it requires more and more. The life of the spirit requires less and less; time is ample and its passage sweet."

~ Annie Dillard ~

The Road Ahead

We've covered a reasonable amount of ground thus far and taken the opportunity to look at our lives from a lot of different perspectives both past and present. Now we invite you to take an even closer look at what you want to do with what lies ahead in this one wild and precious gift called your life.

As we begin this chapter we also remind you of Hillel the Elder's questions — "If not me, then who? If not now, then when?" For as we know, no one can live our lives for us — even though there are plenty of days when we might wish this were possible.

It is also true that none of us — whether we are 5 days old or 50-plus years old — have an unlimited amount of time remaining. In fact, if we compare our lives — which currently average about 77 years in length — to the life of this planet or to that of the solar system, our lives are little more than blinks in the Divine Eye — or, for those otherwise inclined, a minor decimal point in the math of evolutionary history.

Of course, those of us who are in the second half of life tend to be a little more aware of the limits of our time here on this planet. We have watched time speed up and the years move past with what appears to be an accelerated momentum. Indeed, there are many times when we look up from whatever we are doing and find ourselves trying to deal with the fact that it is already December. *"Where has the year gone?"* we ask, or "Is it really possible that I am already 50, 60, or 70?"

Yes, we have experienced a number of milestones, probably more than enough disappointments and losses, plenty of whimsical occurrences, a reasonable amount of wasted times, and a lot of unexpected and wondrous moments and acts of grace in which our own frailties as well as our strengths have been apparent. We are also aware, at least those of us willing to admit it, that a number of things have not always gone the way we wanted them to go, that we missed a number of important opportunities — some by omission, others as a result of our timidity or fear or laziness, and some by life's mysterious design.

We have failed at some important things, succeeded in ways that were sometimes far beyond what we or others expected. And we know, especially in those moments when we are particularly quiet and truthful with ourselves, that our hearts still long for certain experiences and our souls are still more than a little restless over some of the dreams we have held in the quiet of our hearts that are still unexpressed.

So here in this chapter, as you consider some of the things you want to do with the time you have remaining, we encourage you to revisit a few important questions. Isn't it about time...

- You do some of these things your heart still longs to do — time to live out some of your most important dreams?

- You finish some of the major things you started or declare them complete enough and no longer of interest to you?

- You let go of some of the values and practices that you may still be holding that do not work for you?

- You demonstrate a new level of honesty, clarity, and above all caring for this Earth that is your home, for your fellow human beings who travel this path with you, and for all of the living things that reside here?

Making Your List and Checking It Twice

So what are some of the things that are still important to you? We have our list, of course, but before we share it with you, we'd like you to take a few minutes and make your own list. Remember your list can contain:

- Dreams, schemes, and plans you'd like to complete in the years ahead.

- Values you might want to change.

- Habits and practices you'd like to drop.

- ✳ Others you'd like to begin practicing.

- ✳ Practical things that need to be put in order.

- ✳ Places you still want to visit.

- ✳ Talents and skills you may still want to develop.

- ✳ Gifts you want to share with yourself and others.

- ✳ Experiences you want to have, particularly on the inner planes.

- ✳ Legacies you want to create.

- ✳ Healings with friends and loved ones that you want to initiate.

  Etc.

You can do this by yourself by writing the list down in your journal or notebook. Or you can sit down with a friend or colleague and take a few minutes — first you and then them — to make your list out loud so that your friend or colleague can capture it for you.

Once you've developed your list, read it over carefully and then cross off anything on it that you know you really don't care that much to do or are not committed enough to get involved with.

Next prioritize the items on your list that remain. A = Absolutely want to do this. B = Will do this when the A's are done. C = Will do it if I have time.

Our A List

- ✳ Spend more time alone and in silence.

- ✳ Spend more together time in greater intimacy and loving.

- ✳ Write truly meaningful books that touch people's hearts and contribute to their lives.

- ✳ Take time to paint.

- ✳ Set up a new sculpting studio and continue exploring this medium.

- ✳ Share what we know with others in talks and programs.

- ✳ Move beyond the fear of failure, of loss and of death.

- ✳ Practice loving-kindness more frequently each day.

- ✳ Live more fully in each present moment.

- ✸ Give more often to more people in need.

- ✸ Spend more time in nature and gardening.

- ✸ Stop wasting time in conversations and activities that do not uplift us.

- ✸ Trust and surrender more.

- ✸ Laugh more.

- ✸ Learn more (especially how to be).

  Etc.

Moving Beyond Psychological Time

It has been said that as long as we live in the physical world and focus on life through our physical senses, we cannot get beyond the boundaries of physical time. Physical time beats to the 60-second drum, the 60-minute hour, the 24-hour day, the 7-days-a-week rhythm. Physical time is one of the ways we measure both the movement within and passage of our lives.

Psychological time is, however, another phenomenon. It is the arbitrary condition we impose on physical time with our minds and our egos. Psychological time is the measurement of demands, of worries, of past regrets and future fears and anxieties. Psychological time, unlike physical time, is entirely within our control. We can shrink it or expand it or eliminate it entirely by learning to continually bring our focus back to present moment awareness.

Our relationship to and our control over psychological time has been the subject of numerous experiments. Eckhart Tolle explores the subject in his book *The New Earth*. Deepak Chopra and others talk about experiments that were done demonstrating that the rate at which our bodies age has a lot to do with cultural expectations — our beliefs — rather than biological imperatives — the stories that are encoded in our cells.

So if time seems to be a challenge for you, we recommend you pay attention to the difference between physical and psychological time. We recommend that you use your physical time wisely and more efficiently for the things you want to accomplish and learn to experiment more with psychological time.

Life Rule
"We boil at different degrees."

~ Ralph Waldo Emerson

Life Achievement
Robert Frost, one of America's most beloved poets, published *In the Clearing* at **88**.

Life Tool
Today and for the next few days let this question be present in your consciousness — "What do I truly want to do with the rest of my life?" Do not struggle to create an answer. Let the answer slowly unfold itself until it is very clear and your heart knows that it is true.

The Velvet Voice

Tony's Story

Tony Bennett is one of a kind, an original musical magician who has been serenading audiences around the world with his remarkable voice for more than 60 years. These years have not, however, been without their challenges. There was a time when Tony's music was not in vogue and times when he struggled with drugs and alcohol. And yet he weathered these challenges and others and came out the other side.

In an article entitled, "What I learned from Tony Bennett," well-known sports writer and best-selling novelist Mitch Albom had some inspiring things to say. We share his words with you because Tony Bennett demonstrates that it does not matter how old we are, as long as we allow the music of life to flow through us.

"To spend a day with him...is to witness an artist walking through his own mural, amazed and delighted at the colors of his life. What makes Tony Bennett so...satisfied?" Reason 1: "He loves what he does." Reason 2: "He's not a 'things' person." (Bennett says: "I don't own a car or a boat. I don't own a home. I'm on a perpetual vacation.") Reason 3: "He's held firm to his ideals." (Even if he had to endure two decades when his music was out of favor.) Reason 4: "He never forgets where he came from."

Mitch Albom reports that Tony Bennett has sold more than 50 million albums. His artwork hangs in the Smithsonian. He has performed for nine Presidents and the Queen of England. He has been honored by the Grammy Awards, the Kennedy Center, and the United Nations. "But many a public hero has been privately miserable. Bennett's warm, crinkling eyes, boyish smile and relaxed conversation suggests a man who is truly, deeply at peace."

At the time of this writing Tony Bennett is 85 years old.

"We Are Not Going to Take It Anymore!"

"When ancient opinions and rules of life are taken away, the loss cannot possibly be estimated. From that moment we have no compass to govern us, nor can we know distinctly to what port to steer."

~ Edmund Burke ~

Throw Open Those Windows

Remember the film, *Network*? Remember the famous scene in which the fictional television news anchor, Howard Beale, played by Peter Finch, begins to experience what is described by some as a midlife breakdown and by others as a remarkable spiritual breakthrough? No matter how one describes that moment in the film, it captures a very passionate and energetic Howard Beale leaning in close to the camera and telling his viewers he wants them to get up, go over to the window, open it up, stick their head out and shout, *"I've had enough and I'm not going to take it anymore!"* And, of course, the next shot shows people all over New York City doing precisely this.

It is a powerful scene and we both still feel the sense of freedom we felt even if only as members of the theater audience. Well, in this chapter, we are going to ask you to do a lot more than participate vicariously in opening the window of your life and announcing to yourself and to the world that, *"I've had enough and I'm not going to take it anymore!"*

We invite you to feel deeply enough into the words and concepts discussed in this chapter and get in touch with that part of you that resonates with Peter Finch's passion, resonates enough so that you'll be willing to identify and then work with some of the things you are not going to take anymore — whether they involve your own thoughts, beliefs, and habits or those expressed by others that impact you and the world around you.

We suggest you begin by identifying exactly what it is you have had enough of. These things, of course, only you can determine, but one thing we would hope you have had enough of is the pitiful, paltry, prejudicial, limiting, and distorted view the world holds today of what it means to get older. Yes, we'd like you to be troubled and tired enough of the disregard, denial, and outright disrespect shown to those of us who are older that you will get up on your hind legs and bay at the moon of new awareness and possibility. We'd like you to build a bonfire of outrage and throw in all of those outmoded concepts, outdated images, and downright derogatory beliefs about what you and others of us in the 50-and-older crowd can accomplish in the second half of life.

And while you are at it, you might want to pay attention to other things you've had enough of and that you are not going to take anymore. In our case, we have a pretty long list so we are only going to share some of the items on it with you in the hope that they will help you get your process started. As you read our list, please remember, one thing you may have enough of is listening to other people's opinions. And if so, it's time to start articulating what you know rather than what others believe.

In our case we have had enough of individuals, groups, organizations, and governments that:

- Undervalue the experience, skill, and wisdom of people who are getting older.
- Promote the politics of division.
- Want to cut or eliminate the social safety net — Medicare, Medicaid, and Social Security.
- Support religious beliefs that espouse an exclusive and punishing God.
- Protect the right of some to thrive while others suffer.
- Support the production of harmful or inferior products and services.
- Mask hatred and prejudice behind the facade of political correctness and religious piety.
- Shut older people away and consider them a burden.
- Subjugate others in the name of one "ism" or another.
- Withhold drugs from those who need them because of the profit motive.
- Allow our representatives to pass laws which provide them with special powers, special services, and special protections not available to the citizens they represent.

⁕ Defend gun manufacturers who pretend that the right to bear arms means the right to use assault weapons.

⁕ Allow companies that benefit from the U.S. commons, and receive substantial tax breaks to take their jobs and money off-shore.

⁕ Support ministers, priests, and others who champion religious beliefs that distort the foundational precepts of their faith for personal power and money.

⁕ Appoint judges whose personal biases and prejudices limit the public good and who do not serve the common good of all.

⁕ Believe it is alright for some people to live in poverty, to die of hunger or exist in unhealthy conditions, while others have far more than they need.

⁕ Pollute and misuse the Earth's natural resources.

⁕ Condone or practice cruelty to animals.

Etc.

These are some of the things we've had enough of. Obviously, we support political agendas, policies, and organizations that advance programs that are called progressive and that hold that those of us who are more capable and more fortunate have a responsibility to support and uplift those who are not. If you have a different political leaning, however, please do not let our views prevent you from drafting a list of your own.

And here are just a few things we are committed to doing about some of the things on our list:

⁕ We have given birth to AgeNation and The Age of Empowerment, an affiliated 501(c)(3) organization, precisely for this purpose, to change the way Americans view and respond to aging.

⁕ In addition to the work we do through AgeNation and The Age of Empowerment, and the writing of this book, we give our time, money, and support to political candidates who are committed to making a genuine difference in the quality of life in these awkward times. We also write political blogs and support initiatives, organizations, institutions, and individuals that support the continued strengthening of the social safety net.

So please take a few moments and make your list and then identify at least one thing you are willing to do to have a positive impact on things on your list.

Being more proactive is also an important part of crafting a more conscious future for you and for those who will come after you. Finding greater internal alignment is of course the first step, but being proactive is also one of the privileges those of us who are in the second half of life and live in a democracy have. For we have the experience, the time, the resources, and obviously the need.

Life Rule
"The good displeases us when we have not yet grown up to it."

~ Nietzsche

Life Achievement
Giuseppe Verdi composed a new opera at 80.

Life Tool
Allow yourself to feel your feelings — even and especially feelings of righteous indignation. These feelings are an important step to knowing what it is that you have had enough of. So do your best to identify where your world is out of balance and then do your best to identify what you can do to take corrective action. This action might range from a new level of acceptance to making dramatic changes. So experiment with this simple formula: Feel, Identify, and Act. And please remember, the greatest changes we can make are changes to our own beliefs, behaviors, and attitudes.

Dreams vs. Desires

*"Only when we find the spring
Of wisdom in our own life
Can it flow to future generations."*

~ Thich Nhat Hahn ~

Giving Your Best

Since our ability to chart a successful course for the future involves looking more deeply into that portion of our dream that may be unlived or incomplete, we believe it is helpful to be able to differentiate between dreams and desires. It's also important to learn how we can free up the energies that may still be captured in our desires so that we can apply them to fulfilling our dreams.

A desire, in our lexicon, is anything we have wanted to do, have, or be at any time during our lives to date. You know the litany — "I want this. I want that. I want him or her. I want to go there, buy that, experience this, own that, become this or that, and so on." Yes, hundreds, thousands, probably many hundreds of thousands of desires have accumulated thus far in our lives and each has some of our life energy and attention tied up in it.

Why should we concern ourselves with this? Remember the Law of Manifestation — *Energy follows thought, manifestation follows energy.* If you have taken time to test its validity for yourself, you now know that what you focus on, you ultimately manifest. Focus on insignificant, transient, and relatively meaningless things; focus on worry, doubt, and your inability to do something — and that is what you will manifest. Focus on remarkable, life-sustaining things and that will be the result. Remember what Henry Ford said, "Whether you believe you can or you can't, you are right."

Desires vs. Dreams

So it should not surprise any of us that in our restless, acquisitive world, the distinction between desires and dreams has become as blurred as the difference between believing and knowing, looking and seeing, and hearing and listening. Indeed, for many of us these terms have become synonymous and yet the differences between them are enormous. In the case of desires and dreams, they are actually worlds apart.

Desires (you can substitute the word *wants* or *hungers* as well) issue from a perception or belief that there is absence or lack. Desires are the off-spring of emptiness, the illegitimate stepchildren of the insatiable. They arise inside us in an effort to satisfy a hunger that cannot actually be satisfied. In fact, looking for the satisfaction of a desire is a lot like eating the menu instead of the meal. Desires are the balm we hope will heal our wounds and fill the gaps in our emotional body. Desires are mind created and thought driven and often lead us on ill-fated quests that end up in less-than-satisfactory interactions with life.

As a result, following our desires, as anyone who has ever done so can attest, generally does not lead to fulfillment. In fact, satisfying one desire generally gives birth to another larger one. Thus, chasing desires is like the story of the jackass running along after the proverbial carrot dangling from a stick attached to his head.

Unfortunately, especially in our world of constant media bombardment, advertisers, political parties, governments, and others who would like to manipulate our thinking and impact our behaviors tell us otherwise. Ours is a world of constant sell and continuous buy, a world of glitz and glitter in which we worship form, are addicted to consumption, and suffer from spiritual emptiness. Ours is a world in which desires have become not just acceptable, but socially commendable and, when they are fulfilled, the means by which we measure our success. Indeed, we have become so accustomed to giving full vent to our desires, so addicted to acquiring, accumulating, and showing off the stuff that results from their pursuit that we have lost sight of the difference between chasing fool's gold and acquiring the real stuff.

Dreams, by comparison — and we are not referring here to our night dreams, but to the flashes of inspiration and intuition, insights and knowing, that come to us as prompts and messages from our hearts — issue from the right side of our brains. They are the legitimate issue of our souls seeking expression and physical manifestation in this journey that is called life. Dreams are the hints that can, when we are brave enough to follow them, lead us to the discovery of new landscapes and destinations of remarkable individual and collective value.

By comparison to the loud trumpeting and empty posturing of desires, dreams can sometimes be quiet and so subtle that we almost miss them. This subtlety often causes us to doubt their reality — or perhaps it would be more accurate to say that the loud glare of our desires generally obscures them.

For example, perhaps your dream is to be a social activist, a novelist, composer/musician, singer, dancer, painter, or explorer. Perhaps your dream is to invent some remarkable new technology, teach and inspire children, ensure the preservation of a natural landscape, protect wildlife, serve others, or simply lead a life of quiet contemplation and spiritual focus. Perhaps your dream is to be a statesman, a leader, a healer, a nurse or shaman. Perhaps your dream has literally come up from time to time, during your sleep, late at night as you sit and ponder, or in quiet moments during the day — those in-between-the-notes moments — when you least expect it. Perhaps hints surface as daydreams. Perhaps you have seen these hints arise like mirages, there one instant — luminous and enticing — and then gone and almost forgotten the next.

You know what we are talking about! We have all had moments when our Muse has hummed or whispered seductively in our ear. But in a world where there are so many desires fighting for our attention and seducing us away — not just once but again and again — it's easy to brush these promptings of the Muse aside.

Big desires! Little desires. But one thing is certain, our desires have strong voices! There's the desire for recognition, the desire for money, the desire for security and social acceptance, the desire for material abundance, the desire to be safe, the desire for credentials, the desire for fame, etc. So it is no wonder that many of us bypass the soft whisper of our dreams and go for the big brass ring of our desires! After all this is how we've been taught to get attention, applause, and satisfaction. And this is what we've come to believe is the important stuff in life.

So as you continue to explore the course you want to chart going forward, we suggest you stop going for the brass ring and the ever-elusive carrot of desire and focus instead on the authentic look and feel of your deeper dreams for soul fulfillment. Your dreams will open doorways to new ways of living and being that will generate genuine joy, lasting satisfaction, and enduring love. Your dream will lead you to meaning and purpose. Your dream will allow you to harness your potential and fulfill your destiny.

Learning to Live Your Dreams Exercise

So whatever you dream of doing and being, this next exercise will give you a chance to describe and to experience — even if only briefly — aspects of your dream.

You can, if you choose, just describe your dream to yourself in your notebook or journal. There is a tremendous amount of value in doing just that. You can also find someone you care about and trust and tell them about your dream. One caution here! Choose this someone carefully. Remember that many of us pushed down or turned away from our dreams a long time ago because someone or ones in our lives at the time laughed at our dream or told us it was impractical or impossible.

Part One

Whether working alone or with a partner, here are three questions we invite you to answer — repeatedly — until you feel complete:

⊛ What is one dream I still want to experience or manifest in this lifetime?

⊛ How would expressing or manifesting this dream make a difference in my life?

⊛ Would fulfilling this dream contribute to the lives of others?

Part Two

After cycling through these questions long enough to identify several important aspects of your dreams, move to the second part of this exercise. Here you will have an opportunity to let yourself and/or your partner know what it feels and looks and sounds like for you to be a great painter or pianist or social activist — or whatever your dream happens to be.

You can use words, of course, but we also invite you to get your whole body involved in the process and act out the role. Literally stand up in front of your easel or that orchestra or your audience and be that painter, pianist, or activist. Yes, have some fun, get physically involved in communicating your dream to your mirror partner. Literally act out what you are most passionate about doing in the second half of your life.

After you have described one of your most important parts of your dream in your journal, or spoken to and acted that dream out with your partner, then move on to another dream and do the same thing with it.

Part Three — Turning Up the Heat

If you are still game, this part of the exercise will also involve journaling in private or working with a partner.

In this part you will work with three questions:

- ✸ What specific dream do you want to manifest?

- ✸ What will that contribute to your life?

- ✸ What specific action are you going to take to do this?

We invite you to keep answering these questions until you are clear that you have articulated the essential dream you are committed to manifesting in the second half of your life.

A Dream Envisioning

If you participated fully in this dream clarification exercise, we invite you to close your eyes for a moment or two and feel the energy you have created. Then, when you are ready, open your eyes and continue reading.

What you are feeling at this moment is your energy.

It is available to you each and every moment of your life.

All you have to do is stay in touch with your dreams,

with your original and unique passion for life.

This energy is also your resource.

You can invest it in things that are frivolous

or things that are consequential,

things that advance your life

or desires that keep you running in place.

It's your energy,

so for a few moments just surrender to it

and allow it to lead you in the silence to where it wants you to go.

Our Power and Beauty

Before leaving this chapter we want to remind you of the famous Marianne Williamson quote that states that of all of the things that scare us, one of the most daunting is our own beauty, power, and light. Yes, some of us are most afraid of standing out, of shining too brightly. So as you explore your dreams, we are going to ask you to keep this fear of the light in mind.

Life Rule
"It is never too late to be what you might have been."

~ George Eliot

Life Achievement
Nelson Mandela became president of South Africa at 75.

Life Tool
Please pay attention to the difference between your desires and your dreams. And if you want to live the life you were born to live, stop focusing on desires and start living your dreams.

Heroes and Heroines

"There is no use trying," said Alice,
"One can't believe impossible things."

"I dare say you haven't had much practice," said the Queen.
"When I was your age, I always did it for half an hour a day.
Why, sometimes, I've believed as many as
six impossible things before breakfast."

~ Lewis Carroll ~

Motivation and Inspiration

Heroes and heroines lift our spirits, remind us of how the impossible becomes possible, exemplify the best of human accomplishments, motivate and inspire us, prod us out of our complacency, challenge us to go beyond our limits — and that is just the beginning of what heroes and heroines do. Do you have a hero or heroine? We have many. Here are just a few and not in any order:

Leonardo da Vinci	T.S. Eliot
Nelson Mandela	Marcus Aurelius
Hermann Hesse	Anais Nin
Rosa Parks	Jim Thorpe
Carl Jung	Socrates
Ralph Waldo Emerson	Clarence Darrow
Helen Keller	Mother Teresa
Rainer Maria Rilke	Henry Miller
The Dalai Lama	… to name just a few.

Who are some of your heroes and heroines?

Heroes/Heroines Process

In this process you can write in your journal or select a partner. You know the drill. If you elect to work with a partner decide who is Partner A and who is Partner B. Partner A goes first and answers the following questions. If you are doing this by yourself just read the question and then write down your answer.

- ✹ Name one of your personal heroes and heroines.

- ✹ What qualities do they represent?

- ✹ What are some of the lessons you have learned from them?

- ✹ How can you demonstrate these qualities and lessons in your own life?

- ✹ What else can you do to be more of a hero in your own life?

Keep cycling through the questions until you feel complete.

Journaling — What Did You Learn?

Take a few moments to make some notes about what you learned.

Heroes/Heroines

So how can we become heroes and heroines in our own lives? Here are a few comments about things some of us want to do with our lives.

Harry Moody, former deputy director of the Brookdale Center on Aging at Hunter College, advises:

> *"We sacrifice much in becoming responsible adults.*
> *To maintain our place in society, we put our inner lives on hold,*
> *devaluing contact with the sacred in favor of mastering the skills*
> *needed in the everyday utilitarian world."*

Goethe tells us:

> *"Whatever you can do or dream, do it now!"*

Ram Dass advises:

> *"Don't just be a wise elder, be an incarnation of wisdom.*
> *That changes the whole nature of the game.*
> *That's not just a new role, it's a new state of being.*
> *It's the real thing."*

Harry Moody, Goethe, and Ram Dass are encouraging us to become heroes and heroines in our own lives. Not an easy task in a culture like ours that has turned the heroic journey into a pop cliché that we see played out nightly on so many superficial reality shows.

Being heroic is also challenging for us because our culture is dominated by technology and we tend to value information far more than we do wisdom. Information involves the acquisition, organization, and dissemination of facts, a storing of data. But wisdom involves something far more crucial, the emptying and quieting of the mind, the listening within, the application of the heart, and the alchemy of combining reason and feeling, thought and intuition.

As a result wisdom is rare in our culture. Most often what we find are reasonably knowledgeable people who present us with their beliefs, but who too often have not cultivated the quality of mind and the level of experience from which true wisdom arises. Indeed, if there ever was a time that proved the truth of Lao Tsu's comment, this age does.

> *"Those who know, don't say.*
> *Those who say, don't know."*

In ancient cultures, especially indigenous cultures, people celebrated elderhood. Elders were granted respect because they had made the journey and paid their dues in pursuit of their authentic dreams. In short, these were the people who had learned their life lessons and, as a result, had gained genuine wisdom, experience, and compassion they could impart to their people.

So as we make our own passage and prepare for the future, let us aspire to this level of elevated consciousness and greater awareness. And in the process let us contribute to changing the negative images associated with aging in our own culture. Let us instead establish a new and uplifting path ahead for the countless generations that will follow us. And above all let us first be sure that we do our best to continue learning the difference between looking and seeing, hearing and listening, believing and knowing — and certainly the difference between the desires that too often spring from our egos and the dreams that arise from our hearts.

Life Rule
"He who desires, but acts not, breeds illness."

~ William Blake

Life Achievement
Eleanor Roosevelt wrote her autobiography at 78.

Life Tool
Do you remember when you were a child and you wanted to be a hero or a heroine? We invite you to find that place of innocence and hope within yourself and honor it. Let it guide you as you move through your day. For it represents your soul's recognition of its own inherent greatness.

What follows here is a gift we received from a collaborator who worked with us on the final edit of this manuscript. These words came to her after reading this section and we reproduce them here for those who may be moved to read them:

As children, the only thing most of us had to mirror that internal awareness were cartoon representations — like superheroes or faeries and princesses. For these representations were the means we had to live self-transcendent lives.

Now, however, you have begun to identify who your true heroes really are. So let your vision for yourself expand — first, in your imagination. Then, through the action steps you plan to take — let your vision flow out into the very life you lead.

As you do this, you will begin to reconnect more and more with your inner hero and with the energy it takes to live at this elevated level. And as you continue to feel into this energy, visualize yourself receiving wisdom from Source, God, The Divine, or whatever you call the organizing principle of the universe. And if you choose to, receive this energy through the top of your head and allow it to flow through you and be anchored into the center of the Earth.

Next, to keep this moment of true visioning from disappearing like the smoke of a pipe, write it down in full, glorious detail. Then distill it down into an affirmation that you repeat to yourself upon arising each day and before retiring at night.

Finally, make it your resolve to fulfill the vision you were given as your legacy. Let it be the living testament of the life you were born to live; the unique and authentic piece you and only you can leave behind as a gift to others.

Let Passion Lead

"It is not a matter of thinking a great deal, but of
loving a great deal, so do whatever arouses you most to love."

~ St Teresa of Avila ~

A Key to an Extraordinary Future

We have talked about the difference between desires (wants/hungers) and dreams and how the former can lead to the dissipation of our energies and a relatively empty cup while the latter leads to living the lives we were born to live. In this chapter we are going to explore one of the most important qualities we have at our disposal to help us live our dreams. This quality is passion. Yes, your passion will, if you allow it to, lead you to manifest your dreams. Your passion is the grand differentiator, the great discerner, and the extraordinary enabler on your journey into the future.

When we talk about passion we are not, however, talking about lust or greed — two experiences that are often mistaken for passion. Passion is not an overactive restlessness or hunger that leads us to get entangled in desires and that marks so much of life in these challenging times. These cheap and flimsy imitations do not lead us to the fulfillment of our dreams. They are the stepchildren of desire/hunger and lead ultimately to disappointment.

Lust and greed, most especially, like the desires they prompt, are the sirens that draw us toward the rocks of mediocrity with their garish but seductive song. Both emotions have enormous amounts of energy associated with them and so they are easily mistaken for the real thing. For example, although the word *greed* is not generally used in association with spiritual or religious quests, in our experience there are a number of instances where individuals who claim they want enlightenment or religious elevation pursue these quests with the same kind of desperation that motivates the yearning for money, career achievement, sexual satisfaction, or social status.

Lust and greed do not allow us to pursue our dreams from that place of quiet surety within our hearts, nor from a place of surrender and mindfulness. Instead, they come from a place of willfulness — of pushing against what is — from a place that is marked by a kind of desperation and aggression that leads to the abuse of others and that of some of our own most cherished values as well.

The Genuine Article

Passion by comparison has none of these earmarks. Like the difference between knowing and believing, passion is the genuine article. It is authentic and original. It issues from the deepest place of sacredness within us. It can be quiet or it can be bold. It can be subtle or strong. It may not at first feel like something major or even make itself known to us in obvious ways. But like a spring that is only a trickle at its source, our passion can gather strength, power, and momentum. And if we allow ourselves to follow it, it can lead us to an infinite ocean of meaning and purpose.

Yes, passion sometimes begins as a whisper, while at other times it is as a sudden, powerful, and undeniable force that breaks through the fabric of everyday reality and announces its presence. But no matter how it manifests in your life, your willingness to follow it will grant you a second half of life far different and more meaningful than the first half.

Even if the second half of your life is devoted to the same career or avocation that marked the first half, even if you were blessed enough to find your career path early in life and it is the path you will continue to walk for the rest of your life, the difference between letting your passion lead you and running after your desire to succeed is immense.

For example, let us say you are currently a painter or a doctor and you have been practicing your craft for years. Let us say you have worked incredibly hard to achieve a degree of excellence in your practice, but at the same time that you are also aware that as laudable as your achievements are, you still feel a sense of incompleteness or that nagging sense of doubt about whether you are on the right path. You may still feel that you are running after something, as if your life was a race and your objective was still somewhere out there in the distance.

By comparison, embracing your passion and letting that quiet inner knowing emerge will shift your experience. It will allow the strokes of your brush or the diagnostic technique you employ to become even more aligned, natural, and effortless. Passion will grant you access to all sorts of skills — intuition, insight, imagination, genuine knowing — that desire can never grant you. Passion is having. Desire is wanting. Passion is a call. Desire speaks to what is not present, to a kind of lacking and reaching after. And as the old saying goes, you can't want and have at the same time.

Let Passion Lead

So what do you do if you know that your passion does not reside in what you are currently doing in your life? As hard as it may at first seem, our recommendation is to either find a way to bring your passion into what you are doing or let it lead you to your next doing.

Here's how that might look. Let's continue the example of the artist and the doctor. Let us say you began painting because it seemed like a romantic or rebellious thing to do. Perhaps you also were drawn to your painting because it offers the chance for recognition. Let us say you chose to pursue medicine because your father or mother wanted you to or because you believed it was a way to ensure a special status in society and provide a route to financial security. Whatever the reason, you followed this path and now find yourself having achieved some aspects of your goal, but still feeling incomplete. So what can you do? You can keep doing what you are now doing and live with the feeling that something is incomplete or out of alignment or you can change your strategy and explore a different connection, a deeper motivation for what you do.

Let's go a little deeper here. You can, of course, transpose the specifics of art or medicine onto your own career pursuit. As a painter, your brush strokes and colors, while they find an audience, may be less authentic to your vision and thus less vibrant than you wish. They may be a part of a traditional or accepted approach in the genre you have chosen. But you know that they do not advance the art form as much as they allow you to sell your work to designers and some buyers.

As a doctor you know you are competent and that your practice treats people's symptoms. But you also understand that you are not redirecting them to search for the root or cause of their disease, and so instead, are only offering temporary relief.

So this may be a good time to take stock of your situation and look for ways to reinvest your passion into your painting or your medical practice. In the quiet of your own heart ask yourself, "What would it take to give flight to my passion? What would I need to do differently to allow a more authentic, original, and committed form of my art — or my medical practice — to emerge?" Yes, get in touch with your passion and let it guide you to a new and deeper experience.

On the other hand, if you are this painter, that doctor, or someone involved in another career or avocation and you are simply not able to allow your passion to lead you deeper in your career pursuit, you may want to take a sabbatical. Or you may want to start spending some time each day learning to be comfortable in the silence and letting your imagination loose.

In this quiet, what do you find yourself fantasizing about? Perhaps your imagination keeps returning to an idea of what you will do when you retire. Perhaps your fantasy involves cooking or spending your time fly fishing or golfing. Perhaps you think about finally writing that book or those articles you have talked about for years. Perhaps your daydream involves taking a spiritual journey to India, starting a mentorship program for children, or opening a wild animal preserve in Africa, coaching, inventing, or getting more involved in the civic affairs of your community.

Whatever this something is, we'll bet it brings up feelings that are different from those you are currently getting from your painting or medicine or whatever you are doing. So do you go off and become a chef or open that wild animal preserve? If that is what your passion leads you to do, then you will in all likelihood succeed. If it is not your passion leading you, however, but just another desire in disguise, you will probably find that the deeper you go into exploring the hows and the whens of doing this new thing, the less enthusiasm and joy you experience about it.

You see, passion is an inside-out job and not the result of an external focus or motivation. So if you get the inkling that you have been mistaking passion for desire, you would be wise to continue doing whatever you are now doing, and learn to do it from a different place and in a different way. In short, shift your center of attention from your head to your heart. Do what you do — not by following the God of Need or Greed or Fame or Attention — but instead, by giving your allegiance to the God of Connection and Service.

One of the best ways of doing this is to be fully present in each moment. Be the light you are trying to capture, be the color that you are using to express, be the compassion and healing you are trying to prescribe. Literally shift your awareness from result to experience, from projection to realization.

If you legitimately pursue your attempt to bring your passion into your painting, doctoring, or whatever you do, and you do not succeed, then perhaps it really is time to give some long and thoughtful consideration to finding another path. And in the spirit of surrender, trust, and service, perhaps you would be willing to ask within to be guided in that selection instead of trying to figure it out and muscle your way along.

Life Rule

"Absolutely nothing of genuine value in this world has ever been accomplished without passion."

~ George Wilhelm Friedrich Hegel

Life Achievement

Giuseppe Verdi composed his opera *Othello* at 73 and *Falstaff* when he was close to 80.

Life Tool

Close your eyes for a moment or two and ask yourself, "What do I most care about and what would I express in my life if I was not limited or motivated by money, concern about time, or some other obligation or responsibility?" Then open your eyes and write out your answer.

What We Can't Take with Us

"Each of us needs to withdraw from the cares which will not withdraw from us. We need hours of aimless wandering or spates of time sitting on park benches, observing the mysterious world of ants and the canopy of treetops."

~ Maya Angelou ~

Learning to Laugh at Life

For years now we have all heard it said that "you can't take it with you." Unfortunately, based on the way most of us are living today, most do not appear to believe this. Well into our 50s, 60s, 70s or even 80s and 90s, a number of us are still acquiring more, still outwardly focused on accomplishments and form. Far too many of us are also still worrying about our time-shares, what the Joneses think, and how to rebuild our investment portfolios — as if any of these things will ultimately prevent us from facing the real challenges of aging and dying.

Oh yes, some of these things do protect us a little longer or a little better from the life conditions that aging and dying bring up. But we all know that no matter how much money we have or how well balanced our investment portfolios are, no matter how big our houses or how many of them we own, when it is our time to dance the real dance of aging and dying, none of these things will offer us much consolation and absolutely none of them will make the passage with us.

So what is all the huffing and puffing, and the worrying and struggling really about? Isn't it time we stop and look closely at all of the heavy breathing and start remembering that from some perspectives — especially those we experience from a higher altitude — the whole trip down material lane is not only limited but redundant. And although it is hard to say these things in the first half of life when we still believe we must be a part of the push/pull and keep up with our peers, those of us who have run this course certainly ought to be able look out at our efforts with good humor and a more balanced perspective.

We also ought to be able to finally admit the truth of the adage that we have used as the title for this chapter and make a realistic list of the things that we can't take with us.

Things on Our List that We Can't Take with Us

If you are willing to have a little fun and gain a little more perspective on your life, your efforts, and a number of the things you have accumulated to date, we invite you to do this next exercise as a reality check and as a valuable step in creating your course for your future — a course on which you may want to travel light. This may also prove to be a valuable way to consider the kind of legacy you want to leave behind.

To assist you in your personal brainstorming, we will share a few of the things participants in our workshops have come up with:

What We Can't Take with Us

Money	Collections
Cars	Scars
Houses	Warts
Clothing	Breast implants
Jewelry	Long-term health insurance
Bank accounts	College degrees
Artwork	Gold watches
Books	Plaques and awards
Antiques	Options
Mortgages	Pets
Club memberships	People we hate
Deeds of ownership	

If you are inclined, please take a few moments and make your own list of the things you can't take with you when you leave this life.

Things We *Can* Take with Us Creative Brainstorm

Let's do a second brainstorm. To start us off, here is another list people in some of our programs have made of qualities, characteristics, and abilities — the inside stuff — they believe we do take with us in the DNA of our consciousness when we depart planet Earth. In doing this exercise, we invite you to act as if the belief that we are spiritual beings living a physical life is true.

What we know	Anger
What we have done for the greater good	Greed
Grace	Understanding
Healing	Laughter
Love	Wonder
Compassion	Trust
Unpaid spiritual debt	Gratitude
Joy	Courage
Bliss	

You may be surprised by some of the things others have contributed to this list. Some folks believe — with a strong sense of inner knowing — that we do not enter physical existence with a blank slate, or tabula rasa, but with a genetic propensity toward certain types of abilities and conditions and with a reasonable amount of prior history in our DNA. And similarly, some believe when we exit, we carry with us our unprocessed emotions, our habituated and limited beliefs — the unfinished business that we came in agreeing to accomplish. According to many spiritual traditions, these incompletes — along with our victories — are stored in the DNA of our consciousness and go on with us.

What are some of the things you believe you can and will — whether you want to or not — carry with you when you cross the threshold between life and the great unknown?

Life Rule
"Where the spirit does not work with the hand there is no art."
~ Leonardo da Vinci

Life Achievement
Shanadii, granddaughter of Geronimo, still leads groups of people in learning Native American practices and rituals at **88**.

Life Tool
As you go through your day we invite you to continue to pay attention to those things you can and can't take with you. Perhaps you will be encouraged to focus a lot less on the things you can't take with you and a lot more on the things that you can and will.

The Grandmother

Maria's Story

Maria Rizotto was born in Sicily in 1876. She was still young when she fell in love with and married Orazio Caruso. They had two sons, Matthew and Frank, and were building a life on the island when economic challenges became too great and they decided to immigrate to the United States in search of better opportunities.

Although they had relatives in the Boston area, after a while they decided to move to what was, at the time, the small farming community of Fitchburg, Massachusetts. There their family grew — two more sons, Joe and Steve, and then a daughter who they named Mary. Although life was not easy for Maria and Orazio, they managed to care for their family and even put aside a little extra money to buy some land. It was only a few acres but they called it "the farm" and told stories about the day they would build a new home on it.

Unfortunately, Orazio died young and Maria was left with the substantial challenge of raising her five children on her own. With few opportunities to do this in Fitchburg, and relatives still in the Boston area, Maria gathered up her children, her belongings, and the small amount of money she and Orazio had put aside and moved back to that city.

Maria Caruso was my grandmother and she did an outstanding job of raising her family under difficult conditions. Her children grew up to be remarkable and successful people. Each married and had children of their own, and all were involved in successful businesses.

For a number of years two of her sons, Joe and Steve, and their families; as well as my mother, Mary; and my father, George; and my sister and I who carried the same names lived on various floors of the Boston apartment building my grandmother owned and also lived in.

Growing up was quite an experience. The proximity of so many members of my mother's family, and especially my grandmother, made our home environment one of genuine support, constant family interaction, celebration, and joy. In some ways it was not unlike an Italian opera, full of color, drama, and a lot of ceremony.

I remember a number of things about my grandmother — her kindness, her remarkable patience (especially with me and my pranks), and the incredible strength and wisdom that seemed to be an essential and natural part of who she was.

Something else about my grandmother made a deep impression on me. Every day of her adult life until the very end when she was no longer able to walk, she would get up every morning and walk three miles to and from home to her church. She did this in all kinds of New England weather. She did it no matter what others said or tried to do either to support or dissuade her from the practice. She would simply cover her head with a black scarf, bundle up if the weather was cold or inclement, and go off to spend her time in communion with her God.

Knockin' on Heaven's Door

"I thought age was a quiet time. My seventies were interesting and fairly
serene, but my eighties are passionate. I grow more intense as I age... Inside
we flame with a wild life that is almost incommunicable. In silent, hot
rebellion we cry silently, 'I have lived my life, what more is expected of me?'"

~ Florida Scott-Maxwell ~

Dust or Something More

A number of us in the over-50 crowd are familiar with the well-known Bob Dylan song whose title we have borrowed for this chapter. Although Dylan wrote it in the early 1970s for the movie *Pat Garrett & Billy the Kid,* we are broadening the meaning here to refer to those moments that not just Billy but all of us eventually face when we realize that we really are not going to live forever. Moments in which we know that we will soon discover for ourselves if there is a heaven's door and what lies beyond it — oblivion and dissolution or continuation and elevation. Moments when we realize we will know if there is such a thing as reincarnation or if we, as some believe, are a onetime phenomenon who make just one pass at the human drama and then return, as they say, into the dust from which we emerged.

In short, we all must eventually face our own moment on the threshold of what we have come to think of as the end of this physical existence and discover for ourselves a number of things we have been taking on faith most of our lives. For some this direct experience of encountering the unknown occurs earlier, and sometimes frequently, in life as a result of different spiritual practices. For others the unknown is encountered as a result of physical traumas, accidents, or illnesses that prompt what are called out-of-body experiences. For the majority of us, however, the unknown is faced at the time of our transition from this physical existence.

Rather than wait for that opportunity to arise, however, we thought you might like to take advantage of this opportunity to consider this possibility — before your actual moment of transition arrives. We are confident you will find it well worth your while.

What Will You Do?

In this exercise we invite you to act as if the moment of your transition has arrived. We invite you to ask yourself some questions and to write down your answers in your notebook or journal. Having your answers in writing will, we are confident, provide you with the opportunity to reflect back on them and, from time to time, revise some of them, if you are so inclined.

So before you begin, take a few slow, deep breaths. Allow your eyes to close and spend a few minutes quietly following your breath in and out and giving yourself permission to imagine that this is the moment of your transition from this physical plane. Then when you are ready, open your eyes and read and answer each of these questions:

- What are you feeling at this moment?
- Can you say that you have done most of what you came to this Earth to do?
- Are there things you want to say to those you love?
- Are there any incompletes that may impede your transition?
- Where do you think you are going from here?
- Are you committed to staying awake and keeping your focus during your death journey?

We suggest you pay close attention to your answers and wherever there are things that remain incomplete — conversations that are unfinished, attachments that remain, unknowns that are unexamined — decide if there are specific actions you can take to bring these areas into greater balance and make whatever commitment you wish to make inside you to accomplish these objectives.

What Will You Choose?

Having considered some of things you might experience at the moment of your transition and some of the things you might like to do to make your transition easier and more joyful, we thought you might also like to explore some of the other choices you have that will impact the course you are crafting for the future.

Here is a story that may assist you in your process. It is about Baal Shem Tov, a famous 18th century rabbi from the mystical tradition who was being criticized by his fellow rabbis for encouraging singing and freedom on the Sabbath. When questioned by the scholars about his teaching, Baal Shem told this story.

> *Once there was a wonderful wedding in this town. The house where the wedding was taking place was filled with joy and happiness. The musicians played and everyone inside danced with great merriment. Outside a passerby stopped and looked through a window. But all he saw were people jumping about, whirling and leaping, and he walked away from the house muttering to himself that they must all be mad. Just then, one of the men from inside the house opened the windows, which had been closed all this time. The passerby turned once again toward the house, for now he was able to hear the joyous music being played from within.*

From our perspective, this story brings home the point that the beliefs and assumptions we live by either limit us or expand our experience. It reminds us that if we are willing to open the windows of our hearts we will indeed hear the music of life that we may currently be missing.

It also reminds us that there are occasions when one of the other guests in the celebration called our life opens a window for us and provides us with the opportunity to move past our limiting beliefs and erroneous assumptions and experience the joy that is our natural state. Some call this fate, others luck, still others grace. But from our perspective, what matters most is that the music of our souls can be available to all of us if we have the courage and the wit to follow our dream and to celebrate each and every present moment.

So Many Choices, So Little Time

So yes, choices! We have had plenty of them. And we still have many to make. So as you take your next steps and seek to chart a course for the future we invite you to ask yourself these questions:

- 🏵 What are the primary choices I now have in my life?

- 🏵 Will I make them consciously and actively or by default?

- 🏵 What consequences do I think these choices will have on the rest of my life?

What impact will these choices have on the people I love?

  What impact will these choices have on the legacy I will leave?

You can, of course, also make up your own questions. Whatever you do, however, we encourage you to take a few moments to answer these questions and to record your answers. For the life you lead going forward will certainly depend largely on the choices you make today.

Life Rule
"It is not a matter of thinking a great deal, but of loving a great deal, so do whatever arouses you most to love."
~ St. Teresa of Avila

Life Achievement
Ethel Andrus founded AARP at 74.

Life Tool
Moment by moment awareness is the greatest gift we can give ourselves. In this moment we invite you to be conscious of your breath. In this moment be conscious of your body. In this moment listen to the sounds around you. Pay attention to the colors and the scents. Do not move faster than your feelings can follow. Be grateful for it all.

A Legacy & Stewardship of Hope

*"[Elders] are wisdomkeepers who have an ongoing responsibility for
maintaining society's well-being and safeguarding the health of our
ailing planet Earth. They are pioneers in consciousness who practice
contemplative arts from our spiritual traditions to open up greater
intelligence for their late-life vocations. Using tools for inner growth,
such as meditation, journal writing, and life review, elders come to terms
with their mortality, harvest the wisdom of their years,
and transmit a legacy to future generations."*

~ Zalman Schachter-Shalomi & Ronald Miller ~

Legacy and Stewardship

As we head toward home, let's talk just a little more about purpose and
meaning. In doing this we want to go back and review something
we talked about earlier — the fact that in order for us to remain vital and
engaged in our lives, we have to decide what contribution we want to
make and how we want to do this.

In speaking to this question of contribution and legacy, Mother Teresa
once said,

*"We may wonder — 'whom can I love and serve and where is the face of God to
whom I can pray?' The answer is simple. That naked one. That lonely one.
That unwanted one. They are my brothers and my sisters. If we have no peace,
it is because we have forgotten that we belong to each other."*

Unfortunately a number of people in the modern world appear to
have forgotten or perhaps never learned this essential lesson. Indeed,
some look at "that naked one, that lonely one, that unwanted one" and
turn away. Some look at that different one, the one whose skin is darker
or lighter, whose language is unfamiliar to our ears, whose customs and
beliefs seem strange, and pull back into the comfort and seeming safety of
their familiar world. Or, worse yet, they get aggressive or defensive!

Indeed, as we have explored in other sections, for all of our accomplishments, some of us who are part of the over-50 crowd have not always done such a stellar job of supporting and advancing the game of life. In fact, as we discussed earlier, in some very significant ways the condition of the planet we are currently scheduled to leave behind is not better, but in some very primary ways worse than the condition of the one we inherited. So from our perspective, there is still some work to be done before we withdraw from the field. What do you think? When you ask yourself about the legacy you will leave, what is your answer?

Elders in Other Cultures

Many indigenous people believe that each stage of life is designed for different things and that when individuals arrive in the second half of life, it is time for them to take on the mantle of the elder. It is the time to harvest their lessons, share the fruits of this process through the mentoring of younger individuals, focus on their inner spiritual journeys, and become the stewards of the future. In short, they believe the second half of life is a rich and vital time for elders and that elders play a very significant role in the well-being of their communities.

If those of us who are in the second half of life in contemporary industrialized societies wish to regain our privileged role as elders, we will have to follow a similar path. We will have to refine and demonstrate some important qualities — sustainable lifestyles, patience, reflection, a commitment to justice and fairness, integrity, courage, compassion, humor, and the willingness to champion the long view — a perspective that takes into consideration the impact of our current actions many generations into the future.

Maggie Kuhn, the founder of the Gray Panthers, suggests that there are five key roles for elders. From our perspective, these five roles provide us with remarkable choices:

Meditating (reflecting, praying) first and foremost because only by listening to the wisdom of our hearts, only by gaining inner alignment with our essential core values, will any external action be effective. In short, we must stop acting too quickly and in ways that are disconnected from the primary rhythms and wisdom of the universe.

Monitoring second, because only by observing what is going on — seeing as well as looking, and listening as well as hearing — can we know the real state of things sufficiently to create solutions that make genuine sense and promote a greater good.

Mentoring third, because it is not our task to "do it all." Instead, we are meant to share with other generations the fruits of our experience, the wisdom of our failures and our successes. And we are meant to help blend all this experience and wisdom with the new insights, new perspectives, and new energy that other generations bring to the game of life.

Mobilizing fourth because we now have so many of our brothers and sisters who are in the second half of life and whose voices matter. By issuing the call to each other, by reminding each other of our responsibilities and also our privileges, we can make a significant difference in the world.

Motivating fifth because it is by our example and not our words that we can create the greatest good. It is through modeling new sustainable concepts, new values, and more compassionate behavior that those who come after us can gauge the remarkable difference between actions that promote the higher and common good and those we have been practicing that divide humanity and turn brother against brother.

A Better World

At a time when the need for elders, especially in our society, is greater than at any time in history we know we must agree to do the critical work for which the second half of life is intended. And if we remember that we are connected inextricably to all other beings who share this planet — and are responsible, by comission or omission, for everything that occurs — then we can indeed contribute to aligning ourselves more fully to the natural rhythms of life. If we remember that the generations who call themselves older GenXers, Boomers, and Elders will soon oversee the largest transfer of wealth in the history of the world; if we remember that we have all of the experience we need, including the birthing of the major social, cultural, and political changes of the 20th century, then we can begin to remember that we have it in our power to make right our relationship to life and to the world.

How we do this will be one of our challenges. We can, of course, do what other generations before us have done. We can transfer our wealth primarily to members of our families, but in truth, unless we share our values with them, unless we demonstrate a more effective use of our resources, this wealth will not necessarily improve the quality of life for them or for others.

So what other options exist for us? There are many ways in which our heirs can still benefit from the resources we have accumulated, but at the same time, these same resources can be invested in the common good.

Non-profit organizations and causes need our support; special programs that contribute to the well-being of individuals deserve encouragement; and new initiatives that promote greater individual and group empowerment are all worthy of our support. And we can do this through the establishment of land trusts and the use of other giving instruments that make needed contributions for future well-being, scholarship funds that provide options for those deserving of the support, investment funds that offer next chances to those who have innovations worth bringing to life. And these are only a few of the ways we can transfer our wealth; still support the well-being of our heirs; and in the process help make our world better, brighter, more abundant, and more supportive of the common good.

Life Rule
"The artist doesn't see things as they are, but as he is."

~ Anonymous

Life Achievement
Grandma Moses took up painting in her late 70s, when arthritis made it too painful to continue with her needlework. She gained worldwide appreciation and acclaim for her paintings and lived to be 101.

Life Tool
Since no one can live your life for you, the way you live your life, the choices you make, and the characteristics you display will determine if your heart balances with that feather of truth. Please take a few moments to decide what other choices you can make about how you use your talents, the gifts you can make to others, and the kind of legacy you want to leave behind you. Physical time is, after all, ticking. Why not live this moment and every moment you have in a state of joy and grace?

The Best Is yet to Come

"When love and skill work together, expect a masterpiece."

~ John Ruskin ~

Another Gift that Keeps on Giving

In Part Four we spent a reasonable amount of time exploring the topic of living in the now. As we prepare to complete this fifth stage of our journey, we want to return to that conversation, for we believe mindfulness — the intention to live with a greater moment-by-moment awareness — will serve us all as an invaluable key that will open the door to all the best that is yet to come.

We know, of course, that in charting your course for the future, the idea that some of what lies ahead — some of the very real and more challenging aspects of aging and dying — could be included in this "The Best Is yet to Come" chapter may seem strange to you. And yet, if you have taken to heart some of the suggestions, reminders, and recommendations found within the pages of this book, if you have taken the time to participate in some of the exercises and allowed the information about the lives of others to touch and inspire you, then you probably have already begun revisiting some of your values and reshaping some of your priorities in ways that will ensure that what lies ahead — all of it — will not only be acceptable but unique — not only stable but engaging, appropriate, inspiring, and even quite remarkable.

Indeed, the practice of mindfulness is, we believe, one of the genuine gifts that will keep on giving to you and to all who you touch in your life every day for the rest of your life. This intention to live with a greater moment-by-moment awareness will assist you to drink more fully from each experience and every interaction. It will allow you to touch into the essence that each moment contains so that instead of living in a divided house — instead of always trying to perform some feat of bilocation, to be both where you are and where you have been or think you need to be

— you can be present wherever you are and say, as Thich Nhat Hahn, the wise peace activist and mindfulness teacher, reminds us, "I have arrived. I am home."

Yes, the gift of living and of learning in each moment will allow you to move beyond the discomfort of a divided consciousness, and even more than this, it will allow you to live a life that is much freer of worry, doubt, and concern. And the more you are present, especially to each and every one of the opportunities and experiences that will make up this next stage of your life, the more you will be able to do what is in your best interests. The more you will experience that sense of enough — "I am enough and this is enough" — that may have eluded you thus far in your life.

So take a moment here and imagine what this next stage of your life can truly be like if you are able to say, "Whatever I have, whoever I am, whatever I have done — at this very moment — is enough."

Indeed, imagine what it will be like to be able to respond with a genuine conviction, as a good friend of ours often does when asked how she is doing, with the words, "I'm just right!" Just right! What a clear, simple and yet profoundly true statement. For when we are present, when we acknowledge and accept whatever is going on as our reality, we step into what is — what is precisely and indisputably supposed to be going on. Allowing this, dealing fully with its implications, can be such a relief! "I am here. I am now!" "I have arrived. I am home."

As we mentioned earlier, Paracelsus, the 16th century physician and alchemist, advanced the notion that if we truly come to know one aspect of the universe, even just a single leaf, we will come to understand the nature of the universe as a whole. Mark Nepo, a contemporary poet, reminds us of the same thing when he shares the words of the Zen master who said: The greedy one gathered all of the cherries and the simple one tasted all of the cherries in one.

So your key to knowing — not to believing, but to knowing — that the best is yet to come will never be found in having or doing more. Instead you will best glimpse it by reflecting on another Mark Nepo reminder: *"the truth is that one experience taken to heart will satisfy our hunger to be loved [admired, recognized, remembered] by everyone."*

Imagine that! Enough! Satisfaction! Completeness! Fulfillment as close to each of us as our willingness to be present in this moment! Wholeness, individuation, enlightenment, or whatever each of us calls that grace and bliss we seek, is available, not by consuming all of the cherries, not by trying to accumulate more stuff or seeking to be something we are not, but by simply and lovingly being who we authentically are — right here, right now — and savoring it fully.

Life Envisioning —
The Reunion of Past...Present...Future

As we turn toward home, we invite you to participate in one more valuable conversation. It is a conversation you can have with three essential aspects of yourself: your youthful self, your present self, and your future self.

In our experience it can serve as a valuable tool that you can use again and again in the coming years to stay true to the life you were born to live.

To do this, you can go to www.donotgoquietlythebook.com for the "Life Envisioning Guided Process" or you can read along and do the process right here. If you do the latter, just prop the book up on the table in front of you or place it in your lap where you can see it and then begin:

Settle comfortably into your chair
and let the chair support your body
and your body support you.
As you do, begin to notice the natural rhythm of your breath.
Quietly now, focus on the steady flow of air
coming into your body, and going out of your body.
And with each breath, rest in each present moment.
As thoughts come up, just let them drift from view
Instead of focusing on them, follow your own breath —
in and out, in and out,
and now begin this wonderful journey....
Come with me now,
follow my voice to a place
that will be very familiar to you...
walking now, through a quiet forest on a still day...
All around you are tall, old trees —
the kind a young child would take delight in;
all the gentle giants offering their shade
and pine needles to play in —
the kind an older person would go to remember
the great mysteries and simple truths of Life...
You are walking along a path that
hasn't been trodden much of late...
through this wise forest...
deeper now, into the woods.
You notice the subtleties of the creatures here...
a squirrel heralding your arrival;
the cry of a hawk in the distance...

and you keep walking —
the path is easy and smooth —
there is no hurry. No one hurries in this forest.
Step follows step,
breath follows breath
and you notice up ahead,
just a little ways ahead, there's a fork
with two paths...
the one to the right more traveled,
the one to the left hardly noticeable...
You choose the one on the left...
you keep walking effortlessly,
as though you have always known this path...
Not much further ahead
you see a bit of sunlight filtering onto the trail...
there's some kind of opening there...
so you move toward it.
And there, standing in the space
where the light splashes the trail,
the warmth feels good...and you are content...
You see a bigger opening a few more steps ahead...
and you go a little off the path to peer
at what is just on the other side of that big tree...
A clearing...yes, a peaceful, small clearing...
and in the center of that open space,
to your surprise and delight...there is a house...
a sturdy, simple house with rockers on the front porch...
It's a friendly place...one that someone has
taken good care of.
The windows and doors are open...
but you can't tell whose home it is...
And so drawn by curiosity, you decide to at least walk up
to the porch and find out if anybody is here...
Such a familiar place...
there at the front door, you listen...
no sounds of people or pets...
just the easy buzzing of bees along the honeysuckle vine...
and the feeling that you "know" this place...
After a few moments of looking around...
the old and worn farmhouse table in the dining room...
with a pair of half-burnt candles in the center;

the comfortable, overstuffed chair in the living room;
the occasional drip of water from the kitchen faucet...
you decide to go in...and as you cross the threshold,
in a funny kind of way, you feel like you're home.
In front of you is a simple hallway
with a bookshelf and a chair just next to a closed door...
There on that bookshelf you are amazed to find
a whole array of photographs — familiar photographs...
your photos...your family, your friends...
And there you are...very small; and there —
that one to your left — there, yes, that's you...
you a handful of years from now...
You realize — this is a very special place.
You realize that these photos, so accurate,
so real, so confirming...are reminding you of
the story of your life... and so you know it is
time to open the door beside the bookshelf and
through this open door, you walk now...
to find out more about this house
that holds so much for you...
And right there before you is a magnificent, beautiful thing...
so startling, really, it's the only thing in the room...
leaning easily against the strong wall —
there, in the far left corner of the room — an elegant mirror...
probably 8 feet tall and 6 feet wide...
framed with a gold-leaf frame...
And looking back at you from the mirror,
there is this face you know so well...
how simple and stark, and clear...
here in this welcoming space...here you are.
You see yourself here as if for the first time.
Those eyes...windows to your soul
that have witnessed exquisite joy and intolerable sorrows...
the same eyes that have wept at the beauty of Creation
and burned with the frustrations of unanswered questions
and unquenched desires...
Those shoulders that have carried dreams
and burdens, felt the summer breezes and been soaked in the rain...
Your hands...that have touched children's faces
and grasped for love when it felt like it might be leaving...
Those feet that have walked so many, many miles...

that have been on holy ground, been tired...been steady...
So beautiful you are...standing here...You.
It's so quiet here...and peaceful...
and you're startled to hear somewhere nearby,
yes, nearer even now...the sounds of a child's laughter —
the sound of a child, yes...coming into the house...
ever so quietly now almost like a game of hide and seek...
on tiptoes, you start to turn away from the mirror...
but before you can, this little person slips through the doorway
and playfully calls your name...and lovingly...
so happy to see you...this young child comes to you
and hugs you around your legs...
giggling...relaxed, as though they had known
all along that you would come here to meet them...
And as children do, the child looks now to the mirror and says to you,
"Look! Here we are!" And you, realizing with amazement,
how true — yes! "Here we are" — for this little child
is one you know so well...so very well...this little one is you.
Marveling at this magic house,
you reach down to lift the child into your arms
and as you do so, you hear slow, deliberate steps
coming from the hallway —
the steps of an elder...an elder who has come to this place
after waiting a long, long time for your arrival...
a loving elder with clear vision and a longing to visit with you.
At this moment you understand that this visit
is a most important one...
The child is in your arms still...
and this Old One laughs a contented laugh...
and the child too...they so love one another,
know each other so well...
and now this wise ancient soul
takes a place just next to you...an arm around you...
and with the reverence reserved for great rituals,
you look into this Old One's eyes...
you rest in the bliss of a homecoming to this great soul...
and you look back into the mirror now,
and witness the whole picture...
You are all here — you are complete...
All that you've ever longed for, longed to remember
from the time you were so very small is here

in your embrace…and the ache you have had
from your first breath for the wise one
who knows what to do even in the dark…
this ache is satisfied…because you are safely supported,
completely loved — deeply known.
And you, you as you are in this moment…
there you are in the mirror, too.
In all your humanness,
all your longing, your wishes and wants…
here you are — all of you.
And as you stand before yourself,
you witness an amazing thing…
a miracle you will know for always…
as the little one nestles into your arms,
their precious warmth radiates into you…
and your face lightens…
and any aches you'd carried in from your walk
in the forest fade away…
And as your older sage self rests
in the silence of deepest love,
standing there, just next to you,
ever so slightly leaning into your shoulder,
you relax into the deepest core of your being…
You take a breath…all three of you in the mirror —
And now a breeze flutters in through the curtains…
And you turn to look out the open window
and follow that breath from the sky —
and the moving leaves on that tree branch…
and as easily as it came, the breeze fades away…
so your gaze returns to the mirror — to you…
and now, this face looking back at you, smiles…
and the smile turns into a grin and a chuckle, now…
because you get it …
you understand fully…
that little one, and the old wise one…
they are still here,
but they are not as they were before…
Your own feet feel happier…
your heart feels wiser…
there is a wonder in the way you know the world…
an innocence you thought you'd lost long ago…

a peace you have never known quite this way.
You are all accounted for...and you are home.
So you spend a few more moments there
remembering the lines of your face in this mirror,
the joy in the laughter of the child that you
will always carry in your heart,
and when you are ready,
you turn and exit this inner sanctum...
slowly walking down the hall,
past the photos on the bookshelf,
down the hall...to that chair —
the one that looks just right for you.
And so you sit.
And you breathe quietly...
still aware of the sounds around you...
Easy now...slowing, coming back
into the experience of this space
and bringing with you the sense of
contentment and wholeness.
Coming back into this space...
refreshed and renewed.*

*The original version of this envisioning was created by our good friend and colleague, Celeste Krueger-Moulden, for a workshop we jointly facilitated several years ago.

Drawing a Map of Your Future

Having had this opportunity to experience the past, present, and future aspects of yourself, we invite you to take a few moments more and reflect on your experience. We also invite you to consider some of the ground you have covered — on this most recent journey as well as in the pages of this book.

You have had the chance to explore some of the things you have learned, to identify some of the things that are still yours to master, and to examine some of concepts and keys you can practice in living more fully in the present. You have had the opportunity to identify some alternative strategies for the road ahead and consider the kind of legacy you want to leave behind.

Now, if you are inclined, we invite you to take the opportunity to assemble these independent pieces into an actual picture of the future.

You can do this in any way that feels right to you. You can turn to a blank page in your journal and write whatever comes to mind. You can get yourself some large sheets of drawing paper or even a roll of butcher paper and a few boxes of colored markers or crayons. You can sit down at the piano or go into your workshop or garage when you make things. You can turn on your computer and assemble symbols or turn to a canvas with color or ink. You can take photographs, make a visual treasure map from cut-out words and images from magazines, or make a collage of assembled items. You can get up and sing or dance or go for a long walk in the park or woodland that is nearby.

Truly it does not matter the medium or the method you select, the only thing that matters is that you anchor your experience in a way that works for you. The only thing that matters is that you capture images that represent the wishes, hopes, and that special dream you have for your future, for those you love, and for this planet.

These can be expressed in visual images, words of inspiration, prayers and hopes, words of guidance, pledges, commitments, symbols, movements, pictures, sounds, or textures. And remember, whatever you do does not have to be perfect, for the soul does not require perfection, it already has it perfect. The only thing that is necessary is that you allow yourself to express and celebrate what is in your heart and what has genuine meaning for you.

No matter what form your map of your world takes, however, please take a little time to memorialize the magic that you touch into when you know that in the quiet of your own heart you understand that the best is yet to come.

The poet Derek Walcott reinforces this fact in his poem "Love After Death." He suggests that a time will come when you will "greet yourself arriving at your own door." And in this moment "you will love again the stranger who was yourself."

Elderhood

In these pages we have done our best to introduce you to some concepts we believe can prove to be valuable to you on your journey going forward. Now, as they say, the ball is in your court.

So we invite you to make a commitment to yourself to do all that you can do to ensure that this next stage of your life is, indeed, the very best part of your life so that this precious gift of your life becomes a source of inspiration for all who come after you. For the notes you have to sing in this great song called life are notes that only you can add.

You will also find a link on www.donotgoquietlythebook.com to a song written to celebrate AgeNation and this book by the talented Joel Harrison entitled, "The Best Is yet to Come." We know you will enjoy it.

Life Rule
"Only put off until tomorrow what you are willing to die having left undone."
~ Pablo Picasso

Life Achievement
Jessica Tandy won an Oscar for *Driving Miss Daisy* in 1989 at the age of 82.

Life Tool
You will also find a downloadable list of "101 Ways to Live the Life You Were Born to Live" at www.donotgoquietlythebook.com. We invite you to print out a list and post it somewhere that you will see it often or even occasionally.

And in those moments when you feel that you might be getting off course, or other times when you could use a little support, pick something off the list and practice it. No tests, no requirements, just a reminder to keep on living more consciously, to age wisely, and to live the life you were born to live.

Other Programs and Books You Will Value
By George & Sedena Cappannelli

P.E.P.: Personal Energy Program by Sedena C. Cappannelli

This valuable DVD program will provide you with energizing, destressing, and de-aging techniques that will assist you to be vitally alive and healthy for the rest of your life. Experience this combination of contemporary and ancient energy skills to add true PEP to your life. Create wholeness in mind, body, and spirit for your aging-consciously journey. www.donotgoquietlythebook.com and www.agenation.com/store

Say Yes to Change:
25 Keys to Making Change Work for You

In *Say Yes to Change*, George and Sedena Cappannelli, two of the country's leading corporate consultants and personal and executive coaches, provide you with 25 Keys to assist you to make change your ally. www.agenation.com/store

Authenticity: Simple Strategies for Greater Meaning and Purpose at Work and at Home

This is a book for individuals and organizations who want to refine, rediscover, and connect with their sense of meaning and purpose; and who want to use this connection to achieve outstanding levels of performance, greater success, and a genuine sense of contribution. www.agenation.com/store

I Dream of a New America: Keys to Reclaiming the Heart & Soul of Our Nation

A thought-provoking book full of practical recommendations on how we can turn some of the political disharmony and dysfunction that is threatening the foundations of this great democracy and return our nation to a path of greater integrity and commitment to the well-being of all of our citizens. www.agenation.com/store

AgeNation — Our mission is to provide information, inspiration, education, products and services, and opportunities for community and engagement for people who weren't born yesterday. Come spend some time with us at www.AgeNation.com. We are sure you'll be glad you did!

AgeNation
Solutions For People
Who Weren't Born Yesterday

AgeNation is a digital media company. We represent a constituency that will soon be 150 million strong. We weren't born yesterday and we are not dying tomorrow. In fact we have a lot of wonderful living to do and a lot of remarkable things to share with each other and with members of younger generations who will bear the responsibility for tomorrow.

We are also dedicated to making a difference today — in our own lives and in the lives of others. After all, we are the generations who gave birth to some of the great social movements of our time — Civil Rights, Human Rights, Women's Rights, Anti-Nuclear and Environmental Movements. As a result, we know how to get things done. And one thing is clear, we are not done yet. We still have things to learn and time to make things right within ourselves and with others.

So if you would like to learn more about AgeNation, join us at www.agenation.com. Make it your place on the web for terrific information, inspiration, opportunities for engagement, education and entertainment, and a great range of products and services that can help you make the best of this precious gift called your life.

Here are some other things AgeNation offers:

- *The AgeNation Post* provides you with insights and information on 9 major topics from more than 60 world-class experts.

- The AgeNation Radio Network is your source for 8 cutting-edge and informative weekly shows, including *AgeNation Radio Magazine*.

- AgeNation Live produces a broad range of entertainment events as well as inspiring Navigating Your Future conferences and workshops — live and online — featuring some of the leading experts and authors of our time.

- *NEXT, The Digital Magazine for People Who Weren't Born Yesterday* features articles by leading experts on topics you want to know more about.

- AgeNation Consuling and Coaching provides you and your organization with support from some of the leading change agents in the world who can help you better refine your vision, develop new skills, build stronger teams, and better prepare for the world ahead.

- The Council of Wisdom Keepers for the Americas – AgeNation is initiating the formation of a group of leading elders who will collaborate in helping to create a more age-friendly world in which elders once again are honored and offer the wisdom of their experience and guidance in creating a sane and sustainable future.

- www.AgeNation.com for solutions for people who weren't born yesterday.

George and Sedena Cappannelli
www.agenation.com

George and Sedena Cappannelli are authors, world-class consultants, and speakers and co-founders of AgeNation, a digital media company and social enterprise, and The Age of Empowerment, a 501(c)(3) serving vulnerable sections of our aging population.

They are experts on individual, organizational, and societal change, with an outstanding track record serving hundreds of thousands of individuals and hundreds of the world's leading organizations in both the private and public sectors (including Boeing, NASA, Sun MicroSystems, The Disney Company, Oracle, PepsiCo, The LA Times, U.S. Navy, and more).

George and Sedena have hosted their own radio talk shows — *Talk About Your Life* in Phoenix, and currently are on the web with *AgeNation Radio Magazine*. George is also an Emmy Award–winning film and television producer/director; and Sedena, a long-time member of The Screen Actors Guild, has appeared in numerous films, television programs, and theatrical productions.

Sedena is also a television and theatrical producer and the founder of About Life Inc., a company she created to bring personal empowerment to women. Her new Personal Energy Program (P.E.P.) DVD/book set complements the work explored in *Do Not Go Quietly* and introduces a series of ground-breaking wellness and de-aging processes.

In addition, George co-founded The International Integrity Program and served as executive director of The Sedona Institute and a director of The Society for the Advancement of Human Spirit, an organization chaired by the Dalai Lama. He has worked on special projects with Golda Meir, Lech Walesa, Bishop Desmond Tutu, Mother Teresa, and other world leaders. In 1991 George managed the launch of Jerry Brown's U.S. Senate Campaign and has served as a special consultant in the 1992, 1996, and 2008 presidential campaigns. His political blog, *It's About Time* explores the themes covered in his book, *I Dream of a New America*.

Together, George and Sedena are co-authors of two previous books:

Say Yes to Change: 25 Keys to Making Change Work for You

Authenticity: Simple Strategies for Greater Meaning and Purpose at Work and at Home

www.AgeNation.com — www.SayYesToChange.com

www.authenticity.cc — www.Idreamofanewamerica.com

Other Offerings from Agape Media Artists & Authors

Agape Media International (AMI) is dedicated to promoting artists and art forms that uplift the human spirit and inspiring individuals to contribute their own talents to the creation of a world that works for everyone.

Books
Michael Bernard Beckwith | TranscenDance Expanded
Cynthia Occelli | Resurrecting Venus
Dianne Burnett | The Road To Reality
Charles Holt | Intuitive Rebel
Carl Studna | Click! – Choosing Love One Frame At A Time
Michael Bernard Beckwith | The Answer Is You
Michael Bernard Beckwith | 40-Day Mind Fast Soul Feast
Michael Bernard Beckwith | Life Visioning
Michael Bernard Beckwith | Spiritual Liberation

Audio Programs by Michael Bernard Beckwith
The Life Visioning Process
The Life Visioning Life Visioning Kit
The Rhythm Of A Descended Master
Your Soul's Evolution
Living From The Overflow

DVDs
The Answer Is You
Spiritual Liberation, the Movie
Superwise Me!
Living In The Revelation

Music CDs
Music From The PBS Special - The Answer Is You
   feat. Will.I.Am, Siedah Garrett, Niki Haris, Rickie Byars Beckwith,
   Agape International Choir
Jami Lula & Spirit In The House / There's A Healin' Goin' On
Charles Holt | I Am
Charles Holt | Rushing Over Me
Rickie Byars Beckwith | Supreme Inspiration
Ester Nicholson | Child Above The Sun
Ben Dowling | The Path Of Peace
Michael Bernard Beckwith / TranscenDance

Inspirational Cards
Life Lift-Off Cards

Agape Media International

www.agapeme.com
For more information regarding Agape International Spiritual Center in Los Angeles, visit www.agapelive.com